a transparent, repeatable methodology to collaborative analysis—useful in areas well beyond the U.S. Intelligence Community."

—Jim Dubik, Senior Fellow at the Institute for the Study of War and also the Institute of Land Warfare; President and CEO of Dubik Associates, LLC

"Many observers, including me, have noted that intelligence analysis as practiced during the Cold War made little use of formal methods. Recent blue-ribbon panels convened to study intelligence failures have called for greater rigor, and there is no team better than the authors of this book to provide a cookbook of techniques. Heuer all but created the subject, and Pherson is a longtime practitioner, methodologist, and teacher. The book will be most valuable to practitioners, for whom it should become a touchstone for any time they need to ask themselves, 'what if?'"

—Greg Treverton, Director of RAND's Center for Global Risk and Security; former Vice Chair of the National Intelligence Council

"Seeking to overcome the perceptual blocks and analytic pathologies identified by Richards Heuer in his seminal work *The Psychology of Intelligence Analysis*, this is the most constructive and probably the most important book on intelligence analysis ever written. It should be compulsory reading for all analysts in the Intelligence Community as well as all future analysts. Systematic adoption of the structured analytic techniques identified in this volume will not only improve the quality of analysis but also make it less likely that the United States will be the victim of a strategic surprise. The authors have developed techniques that, if put into practice, might take many analysts out of their comfort zones, but will significantly enhance the value and impact of intelligence products."

—Phil Williams, Posvar Chair of International Security Studies, Graduate School of Public and International Affairs, University of Pittsburgh

"When it comes to intelligence analysis, Randy Pherson has no equal. He kept an audience of 150 of our clients spellbound for six hours."

—Kiril Sokoloff, President, 13D Research (USVI) LLC

STRUCTURED ANALYTIC TECHNIQUES *for* INTELLIGENCE ANALYSIS

STRUCTURED ANALYTIC
TECHNIQUES *for*
INTELLIGENCE ANALYSIS

By
Richards J. Heuer Jr.
and
Randolph H. Pherson

CQ PRESS

A Division of SAGE
Washington, D.C.

CQ Press
2300 N Street, NW, Suite 800
Washington, DC 20037

Phone: 202-729-1900; toll-free, 1-866-4CQ-PRESS (1-866-427-7737)

Web: www.cqpress.com

Versions of twelve of the analytical techniques published in this volume (ACH, alternative futures analysis, brainstorming, deception detection, devil's advocacy, indicators, key assumptions check, outside-in thinking, quadrant crunching, red cell analysis, team a/team b analysis and debate, and what if? analysis) were published by Randolph H. Pherson in *The Handbook of Analytical Techniques* (2005) on behalf of the government under contract number 2003*N(Y)481500*000. Techniques published here under those names have been substantially refocused, refined, and improved.

Cover design: Jeffrey Everett/El Jefe Designs
Cover image: istock.com
Interior design: Judy Myers
Composition: C&M Digitals (P) Ltd.

∞ The paper used in this publication exceeds the requirements of the American National Standard for Information Sciences—Permanence of Paper for Printed Library Materials, ANSI Z39.48–1992.

Printed and bound in the United States of America

16   15   14   13   12   2   3   4   5   6

Library of Congress Cataloging-in-Publication Data

Heuer, Richards J., Jr.
Structured analytic techniques for intelligence analysis / by Richards J. Heuer, Jr., and Randolph H. Pherson.
      p. cm.
   Includes bibliographical references.
   ISBN 978-1-60871-018-8 (alk. paper)

1. Intelligence service—United States. 2. Intelligence service—Methodology. I. Pherson, Randolph H. II. Title.

   JK468.I6H478 2010
   327.12—dc22

                                                                                    2009033571

CONTENTS

Figures   xi

Foreword by John McLaughlin   xiv

Preface   xvi

1. **Introduction and Overview**   3

   1.1   Our Vision   4

   1.2   The Value of Team Analysis   6

   1.3   The Analyst's Task   7

   1.4   History of Structured Analytic Techniques   8

   1.5   What's in This Book?   10

   1.6   Agenda for the Future   13

2. **Building a Taxonomy**   19

   2.1   Four Categories of Analytic Methods   21

   2.2   Taxonomy of Structured Analytic Techniques   24

3. **Criteria for Selecting Structured Techniques**   29

   3.1   Selection of Techniques for This Book   29

   3.2   Techniques Every Analyst Should Master   30

   3.3   Common Errors in Selecting Techniques   33

   3.4   One Project, Multiple Techniques   34

   3.5   Structured Technique Selection Guide   34

4. **Decomposition and Visualization**   41

   *4.1   Getting Started Checklist   45

   *4.2   Customer Checklist   47

   *4.3   Issue Redefinition   49

   *4.4   Chronologies and Timelines   52

＊ *= technique*

* 4.5	Sorting	56
* 4.6	Ranking, Scoring, Prioritizing	59
* 4.7	Matrices	64
* 4.8	Network Analysis	68
* 4.9	Mind Maps and Concept Maps	76
* 4.10	Process Maps and Gantt Charts	82
5.	**Idea Generation**	**89**
* 5.1	Structured Brainstorming	92
* 5.2	Virtual Brainstorming	97
* 5.3	Nominal Group Technique	99
* 5.4	Starbursting	102
* 5.5	Cross-Impact Matrix	104
* 5.6	Morphological Analysis	108
* 5.7	Quadrant Crunching	111
6.	**Scenarios and Indicators**	**119**
* 6.1	Scenarios Analysis	122
* 6.1.1	*The Method: Simple Scenarios*	125
* 6.1.2	*The Method: Alternative Futures Analysis*	126
* 6.1.3	*The Method: Multiple Scenarios Generation*	128
* 6.2	Indicators	132
* 6.3	Indicators Validator	140
7.	**Hypothesis Generation and Testing**	**147**
* 7.1	Hypothesis Generation	150
* 7.1.1	*Simple Hypotheses*	151
* 7.1.2	*The Method: Multiple Hypotheses Generator*	153
* 7.1.3	*The Method: Quadrant Hypothesis Generation*	155

* = technique

7.2   Diagnostic Reasoning   158

7.3   Analysis of Competing Hypotheses   160

7.4   Argument Mapping   170

7.5   Deception Detection   173

8.   Assessment of Cause and Effect   **179**

8.1   Key Assumptions Check   183

8.2   Structured Analogies   189

8.3   Role Playing   193

8.4   Red Hat Analysis   197

8.5   Outside-In Thinking   201

8.6   Policy Outcomes Forecasting Model   204

8.7   Prediction Markets   209

9.   Challenge Analysis   **215**

9.1   Premortem Analysis   221

9.2   Structured Self-Critique   226

9.3   What If? Analysis   231

9.4   High Impact/Low Probability Analysis   235

9.5   Devil's Advocacy   240

9.6   Red Team Analysis   243

9.7   Delphi Method   245

10.   Conflict Management   **253**

10.1   Adversarial Collaboration   256

10.2   Structured Debate   262

11.   Decision Support   **267**

11.1   Complexity Manager   271

11.2   Decision Matrix   279

✳ = technique

11.3   Force Field Analysis   281

11.4   Pros-Cons-Faults-and-Fixes   284

11.5   SWOT Analysis   288

12. Practitioner's Guide to Collaboration   293

12.1   Social Networks and Analytic Teams   294

12.2   Dividing the Work   298

12.3   Common Pitfalls with Small Groups   300

12.4   Benefiting from Diversity   301

12.5   Advocacy vs. Objective Inquiry   303

12.6   Leadership and Training   305

13. Evaluation of Structured Analytic Techniques   309

13.1   Establishing Face Validity   310

13.2   Limits of Empirical Testing   312

13.3   A New Approach to Evaluation   319

13.4   Recommended Research Program   321

14. Vision of the Future   327

14.1   Structuring the Data   330

14.2   Analyzing the Data   330

14.3   Conclusions Drawn from This Analysis   339

14.4   Imagining the Future: 2015   340

＊ = *technique*

FIGURES

2.0	Taxonomy Outline	20
4.3	Issue Redefinition Example	51
4.4	Timeline Estimate of Missile Launch Date	55
4.6a	Paired Comparison Matrix	61
4.6b	Weighted Ranking Matrix	63
4.7	Rethinking the Concept of National Security: A New Ecology	66
4.8a	Social Network Analysis: The September 11 Hijackers	70
4.8b	Social Network Analysis: September 11 Hijacker Key Nodes	73
4.8c	Social Network Analysis	74
4.9a	Concept Map of Concept Mapping	77
4.9b	Mind Map of Mind Mapping	78
4.10	Gantt Chart of Terrorist Attack Planning	84
5.1	Picture of Brainstorming	94
5.4	Starbursting Diagram of a Lethal Biological Event at a Subway Station	103
5.5	Cross-Impact Matrix	106
5.6	Morphological Analysis: Terrorist Attack Options	110
5.7a	Quadrant Crunching: Creating a Set of Stories	113
5.7b	Terrorist Attacks on Water Systems: Flipping Assumptions	114
5.7c	Terrorist Attacks on Water Systems: Sample Matrices	114
5.7d	Selecting Scenarios	115
6.1.1	Simple Scenarios	126
6.1.2	Alternative Futures Analysis: Cuba	127
6.1.3a	Multiple Scenarios Generation: Future of the Iraq Insurgency	129
6.1.3b	Future of the Iraq Insurgency: Using Spectrums to Define Potential Outcomes	130
6.1.3c	Selecting Attention-deserving and Nightmare Scenarios	131

6.2a	Descriptive Indicators of a Clandestine Drug Laboratory	133
6.2b	Using Indicators to Track Emerging Scenarios in Zambria	135
6.2c	Zambria Political Instability Indicators	138
6.3a	Indicators Validator Model	140
6.3b	Indicators Validator Process	142
7.1.1	Simple Hypothesis Generation	152
7.1.2	Hypothesis Generator: Generating Permutations	154
7.1.3	Quadrant Hypothesis Generation: Four Hypotheses on the Future of Iraq	156
7.3a	ACH: Entering and Coding Evidence	164
7.3b	ACH: Sorting Evidence for Diagnosticity	165
7.3c	Showing Levels of Disagreement with Collaborative ACH	166
7.4	Argument Mapping: Does North Korea Have Nuclear Weapons?	172
8.1	Key Assumptions Check: The Case of Wen Ho Lee	187
8.4	Using Red Hat Analysis to Catch Bank Robbers	200
8.5	Inside-Out Analysis vs. Outside-In Approach	202
8.6	Zambria Energy Investment Diagram	206
9.1	Structured Self-Critique: Key Questions	225
9.3	What If? Scenario: India Makes Surprising Gains from the Global Financial Crisis	233
9.4	High Impact/Low Probability Scenario: Conflict in the Arctic	238
9.7	The Delphi Technique	248
11.1	Variables Affecting Future Use of Structured Analysis	275
11.2	Example of a Decision Matrix	279
11.3	Force Field Analysis: Removing Abandoned Cars from City Streets	282
11.4	Pros-Cons-Faults-and-Fixes Analysis	285
11.5	SWOT Analysis	289
12.1a	Traditional Analytic Team	295
12.1b	Special Project Team	296
12.2	Wikis as Collaboration Enablers	298

12.5	Advocacy vs. Inquiry in Small-Group Processes	303
12.6	Effective Small-Group Roles and Interactions	305
13.3	Three Approaches to Evaluation	319
14.1	Variables Affecting Future Use of Structured Analysis	330

FOREWORD

John McLaughlin

Senior Research Fellow, Paul H. Nitze School of Advanced International Studies, Johns Hopkins University

Former Deputy Director, Central Intelligence Agency and Acting Director of Central Intelligence

As intensively as America's Intelligence Community has been studied and critiqued, little attention has typically been paid to intelligence analysis. Most assessments focus on such issues as overseas clandestine operations and covert action, perhaps because they accord more readily with popular images of the intelligence world.

And yet, analysis has probably never been a more important part of the profession—or more needed by policymakers. In contrast to the bipolar dynamics of the Cold War, this new world is strewn with failing states, proliferation dangers, regional crises, rising powers, and dangerous nonstate actors—all at play against a backdrop of exponential change in fields as diverse as population and technology.

To be sure, there are still precious secrets that intelligence collection must uncover—things that are knowable and discoverable. But this world is equally rich in mysteries having to do more with the future direction of events and the intentions of key actors. Such things are rarely illuminated by a single piece of secret intelligence data; they are necessarily subjects for analysis.

Analysts charged with interpreting this world would be wise to absorb the thinking in this book by Richards Heuer and Randy Pherson and in Heuer's earlier work *The Psychology of Intelligence Analysis*. The reasons are apparent if one considers the ways in which intelligence analysis differs from similar fields of intellectual endeavor.

Intelligence analysts must traverse a minefield of potential errors.

* First, they typically must begin addressing their subjects where others have left off; in most cases the questions they get are about what happens next, not about what is known.

* Second, they cannot be deterred by lack of evidence. As Heuer pointed out in his earlier work, the essence of the analysts' challenge is having to deal with ambiguous situations in which information is never complete

and arrives only incrementally—but with constant pressure to arrive at conclusions.

* Third, analysts must frequently deal with an adversary that actively seeks to deny them the information they need and is often working hard to deceive them.

* Finally, analysts, for all of these reasons, live with a high degree of risk— essentially the risk of being wrong and thereby contributing to ill-informed policy decisions.

The risks inherent in intelligence analysis can never be eliminated, but one way to minimize them is through more structured and disciplined thinking about thinking. On that score, I tell my students at the Johns Hopkins School of Advanced International Studies that the Heuer book is probably the most important reading I give them, whether they are heading into the government or the private sector. Intelligence analysts should reread it frequently. In addition, Randy Pherson's work over the past six years to develop and refine a suite of structured analytic techniques offers invaluable assistance by providing analysts with specific techniques they can use to combat mindsets, groupthink, and all the other potential pitfalls of dealing with ambiguous data in circumstances that require clear and consequential conclusions.

The book you now hold augments Heuer's pioneering work by offering a clear and more comprehensive menu of more than fifty techniques to build on the strategies he earlier developed for combating perceptual errors. The techniques range from fairly simple exercises that a busy analyst can use while working alone—the assumptions checklist, the Indicators Validator, or What If? Analysis—to more complex techniques that work best in a group setting—structured brainstorming, Analysis of Competing Hypotheses, or what the authors call "Premortem Analysis."

The key point is that all analysts should do something to test the conclusions they advance. To be sure, expert judgment and intuition have their place—and are often the foundational elements of sound analysis—but analysts are likely to minimize error to the degree they can make their underlying logic explicit in the ways these techniques demand.

Just as intelligence analysis has seldom been more important, the stakes in the policy process it informs have rarely been higher. Intelligence analysts these days therefore have a special calling, and they owe it to themselves and to those they serve to do everything possible to challenge their own thinking and to rigorously test their conclusions. The strategies offered by Richards Heuer and Randy Pherson in this book provide the means to do precisely that.

PREFACE

Origin and Purpose

The investigative commissions that followed the terrorist attacks of 2001 and the erroneous 2002 National Intelligence Estimate on Iraq's weapons of mass destruction clearly documented the need for a new approach to intelligence analysis. Attention focused initially on the need for "alternative analysis"—techniques for questioning conventional wisdom by identifying and analyzing alternative explanations or outcomes. This approach was later subsumed by a broader effort to transform the tradecraft of intelligence analysis by using what have become known as structured analytic techniques. Structured analysis involves a step-by-step process that externalizes an individual analyst's thinking in a manner that makes it readily apparent to others, thereby enabling it to be shared, built on, and critiqued by others. When combined with the intuitive judgment of subject matter experts, such a structured and transparent process can significantly reduce the risk of analytic error.

Our current high-tech, global environment increasingly requires collaboration among analysts with different areas of expertise and different organizational perspectives. Structured analytic techniques are ideal for this interaction. Each step in a technique prompts relevant discussion and, typically, this generates more divergent information and more new ideas than any unstructured group process. The step-by-step process of structured analytic techniques structures the interaction among analysts in a small analytic group or team in a way that helps to avoid the multiple pitfalls and pathologies that often degrade group or team performance.

Progress in the development and use of structured analytic techniques has been slow but steady—in our view, too slow and too steady. We need a big jolt forward. We hope this book provides that jolt. By defining the domain of structured analytic techniques, providing a manual for using and testing these techniques, and outlining procedures for evaluating and validating these techniques, this book lays the groundwork for continuing improvement of how analysis is done, both within the Intelligence Community and beyond.

As the use of structured analytic techniques becomes more widespread, we anticipate that the ways these techniques are used will continue to change. Our goal is to keep up with these changes in future editions, so we welcome your suggestions, at any time, for updating the book or otherwise enhancing its utility. To facilitate the use of these techniques, a companion book of case studies and exercises for practicing and teaching structured analytic techniques is forthcoming.

Audience for This Book

This book is for practitioners, managers, teachers, and students of intelligence analysis and foreign affairs in both the public and private sectors. Managers, commanders, action officers, planners, and policymakers who depend upon input from analysts to help them achieve their goals should also find it useful. Academics who specialize in qualitative methods for dealing with unstructured data will be interested in this pathbreaking book as well.

Many of the techniques described here relate to strategic, all-source intelligence, but there is ample information on techniques of interest to tactical military, law enforcement, counterterrorism, and competitive intelligence analysts as well as business consultants and financial planners with a global perspective. Many techniques developed for these related fields have been adapted for use in intelligence analysis, and now we are starting to see the transfer of knowledge going in the other direction. Techniques such as Analysis of Competing Hypotheses, Key Assumptions Check, and Quadrant Crunching developed specifically for intelligence analysis are now being adapted for use in other fields. New techniques that the authors developed to fill gaps in what is currently available for intelligence analysis are being published for the first time in this book and have broad applicability.

Content and Design

The first three chapters describe structured analysis in general, how it fits into the spectrum of methods used by intelligence analysts, and how to select which techniques are most suitable for your analytic project. The next eight chapters describe when, why, and how to use each of the techniques contained in this volume. The final chapters discuss the integration of these techniques in a collaborative team project, research needed to evaluate key techniques, and a vision of how these techniques are likely to be used in the year 2015.

We designed the book for ease of use and quick reference. The spiral binding allows analysts to have the book open while they follow step-by-step instructions for each technique. We grouped the techniques into logical categories based on a taxonomy we devised. Tabs separating each chapter contain a table of contents for the selected chapter. Each technique chapter starts with a description of that technique category and then provides a one-paragraph summary of each technique covered in that chapter.

The Authors

Richards J. Heuer Jr. is best known for his book *Psychology of Intelligence Analysis* and for developing and then guiding automation of the Analysis of Competing

Hypotheses technique. Both are being used to teach and train intelligence analysts throughout the Intelligence Community and in a growing number of academic programs on intelligence or national security. Long retired from the Central Intelligence Agency (CIA), Mr. Heuer has been associated with the Intelligence Community in various roles for more than five decades and has written extensively on personnel security, counterintelligence, deception, and intelligence analysis. He has an A.B. in philosophy from Williams College and an M.A. in international relations from the University of Southern California, and he has pursued other graduate studies at the University of California at Berkeley and the University of Michigan.

Randolph H. Pherson, president of Pherson Associates, LLC, teaches advanced analytic tools and techniques to analysts throughout the Intelligence Community and the private sector. He collaborated with Richards Heuer in developing and launching the Analysis of Competing Hypotheses (ACH) software tool and developed several analytic techniques for the CIA's Sherman Kent School. Mr. Pherson completed a 28-year career with the Intelligence Community in 2000, last serving as National Intelligence Officer (NIO) for Latin America. Previously at the CIA, he conducted and managed the production of intelligence analysis on topics including southern Africa, Iran, Cuba, and Latin America; served on the Inspector General's staff; and sponsored the development of collaborative networks. Mr. Pherson received his A.B. from Dartmouth College and an M.A. in international relations from Yale University.

Acknowledgments

Richards Heuer is grateful to William Reynolds of Least Squares Software for pointing out the need for a taxonomy of analytic methods and generating financial support through the ODNI/IARPA PAINT program for the initial work on what subsequently evolved into chapters 1 and 2 of this book. He is also grateful to the CIA's Sherman Kent School for Intelligence Analysis for partial funding of what evolved into parts of chapters 3 and 12. This book as a whole, however, has not been funded by the Intelligence Community.

Both authors recognize the large contribution to this book made by individuals who devoted their time to review all or large portions of the draft text. These are J. Scott Armstrong, editor of *Principles of Forecasting: A Handbook for Researchers and Practitioners*, professor at the Wharton School, University of Pennsylvania; Sarah Miller Beebe, a Russian specialist who previously served as a CIA analyst and on the National Security Council staff and is now associated with Pherson Associates, LLC; Jack Davis, noted teacher and writer on intelligence analysis, a retired senior CIA officer, and now an independent contractor with the CIA; Robert R. Hoffman, noted author of books on naturalistic decision making, Institute for

Human & Machine Cognition; Marilyn B. Peterson, senior instructor at the Defense Intelligence Agency, former president of the International Association of Law Enforcement Intelligence Analysts, and current chair of the International Association for Intelligence Education; and Cynthia Storer, a counterterrorism specialist and former CIA analyst now associated with Pherson Associates, LLC. Their thoughtful critiques, recommendations, and edits as they reviewed this book were invaluable.

Valuable comments, suggestions, and assistance were also received from many others during the development of this book, including the following: Todd Bacastow, Michael Bannister, Aleksandra Bielska, Arne Biering, Jim Bruce, Hrair Cabayan, Ray Converse, Steve Cook, John Donelan, Averill Farrelly, Stanley Feder, Michael Fletcher, Roger George, Jay Hillmer, Terri Lange, Darci Leonhart, Mark Lowenthal, Elizabeth Manak, Stephen Marrin, William McGill, David Moore, Mary O'Sullivan, Emily Patterson, Amanda Pherson, Kathy Pherson, Steve Rieber, Grace Scarborough, Alan Schwartz, Marilyn Scott, Gudmund Thompson, Kristan Wheaton, and Adrian "Zeke" Wolfberg.

The CQ Press team headed by editorial director Charisse Kiino and acquisitions editor Elise Frasier did a marvelous job in managing the production of this book and getting it out on a quick schedule. Copy editor Ann Davies, production editor Lorna Notsch, and designer Judy Myers all earned high fives for the quality of their work.

The ideas, interest, and efforts of all the above contributors to this book are greatly appreciated, but the responsibility for any weaknesses or errors rests solely on the shoulders of the authors.

Disclaimer

1

Introduction
and
Overview

1

Introduction and Overview

1.1 Our Vision   [4]

1.2 The Value of Team Analysis   [6]

1.3 The Analyst's Task   [7]

1.4 History of Structured Analytic Techniques   [8]

1.5 What's in This Book?   [10]

1.6 Agenda for the Future   [13]

CHAPTER 1

Introduction and Overview

Analysis in the U.S. Intelligence Community is currently in a transitional stage, evolving from a mental activity done predominantly by a sole analyst to a collaborative team or group activity.[1] The driving forces behind this transition include the following:

* The growing complexity of international issues and the consequent requirement for multidisciplinary input to most analytic products.[2]

* The need to share more information more quickly across organizational boundaries.

* The dispersion of expertise, especially as the boundaries between analysts, collectors, and operators become blurred.

* And the need to identify and evaluate the validity of alternative mental models.

This transition is being enabled by advances in technology, such as the Intelligence Community's Intellipedia and new A-Space collaborative network, "communities of interest," the mushrooming growth of social networking practices among the upcoming generation of analysts, and the increasing use of structured analytic techniques that guide the interaction among analysts.

---

1. *Vision 2015: A Globally Networked and Integrated Intelligence Enterprise* (Washington, D.C.: Director of National Intelligence, 2008).

2. National Intelligence Council, *Global Trends 2025: A Transformed World* (Washington, D.C.: U.S. Government Printing Office, November 2008).

1.1 OUR VISION

This book defines the role and scope of structured analysis as a distinct form of intelligence analysis methodology that provides a step-by-step process for analyzing the kinds of incomplete, ambiguous, and sometimes deceptive information that analysts must deal with. As described later in this chapter, the concept of structured analysis and the practice of broadly and consistently applying structured techniques are relatively new in the Intelligence Community.

Structured analysis is a mechanism by which internal thought processes are externalized in a systematic and transparent manner so that they can be shared, built on, and easily critiqued by others. Each technique leaves a trail that other analysts and managers can follow to see the basis for an analytic judgment. These techniques are commonly used in a collaborative team or group effort in which each step of the analytic process exposes analysts to divergent or conflicting perspectives. This transparency also helps ensure that differences of opinion among analysts are heard and seriously considered early in the analytic process. Analysts have told us that this is one of the most valuable benefits of any structured technique.

Structured analysis helps analysts ensure that their analytic framework—the foundation upon which they form their analytic judgments—is as solid as possible. By helping break down a specific analytic problem into its component parts and specifying a step-by-step process for handling these parts, structured analytic techniques help to organize the amorphous mass of data with which most analysts must contend. This is the basis for the terms *structured analysis* and *structured analytic techniques*. Such techniques make an analyst's thinking more open and available for review and critique than the traditional approach to analysis. It is this transparency that enables the effective communication at the working level that is essential for interoffice and interagency collaboration.

These are called "techniques" because they usually guide the analyst in thinking about a problem rather than provide the analyst with a definitive answer as one might expect from a method. Structured analytic techniques in general, however, do form a methodology—a set of principles and procedures for qualitative analysis of the kinds of uncertainties that intelligence analysts must deal with on a daily basis.

This book is a logical follow-on to Richards Heuer's book, *Psychology of Intelligence Analysis*,[3] which describes the cognitive limitations and pitfalls typically encountered by intelligence analysts. Many readers of that book were discouraged

---

3. Richards J. Heuer Jr., *Psychology of Intelligence Analysis* (Washington, D.C.: CIA Center for the Study of Intelligence, 1999), reprinted by Pherson Associates, LLC, 2007.

to learn of the scope of human cognitive limitations and the multitude of pitfalls encountered when analysts must cope with incomplete, ambiguous, and often deceptive information. As one reader said, "It makes you wonder if it is possible to ever get anything right!"

There is, of course, no formula for always getting it right, but the use of structured techniques can reduce the frequency and severity of error. These techniques can help analysts mitigate the proven cognitive limitations, side-step some of the known analytic pitfalls, and explicitly confront the problems associated with unquestioned mental models (also known as mindsets). They help analysts think more rigorously about an analytic problem and ensure that preconceptions and assumptions are not taken for granted but are explicitly examined and tested.[4]

Discussions within the Intelligence Community and in the literature on intelligence analysis commonly refer to an analytic "mindset" as a principal source of analytic failure. A mindset "can be defined as the analyst's mental model or paradigm of how government and group processes usually operate in country 'X' or on issue 'Y.'"[5] This is a key concept in understanding intelligence analysis. We, along with most analysts, have used the term "mindset" for many years. We have now decided, however, to use the term "mental model" instead. The term "mindset" has a negative connotation for many people. It implies that if analysts were not so "set" in their ways, they would not make so many mistakes. But a mindset is neither good nor bad; it is unavoidable.

Intelligence analysts, like humans in general, do not start with an empty mind. Whenever people try to make sense of events, they begin with some body of experience or knowledge that gives them a certain perspective or viewpoint which we are calling a mental model. Intelligence specialists who are expert in their field have well developed mental models. Their mental model tells them, sometimes subconsciously, what to look for, what is important, and how to interpret what they see. This mental model formed through education and experience serves a valuable function, as it is what enables an analyst to provide on a daily basis reasonably accurate assessments or estimates about what is happening or is likely to happen.

Why does it matter whether one uses the term "mindset" or "mental model"? It matters because it may affect how one tries to solve a problem. If an analyst's mindset is seen as the problem, one tends to blame the analyst for being inflexible or outdated in his or her thinking. That may be valid in individual cases, as analysts

---

4. Judgments in this and the next sections are based on our personal experience and anecdotal evidence gained in work with or discussion with other experienced analysts. As we will discuss in chapter 13, there is a need for systematic research on these and other benefits believed to be gained through the use of structured analytic techniques.

5. Jack Davis, "Why Bad Things Happen to Good Analysts," in *Analyzing Intelligence: Origins, Obstacles, and Innovations,* ed. Roger Z. George and James B. Bruce (Washington, D.C.: Georgetown University Press, 2008), 160.

do vary considerably in their ability and willingness to question their own thinking. However, if one recognizes that all analysis is based on fallible mental models of a complex and uncertain world, one might approach the problem differently. One might recognize that greater accuracy is best achieved through collaboration among analysts who bring diverse viewpoints to the table and the use of structured analytic techniques that assess alternative explanations or outcomes.

To put this book in perspective, it is noted that analytic methods are important, but method alone is far from sufficient to ensure analytic accuracy or value. Method must be combined with substantive expertise and an inquiring and imaginative mind. And these, in turn, must be supported and motivated by the organizational environment in which the analysis is done.

1.2 THE VALUE OF TEAM ANALYSIS

Our vision for the future of intelligence analysis dovetails with that of the Director of National Intelligence's *Vision 2015,* in which intelligence analysis increasingly becomes a collaborative enterprise, with the focus of collaboration shifting "away from coordination of draft products toward regular discussion of data and hypotheses early in the research phase."[6] This is a major change from the traditional concept of analysis as largely an individual activity and coordination as the final step in the process.

In the collaborative enterprise envisaged by the Director of National Intelligence, structured analytic techniques are a *process* by which collaboration occurs. Just as these techniques provide structure to our individual thought processes, they can also structure the interaction of analysts within a small team or group. Because the thought process in these techniques is transparent, each step in the technique prompts discussion within the team. Such discussion can generate and evaluate substantially more divergent information and new information than can a group that does not use a structured process. When a team is dealing with a complex issue, the synergy of multiple minds using structured analysis is usually more effective than is the thinking of a lone analyst.

Team-based analysis can, of course, bring with it a new set of challenges comparable to the cognitive limitations and pitfalls faced by the individual analyst. However, the well-known group process problems can be minimized by use of structured techniques that guide the interaction among members of a team or group. This helps to keep discussions from getting sidetracked and elicits alternative views from all team members. Analysts have also found that use of a structured process helps to depersonalize arguments when there are differences

---

6. Ibid., 13.

of opinion. Fortunately, today's technology and social networking programs make structured collaboration much easier than it has ever been in the past.

1.3 THE ANALYST'S TASK

It is one thing to say that analysts *should* use structured analytic techniques to help overcome the cognitive pitfalls that lead to analytic failure. It is another matter altogether for analysts to learn to select, understand, and actually use structured analytic techniques—and to use them well. That is what this book is about. From the several hundred techniques that might have been included here, we developed a taxonomy for a core group of fifty techniques that appear to be the most useful for the Intelligence Community, but also useful for those engaged in related analytic pursuits in academia, business, law enforcement, finance, and medicine. This list, however, is not static. It is expected to increase or decrease as new techniques are identified and others are tested and found wanting. Some training programs may have a need to boil down their list of techniques to the essentials required for one particular type of analysis. No one list will meet everyone's needs. However, we hope that having one fairly comprehensive list and common terminology available to the growing community of analysts now employing structured analytic techniques will help to facilitate the discussion and use of these techniques in projects involving collaboration across organizational boundaries.

The most common criticism of structured analytic techniques is, "I don't have enough time to use them." The experience of many analysts shows that this criticism is not justified. Many techniques take very little time. Anything new does take some time to learn, but, once learned, the use of structured analytic techniques often saves analysts time. It can enable the individual analyst to work more efficiently, especially at the start of a project when the analyst may otherwise flounder a bit in trying to figure out how to proceed. Structured techniques usually aid group processes by improving communication as well as enhancing the collection and interpretation of evidence. And in the end, a structured technique usually produces a product in which the reasoning behind the conclusions is more transparent and readily accepted than one derived from other methods. This generally saves time by expediting review by supervisors and editors and thereby compressing the coordination process.[7]

There is reason to suspect that the "don't have time" explanation may mask deeper concerns by analysts. In-depth interviews of fifteen Defense Intelligence Agency analysts concerning their use of Intellipedia found that whether or not an

---

7. Again, these statements are our professional judgments based on discussions with working analysts using structured analytic techniques. Research by the Intelligence Community on the benefits and costs associated with all aspects of the use of structured analytic techniques is strongly recommended, as is discussed in chapter 13.

analyst contributed to Intellipedia was determined by "a more profound rationale than being a member of a particular age group." Some older analysts contributed and some from the younger generation did not. The Defense Intelligence Agency's Knowledge Lab hypothesized that this depends in part on how analysts view their responsibility to the customer.

> For example, if an analyst believes that the customer is better served when the uncertainty and diversity associated with knowledge is revealed to the customer, then the analyst is more likely to share and collaborate throughout the knowledge creation process. If the analyst believes that the customer is better served by being certain about what is delivered, then the analyst is more likely to wait until near the final stage of product delivery before sharing. For the former, collaborative behavior is not constrained by a need for ownership. For the latter, collaborative behavior is constrained by ownership needs.[8]

We note that willingness to share in a collaborative environment is also conditioned by the sensitivity of the information that one is working with.

1.4 HISTORY OF STRUCTURED ANALYTIC TECHNIQUES

The first use of the term "Structured Analytic Techniques" in the Intelligence Community was in 2005. However, the origin of the concept goes back to the 1980s, when the eminent teacher of intelligence analysis, Jack Davis, first began teaching and writing about what he called "alternative analysis."[9] The term referred to the evaluation of alternative explanations or hypotheses, better understanding of other cultures, and analyzing events from the other country's point of view rather than by mirror imaging. In the mid-1980s some initial efforts were made to initiate the use of more alternative analytic techniques in the CIA's Directorate of Intelligence. Under the direction of Robert Gates, then CIA Deputy Director for Intelligence, analysts employed several new techniques to generate scenarios of dramatic political change, track political instability, and anticipate military coups. Douglas MacEachin, Deputy Director for Intelligence from 1993 to 1996, supported new standards for systematic and transparent analysis that helped pave the path to further change.[10]

---

8. Nancy M. Dixon and Laura A. McNamara, "Our Experience with Intellipedia: An Ethnographic Study at the Defense Intelligence Agency." February 5, 2008. https://cfwebprod.sandia.gov/cfdocs/CCIM/docs/DixonMcNamara.pdf.

9. Information on the history of the terms "alternative analysis" and "structured analytic techniques" is based on information provided by Jack Davis, Randy Pherson, and Roger Z. George, all of whom were key players in developing and teaching these techniques at the CIA.

10. See Heuer, *Psychology of Intelligence Analysis*, xvii–xix.

The term "alternative analysis" became widely used in the late 1990s after Adm. David Jeremiah's postmortem analysis of the Intelligence Community's failure to foresee India's 1998 nuclear test, a U.S. congressional commission's review of the Intelligence Community's global missile forecast in 1998, and a report from the CIA Inspector General that focused higher level attention on the state of the Directorate of Intelligence's analytic tradecraft. The Jeremiah report specifically encouraged increased use of what it called "red team" analysis.

When the Sherman Kent School for Intelligence Analysis at the CIA was created in 2000 to improve the effectiveness of intelligence analysis, John McLaughlin, then Deputy Director for Intelligence, tasked the school to consolidate techniques for doing what was then referred to as "alternative analysis." In response to McLaughlin's tasking, the Kent School developed a compilation of techniques, and the CIA's Directorate of Intelligence started teaching these techniques in a class that later evolved into the Advanced Analytic Tools and Techniques Workshop. The course was subsequently expanded to include analysts from the Defense Intelligence Agency and other elements of the Intelligence Community.

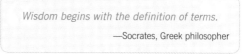

Wisdom begins with the definition of terms.

—Socrates, Greek philosopher

The various investigative commissions that followed the surprise terrorist attacks of September 11, 2001, and then the erroneous analysis of Iraq's possession of weapons of mass destruction, cranked up the pressure for more alternative approaches to intelligence analysis. For example, the Intelligence Reform Act of 2004 assigned to the Director of National Intelligence "responsibility for ensuring that, as appropriate, elements of the intelligence community conduct alternative analysis (commonly referred to as 'red-team' analysis) of the information and conclusions in intelligence analysis."

Over time, however, analysts who misunderstood or resisted this approach came to interpret alternative analysis as simply meaning an alternative to the normal way that analysis is done, implying that these alternative procedures are needed only occasionally in exceptional circumstances when an analysis is of critical importance. Kent School instructors had to explain that the techniques are not alternatives to traditional analysis, but that they are central to good analysis and should be integrated into the normal routine—instilling rigor and structure into the analysts' everyday work process.

In 2004, when the Kent School decided to update its training materials based on lessons learned during the previous several years, Randy Pherson and Roger Z. George were among the drafters. "There was a sense that the name alternative analysis was too limiting and not descriptive enough. At least a dozen different analytic techniques were all rolled into one term, so we decided to find a name that was more encompassing and suited this broad array of approaches to analysis."[11] Kathy Pherson is credited with coming up with the name "structured analytic techniques" during a dinner table conversation with her husband, Randy. Roger George organized the techniques into three categories: diagnostic techniques, contrarian techniques, and imagination techniques. The term "structured analytic techniques" became official in June 2005, when updated training materials were formally approved.

The Directorate of Intelligence's senior management became a strong supporter of the structured analytic techniques and took active measures to facilitate and promote this approach. The term is now used throughout the Intelligence Community—and increasingly in academia and allied intelligence services overseas. Senior analysts with whom we have spoken believe the term "alternative analysis" should be relegated to past history. It is often misunderstood, and, even when understood correctly, it covers only part of what is now regarded as structured analytic techniques.

One thing cannot be changed, however, in the absence of new legislation. The Director of National Intelligence (DNI) is still responsible under the Intelligence Reform Act of 2004 for ensuring that elements of the Intelligence Community conduct alternative analysis. For purposes of compliance with this act of Congress, the DNI interprets the law as applying to both alternative analysis and structured analytic techniques.[12] We recommend avoiding use of the term "alternative analysis" in any other context.

1.5 WHAT'S IN THIS BOOK?

Chapter 2 ("Building a Taxonomy") defines the domain of structured analytic techniques by describing how it differs from three other major categories of intelligence analysis methodology. It presents a taxonomy with eight distinct categories of structured analytic techniques. The categories are based on how each set of techniques contributes to better intelligence analysis.

Chapter 3 ("Selecting Structured Techniques") describes the criteria we used for selecting techniques for inclusion in this book, discusses which techniques might be learned first and used the most, and provides a guide for matching techniques to analyst needs. Analysts using this guide answer twelve abbreviated questions about what the analyst wants or needs to do. An affirmative answer to any question directs the analyst to the appropriate chapter(s) where the analyst can quickly zero in on the most appropriate technique(s).

---

11. Personal communication to Richards Heuer from Roger Z. George, October 9, 2007.

12. E-mail to Richards Heuer from Steven Rieber, ODNI/AIS, October 9, 2007.

Chapters 4 through 11 each describe one taxonomic category of techniques, which taken together cover fifty different techniques. Each of these chapters starts with a description of that particular category of techniques and how it helps to mitigate known cognitive limitations or pitfalls that cause analytic errors. It then provides a one-paragraph overview of each technique. This is followed by a detailed discussion of each technique including when to use it, value added, potential pitfalls when appropriate, the method, relationship to other techniques, and sources.

Readers who go through these eight chapters of techniques from start to finish may perceive some overlap. This repetition is for the convenience of those who use this book as a reference book and seek out individual sections or chapters. The reader seeking only an overview of the techniques as a whole can save time by reading the introduction to each technique chapter, the one-paragraph overview of each technique, and the full descriptions of only those specific techniques that pique the reader's interest.

Highlights of the eight chapters of techniques are as follows:

* Chapter 4 ("Decomposition and Visualization") covers the basics such as Checklists, Sorting, Ranking, Classification, several types of Mapping, Matrices, and Networks.

* Chapter 5 ("Idea Generation") presents several types of brainstorming. That includes Nominal Group Technique, a form of brainstorming that has been used rarely in the Intelligence Community but should be used when there is concern that a brainstorming session might be dominated by a particularly aggressive analyst or constrained by the presence of a senior officer. A Cross-Impact Matrix supports a group learning exercise about the relationships in a complex system.

* Chapter 6 ("Scenarios and Indicators") covers three scenario techniques and the Indicators used to monitor which scenario seems to be developing. There is a new technique called the Indicators Validator developed by Randy Pherson.

* Chapter 7 ("Hypothesis Generation and Testing") includes three techniques for hypothesis generation, Diagnostic Reasoning, Analysis of Competing Hypotheses, Argument Mapping, and Deception Detection.

* Chapter 8 ("Assessment of Cause and Effect") includes the widely used Key Assumptions Check and an important new technique called Structured Analogies, which comes from the literature on forecasting the

future. Other techniques of particular interest include Role Playing, Red Hat Analysis, Outside-In Thinking, and a policy forecasting model.

* Chapter 9 ("Challenge Analysis") helps analysts break away from an established mental model to imagine a situation or problem from a different perspective. Two important new techniques developed by the authors, Premortem Analysis and Structured Self-Critique, give analytic teams viable ways to imagine how their own analysis might be wrong. What if? Analysis and High Impact/Low Probability Analysis are tactful ways to suggest that the conventional wisdom could be wrong. Devil's Advocacy, Red Team Analysis, and the Delphi Method can be used by management to actively seek alternative answers.

* Chapter 10 ("Conflict Management") explains that confrontation between conflicting opinions is to be encouraged, but it must be managed so that it becomes a learning experience rather than an emotional battle. Two new techniques are introduced, including Adversarial Collaboration (actually a family of techniques) and an original approach to Structured Debate in which debaters refute the opposing argument rather than supporting their own.

* Chapter 11 ("Decision Support") includes four techniques, including Decision Matrix, that help managers, commanders, planners, and policymakers make choices or tradeoffs between competing goals, values, or preferences. This chapter also includes Richards Heuer's new Complexity Manager technique.

As previously noted, analysis in the U.S. Intelligence Community is now in a transitional stage from a mental activity performed predominantly by a sole analyst to a collaborative team or group activity. Chapter 12, entitled "Practitioner's Guide to Collaboration," discusses, among other things, how to include in the analytic process the rapidly growing social networks of area and functional specialists who are geographically distributed throughout the Intelligence Community. It proposes that most analysis be done in two phases: a divergent analysis or creative phase with broad participation by a social network using a wiki, followed by a convergent analysis phase and final report done by a small analytic team.

How can we know that the use of structured analytic techniques does, in fact, provide the claimed benefits for intelligence analysis? As we discuss in chapter 13 ("Evaluation of Structured Analytic Techniques"), there are two approaches to answering this question—logical reasoning and empirical research. The logical reasoning approach starts with the large body of psychological research on the limitations of human memory and perception and pitfalls in human thought processes. If a structured analytic technique is specifically intended to mitigate or avoid one of the proven problems in human thought processes, and that technique appears to be successful in doing so, that technique can be said to have "face validity." The growing popularity of several of these techniques would argue that they are perceived by analysts—and their customers—as providing distinct added value in a number of different ways. Although these are strong arguments, the Intelligence Community has not yet done the research or surveys needed to document them.

Another approach to evaluation of these techniques is empirical testing. This is often done by constructing experiments that compare analyses in which a specific technique is used with comparable analyses in which the technique is not used. Our research found that such testing done outside the Intelligence Community is generally of limited value, as the experimental conditions varied significantly from the conditions under which the same techniques are used in the Intelligence Community. Chapter 13 proposes a broader approach to the validation of structured analytic techniques. It calls for structured interviews, observation, and surveys in addition to experiments conducted under conditions that closely simulate how these techniques are used in the Intelligence Community. Chapter 13 also recommends formation of a separate organizational unit to conduct such research as well as other tasks to support the use of structured analytic techniques throughout the Intelligence Community.

The final chapter, "Vision of the Future," begins by using a new structured technique, Complexity Manager, to analyze the prospects for future growth in the use of structured analytic techniques during the next five years, until 2015. It identifies and discusses the interactions between ten variables that will either support or hinder the growing use of structured techniques during this time frame. The DNI paper, *Vision 2015: A Globally Networked and Integrated Intelligence Enterprise,* presented a vision for what should be in place in the year 2015. The second part of this final chapter asks the reader to imagine it is now 2015. It then provides an imaginary description of how structured analysis is being done at that time and discusses how these changes came about.

1.6 AGENDA FOR THE FUTURE

A principal theme of this book is that structured analytic techniques facilitate effective collaboration among analysts. These techniques guide the dialogue among analysts with common interests as they share evidence and alternative perspectives on the meaning and significance of this evidence. Just as these techniques provide structure to our individual thought processes, they also structure the interaction of analysts within a small team or group. Because structured techniques are designed to generate and evaluate divergent information and new ideas, they can help avoid the common pitfalls and pathologies that commonly beset other small group processes. In other words, structured analytic techniques are enablers of collaboration. These techniques and collaboration fit together like hand in glove, and they should be promoted and developed together.

To promote greater interagency collaboration and use of structured analysis at the working level, the top levels of the Intelligence Community must set a good example. One high-profile way to do this is to make the National Intelligence Council (NIC) a centerpiece for analytic transformation. The NIC produces the Intelligence Community's most important projects. It needs interagency collaboration as well as coordination for all its products, and the use of structured analytic techniques should play a significant role in preparing most if not all of these products. One often hears it said that the current procedure for coordinating national estimates at the end of the analytic process needs to be replaced, or at least supplemented, with collaboration throughout the process leading up to the final coordination meeting.

To implement such a change, we propose that the Director of National Intelligence (DNI) create a new position in the NIC, or under the DNI for Analysis (DNI/A), with the functions of a vice chair or deputy for analytic tradecraft. The new vice chair, or whatever this person is called, would help to plan and oversee the appropriate use of collaboration and structured analytic techniques early and throughout the estimative process. New members of the NIC without prior experience with structured analytic techniques will need some training to acquaint them with these tools. The vice chair should also be responsible for initiating and managing a program for after-action review of lessons learned after each major paper or project produced under the auspices of the DNI/A or the NIC, including National Intelligence Estimates. After identifying lessons learned, the vice chair should then be responsible for ensuring that these lessons are applied in subsequent Intelligence Community projects. Making the same organization responsible for both the learning process and the implementation of what is learned is the most effective approach to organizational learning.[13]

The creation of a new center for analytic tradecraft within the DNI/A would be another important step on the agenda for change. It would provide a much-needed institutional foundation for the continuing improvement of

---

13. Nancy M. Dixon, "The Problem and the Fix for the US Intelligence Agencies' Lessons Learned," July 1, 2009, www.nancydixonblog .com.

analytic tradecraft and collaboration. The center should have the following responsibilities:

* Implementing the research program described in chapter 13 for testing the validity and value of existing analytic techniques and for developing and testing new tools and techniques. This would be its primary responsibility.

* Providing guidance and assistance as needed to tradecraft cells throughout the Intelligence Community. The tradecraft cells created by the CIA set an excellent example, and comparable cells should be created to serve similar functions throughout the Intelligence Community.

* Establishing and managing an Intelligence Community–wide knowledge management system for the creation, capture, storage, and sharing of lessons learned about analytic techniques and methods. The tradecraft cells throughout the Intelligence Community should play a key role in the collection and dissemination of lessons learned.

* Encouraging the formation of analytic "communities of interest" and ensuring that they have appropriate technical support.

A further suggestion is that the vice chair of the NIC for analytic tradecraft be dual-hatted, also holding the position of chief or deputy chief of the proposed new center for analytic tradecraft. This would ensure that the NIC has appropriate support for its use of tradecraft, while also ensuring that the research program of the new center will be guided in a direction most directly relevant to the needs of the working analyst.

These recommendations are supported by recent research sponsored by the Defense Intelligence Agency on the implementation (actually failure to implement) of lessons learned. This research found a "disconnect between gathering lessons and implementing them" in the Intelligence Community in general and in the Defense Intelligence Agency in particular. It concluded that lessons learned from research are far more likely to be implemented if those responsible for implementing the findings are directly involved in the research that develops the findings and recommendations.[14] We have tried to follow that sound guidance in making our recommendations. Relevant findings of this study are discussed in more detail in the final section of chapter 13.

---

14. Ibid.

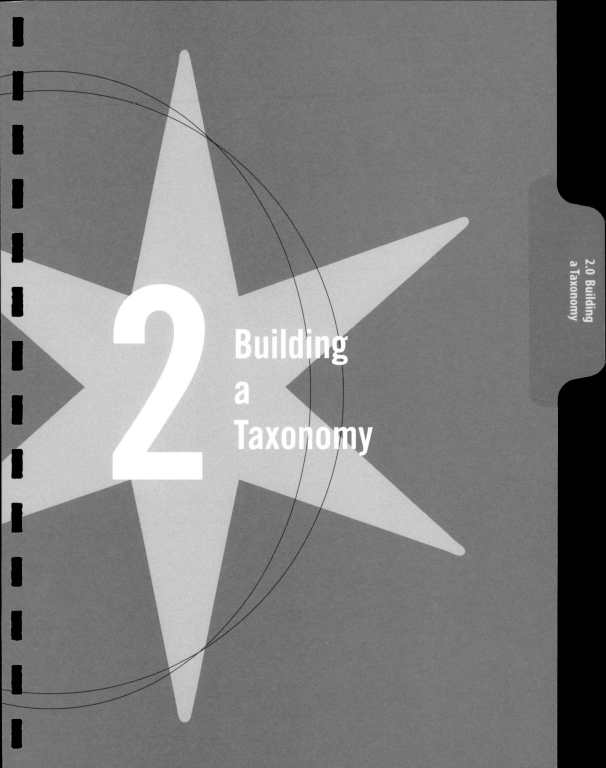

2

Building
a
Taxonomy

2

Building a Taxonomy

2.1 Four Categories of Analytic Methods   [21]

2.2 Taxonomy of Structured Analytic Techniques   [24]

CHAPTER 2

Building a Taxonomy

A taxonomy is a classification of all elements of the domain of information or knowledge. It defines a domain by identifying, naming, and categorizing all the various objects in this space. The objects are organized into related groups based on some factor common to each object in the group. This book presents a taxonomy that defines the domain of structured analysis, which is but one part of the larger domain of intelligence analysis methods in general.

Figure 2.0 shows four broad categories of analytic methods. The focus of this book, the structured analysis category, is broken down further into eight categories. This chapter describes the rationale for these four broad categories and identifies the eight categories of structured analysis.

The word taxonomy comes from the Greek *taxis* meaning arrangement, division, or order and *nomos* meaning law. Classic examples of a taxonomy are Carolus Linnaeus's hierarchical classification of all living organisms by kingdom, phylum, class, order, family, genus, and species that is widely used in the biological sciences, and the periodic table of elements used by chemists. A library catalogue is also considered a taxonomy, as it starts with a list of related categories that are then progressively broken down into finer categories.

Development of a taxonomy is an important step in organizing knowledge and furthering the development of any particular discipline. Rob Johnston developed a taxonomy of variables that influence intelligence analysis but did not go into any depth on analytic techniques or methods. He noted that "a taxonomy differentiates domains by specifying the scope of inquiry, codifying naming

| Figure 2.0 | Taxonomy Outline |

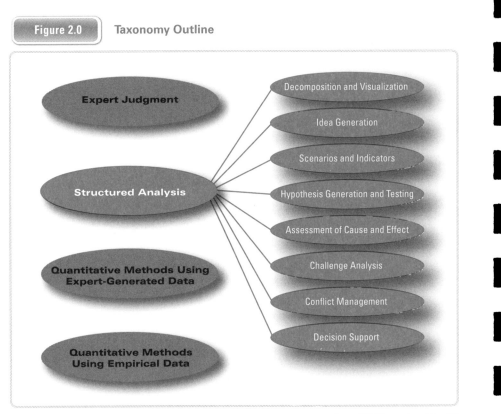

Source: 2009 Pherson Associates, LLC.

conventions, identifying areas of interest, helping to set research priorities, and often leading to new theories. Taxonomies are signposts, indicating what is known and what has yet to be discovered."[1]

Robert Clark has described a taxonomy of intelligence sources.[2] He also categorizes some analytic techniques commonly used in intelligence analysis, but not to the extent of creating a taxonomy. To the best of our knowledge, a taxonomy of analytic methods for intelligence analysis has not previously been developed, although taxonomies have been developed to classify research methods used in forecasting,[3]

---

1. Rob Johnston, *Analytic Culture in the U.S. Intelligence Community* (Washington, D.C.: CIA Center for the Study of Intelligence, 2005), 34.

2. Robert M. Clark, *Intelligence Analysis: A Target-Centric Approach*, 2nd ed. (Washington, D.C.: CQ Press, 2007), 84.

3. Forecasting Principles Web site, www.forecastingprinciples.com/files/pdf/methodsselectionchart.pdf.

operations research,[4] information systems,[5] visualization tools,[6] electronic commerce,[7] knowledge elicitation,[8] and cognitive task analysis.[9]

After examining taxonomies of methods used in other fields, we found that there is no single right way to organize a taxonomy—only different ways that are more or less useful in achieving a specified goal. In this case, our goal is to gain a better understanding of the domain of structured analytic techniques, investigate how these techniques contribute to providing a better analytic product, and consider how they relate to the needs of analysts. The objective has been to identify various techniques that are currently available, identify or develop additional potentially useful techniques, and help analysts compare and select the best technique for solving any specific analytic problem. Standardization of terminology for structured analytic techniques will facilitate collaboration across agency boundaries during the use of these techniques.

2.1 FOUR CATEGORIES OF ANALYTIC METHODS

Intelligence analysts employ a wide range of methods to deal with an even wider range of subjects. Although this book focuses on the developing field of structured analysis, it is necessary to identify some initial categorization of all the methods in order to see where structured analysis fits in. Many researchers write of only two general approaches to analysis: qualitative vs. quantitative, intuitive vs. empirical, or intuitive vs. scientific. Others might grant that there are three—intuitive, structured, and scientific.

> *The first step of science is to know one thing from another. This knowledge consists in their specific distinctions; but in order that it may be fixed and permanent, distinct names must be given to different things, and those names must be recorded and remembered."*
>
> —Carolus Linnaeus, *Systema Naturae* (1738)

Whether intelligence analysis is, or should be, an art or science is one of the long-standing debates in the literature on intelligence analysis. As we see it, intelligence analysis has aspects of both

---

4. Russell W. Frenske, "A Taxonomy for Operations Research," *Operations Research* 19, no. 1 (January–February 1971).

5. Kai R. T. Larson, "A Taxonomy of Antecedents of Information Systems Success: Variable Analysis Studies," *Journal of Management Information Systems* 20, no. 2 (Fall 2003).

6. Ralph Lengler and Martin J. Epler, "A Periodic Table of Visualization Methods," undated, www.visual-literacy.org/periodic_table/periodic_table.html.

7. Roger Clarke, *Appropriate Research Methods for Electronic Commerce* (Canberra, Australia: Xanax Consultancy Pty Ltd., 2000), http://anu.edu.au/people/Roger.Clarke/EC/ResMeth.html.

8. Robert R. Hoffman, Nigel R. Shadbolt, A. Mike Burton, and Gary Klein, "Eliciting Knowledge from Experts," *Organizational Behavior and Human Decision Processes* 62 (May 1995): 129–158.

9. Robert R. Hoffman and Laura G. Militello, *Perspectives on Cognitive Task Analysis: Historical Origins and Modern Communities of Practice* (Boca Raton, Fla.: CRC Press/Taylor and Francis, 2008); and Beth Crandall, Gary Klein, and Robert R. Hoffman, *Working Minds: A Practitioner's Guide to Cognitive Task Analysis* (Cambridge, Mass.: MIT Press, 2006).

spheres. The range of activities that fall under the rubric of intelligence analysis spans the entire range of human cognitive abilities, and it is not possible to divide it into just two categories, art and science, or to say that it is only one or the other. The extent to which any part of intelligence analysis is either art or science is entirely dependent upon how one defines "art" and "science."

The taxonomy described here posits four functionally distinct methodological approaches to intelligence analysis. These approaches are distinguished by the nature of the analytic methods used, the type of quantification if any, the type of data that are available, and the type of training that is expected or required. Although each method is distinct, the borders between them can be blurry.

*   Expert judgment: This is the traditional way most intelligence analysis has been done. When done well, expert judgment combines subject matter expertise with critical thinking. Evidentiary reasoning, historical method, case study method, and reasoning by analogy are included in the expert judgment category.[10] *The key characteristic that distinguishes expert judgment from structured analysis is that it is usually an individual effort in which the reasoning remains largely in the mind of the individual analyst until it is written down in a draft report.* Training in this type of analysis is generally provided through postgraduate education, especially in the social sciences and liberal arts, and often along with some country or language expertise.

*   Structured analysis: Each structured analytic technique involves a step-by-step process that externalizes the analyst's thinking in a manner that makes it readily apparent to others, thereby enabling it to be reviewed, discussed, and critiqued piece by piece, or step by step. For this reason, structured analysis often becomes a collaborative effort in which the transparency of the analytic process exposes participating analysts to divergent or conflicting perspectives. This type of analysis is believed to mitigate the adverse impact on analysis of known cognitive limitations and pitfalls. Frequently used techniques include Structured Brainstorming, Scenarios, Indicators, Analysis of Competing Hypotheses, and Key Assumptions Check. Structured techniques can be used by analysts who have not been trained in statistics, advanced mathematics, or the hard sciences. For most analysts, training in structured analytic techniques is obtained only within the Intelligence Community. This situation is now changing, however; quite a few colleges and universities have initiated programs in intelligence or homeland security analysis, and some of the course curricula include structured techniques, such as Analysis of Competing Hypotheses.

10. Reasoning by analogy can also be a structured technique called Structured Analogies, as described in chapter 8.

✳ Quantitative methods using expert-generated data: Analysts often lack the empirical data needed to analyze an intelligence problem. In the absence of empirical data, many methods are designed to use quantitative data generated by expert opinion, especially subjective probability judgments. Special procedures are used to elicit these judgments. This category includes methods such as Bayesian inference, dynamic modeling, and simulation. Training in the use of these methods is provided through graduate education in fields such as mathematics, information science, operations research, business, or the sciences.

✳ Quantitative methods using empirical data: Quantifiable empirical data are so different from expert-generated data that the methods and types of problems the data are used to analyze are also quite different. Econometric modeling is one common example of this method. Empirical data are collected by various types of sensors and are used, for example, in analysis of weapons systems. Training is generally obtained through graduate education in statistics, economics, or the hard sciences.

No one of these methods is better or more effective than another. All are needed in various circumstances to optimize the odds of finding the right answer. The use of multiple methods during the course of a single analytic project should be the norm, not the exception. For example, even a highly quantitative technical analysis may entail assumptions about motivation, intent, or capability that are best handled with expert judgment and/or structured analysis. One of the structured techniques for idea generation might be used to identify the variables to be included in a dynamic model that uses expert-generated data to quantify these variables.

Of these four methods, structured analysis is the new kid on the block, so to speak; so it is useful to consider how it relates to the other methods, especially how it relates to expert judgment. Expert judgment combines subject-matter expertise and critical thinking in an activity that takes place largely in an analyst's head. Although the analyst may gain input from others, the analytic product is frequently perceived as the product of a single analyst, and the analyst tends to feel "ownership" of his or her analytic product. The work of a single analyst is particularly susceptible to the wide range of cognitive pitfalls described in *Psychology of Intelligence Analysis*.[11]

Structured analysis follows a step-by-step process that can be used by an individual analyst, but it is done more commonly as a group process, as that is

---

11. Richards J. Heuer Jr., *Psychology of Intelligence Analysis* (Washington, D.C.: CIA Center for the Study of Intelligence, 1999), reprinted by Pherson Associates, LLC, 2007.

how the principal benefits are gained. As we discussed in the previous chapter, structured techniques guide the dialogue between analysts with common interests as they work step-by-step through an analytic problem. The critical point is that this approach exposes participants with various types and levels of expertise to alternative ideas, evidence, or mental models early in the analytic process. It can help the experts avoid some of the common cognitive pitfalls. The structured group process that identifies and assesses alternative perspectives can also help to avoid "groupthink," the most common problem of small-group processes.

When used by a group or a team, structured techniques can become a mechanism for information sharing and group learning that helps to compensate for gaps or weaknesses in subject-matter expertise. This is especially useful for complex projects that require a synthesis of multiple types of expertise.

2.2 TAXONOMY OF STRUCTURED ANALYTIC TECHNIQUES

Structured techniques have been used by Intelligence Community methodology specialists and some analysts in selected specialties for many years, but the broad and general use of these techniques by the average analyst is a relatively new approach to intelligence analysis. The driving forces behind the development and use of these techniques are (1) an increased appreciation of cognitive limitations and pitfalls that make intelligence analysis so difficult, (2) prominent intelligence failures that have prompted reexamination of how intelligence analysis is generated, (3) policy support and technical support for interagency collaboration from the Office of the Director of National Intelligence, and (4) a desire by policymakers who receive analysis that it be more transparent as to how the conclusions were reached.

Considering that the Intelligence Community started focusing on structured techniques in order to improve analysis, it is fitting to categorize these techniques by the various ways they can help achieve this goal. Structured analytic techniques can mitigate some of the human cognitive limitations, side-step some of the well-known analytic pitfalls, and explicitly confront the problems associated with unquestioned assumptions and mental models. They can ensure that assumptions, preconceptions, and mental models are not taken for granted but are explicitly examined and tested. They can support the decision-making process, and the use and documentation of these techniques can facilitate information sharing and collaboration.

A secondary goal when categorizing the structured techniques was to correlate categories with different types of common analytic tasks. This makes it possible to match specific techniques to individual analyst's needs, as will be discussed in chapter 3. There are, however, some techniques that fit comfortably in several categories because they serve multiple analytic functions.

The eight categories of structured analytic techniques, which are listed below, are described in detail in chapters 4–11. The introduction to each chapter describes how that specific category of techniques helps to improve analysis.

Decomposition and Visualization (chapter 4)

Assessment of Cause and Effect (chapter 8)

Idea Generation (chapter 5)

Challenge Analysis (chapter 9)

Scenarios and Indicators (chapter 6)

Conflict Management (chapter 10)

Hypothesis Generation and Testing (chapter 7)

Decision Support (chapter 11)

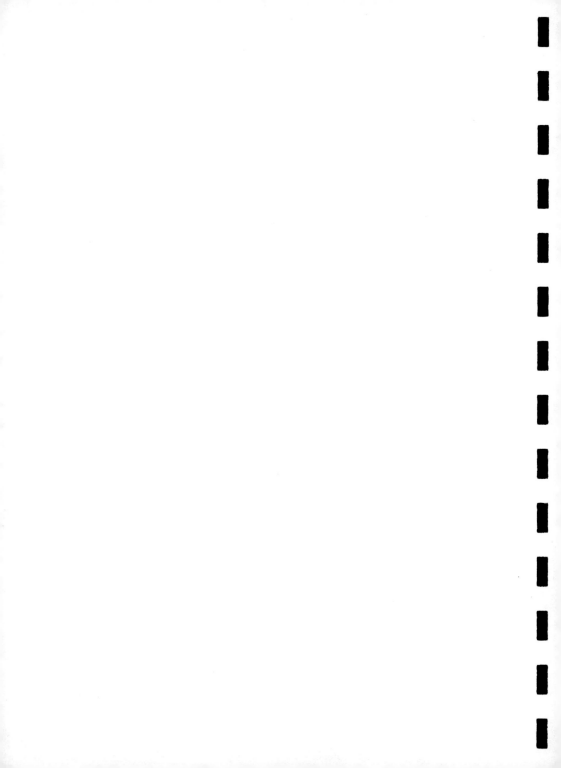

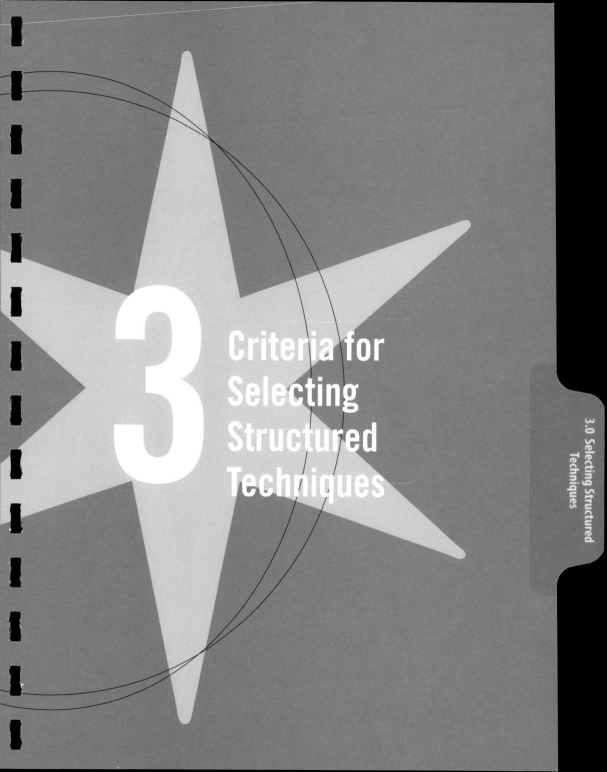

3 Criteria for Selecting Structured Techniques

3

Criteria for Selecting Structured Techniques

3.1 Selection of Techniques for This Book   [29]

3.2 Techniques Every Analyst Should Master   [30]

3.3 Common Errors in Selecting Techniques   [33]

3.4 One Project, Multiple Techniques   [34]

3.5 Structured Technique Selection Guide   [34]

Criteria for Selecting Structured Techniques

This chapter provides analysts with a practical guide to identifying the various techniques that are most likely to meet their needs. It also:

* Describes the criteria and process we used for selecting techniques to be included in this book.

* Identifies a small set of techniques that are used or should be used most frequently and that every intelligence analyst should know. These may be of assistance to instructors who must be selective in determining which techniques to teach.

* Lists a number of common mistakes analysts make when deciding which technique or techniques to use for a specific project.

* Discusses the use of multiple techniques for a single project.

3.1 SELECTION OF TECHNIQUES FOR THIS BOOK

The techniques discussed in the following eight chapters are limited to ones that meet the definition of structured analytic techniques as described in chapter 2. Although the focus is on techniques for all-source political and strategic intelligence analysis, many of the techniques described in this book have wide applicability to tactical military analysis, law enforcement intelligence analysis, homeland security, business consulting, financial planning, and complex decision making in any field. The book focuses on techniques that can be used by a single analyst working alone or preferably with a small group or team of analysts. Usually all the analyst needs is a keyboard or just pen and paper, though software is often useful.

Techniques that require a major project of the type usually outsourced to an outside expert or company are not included. Several interesting techniques that were recommended to us were not included for this reason. A number of techniques that tend to be used *exclusively* for a single type of analysis, such as tactical military, law enforcement, or business consulting, have not been included.

In this collection of techniques we build on work previously done in the Intelligence Community. Nineteen of the techniques described here were previously written up in training materials used either by the CIA's Sherman Kent School for Intelligence Analysis or the Defense Intelligence Agency, but in most cases we have edited those techniques for this book. Many of those techniques were originally developed or refined by one of the authors, Randy Pherson, when he was teaching structured techniques at the Sherman Kent School and elsewhere in the Intelligence Community.

Fifteen techniques were newly created or adapted to intelligence analyst needs by either Richards Heuer or Randy Pherson to fill perceived needs and gaps in what was available. To select the most appropriate additional techniques for inclusion in this book, Heuer reviewed a large number of books and Web sites dealing with intelligence analysis methodology, qualitative methods in general, decision making, problem solving, competitive intelligence, law enforcement intelligence, forecasting or futures research, and social science research in general. Given the immensity of this literature, there can be no guarantee that nothing was missed. For some techniques, Heuer drew on his personal experience from thirty years ago when he headed a CIA unit responsible for identifying and testing new analytic methods.

We provide specific guidance on how to use each technique, but this guidance is not written in stone. There is more than one way to implement many of these techniques, and some techniques are known by several different names. The leader of one analytic tradecraft cell told one of the authors that he seldom uses a technique the same way twice. He adapts techniques to the requirements of the specific problem, and his ability to do that effectively is a measure of his experience.

The names of some techniques are normally capitalized while many are not. For consistency and to make them stand out, the names of all techniques described in this book are capitalized.

3.2 TECHNIQUES EVERY ANALYST SHOULD MASTER

The average intelligence analyst is not expected to know how to use every technique in this book. All analysts should, however, understand the functions performed by various types of techniques and recognize the analytic circumstances in which it is advisable to use them. An analyst can gain this knowledge by reading the introductions to each of the technique chapters and the one-paragraph overviews of each technique. Tradecraft or methodology specialists should be available to assist when needed in the actual implementation of these techniques. The CIA, for example, has made good progress in supporting such techniques through its tradecraft cells.

There are, however, a small number of core techniques that beginning analysts should be trained to use, because they are needed so frequently and are widely applicable across the various types of intelligence analysis—strategic, tactical, law enforcement, and business. These core techniques are identified and described briefly in the following paragraphs.

Structured Brainstorming (chapter 5): Perhaps the most commonly used technique, Structured Brainstorming is a simple exercise often employed at the beginning of an analytic project to elicit relevant information or insight from a small group of knowledgeable analysts. The group's goal might be to identify a list of such things as relevant variables, driving forces, a full range of hypotheses, key players or stakeholders, available evidence or sources of information, potential solutions to a problem, potential outcomes or scenarios, potential responses by an adversary or competitor to some action or situation, or, for law enforcement, potential suspects or avenues of investigation. Analysts should be aware of Nominal Group Technique as an alternative to Structured Brainstorming when there is concern that a regular brainstorming session may be dominated by a senior officer or that junior personnel may be reluctant to speak up.

Cross-Impact Matrix (chapter 5): If the brainstorming identifies a list of relevant variables, driving forces, or key players, the next step should be to create a Cross-Impact Matrix and use it as an aid to help the group visualize and then discuss the relationship between each pair of variables, driving forces, or players. This is a learning exercise that enables a team or group to develop a common base of knowledge about, for example, each variable and how it relates to each other variable. It is a very simple but effective learning exercise that will be new to most intelligence analysts.

Key Assumptions Check (chapter 8): One of the most commonly used techniques is the Key Assumptions Check, which requires analysts to explicitly list and question the most important working assumptions underlying their analysis. Any explanation of current events or estimate of future developments requires the interpretation of incomplete, ambiguous, or potentially deceptive evidence. To fill in the gaps, analysts typically make assumptions about such things as another country's intentions or capabilities, the way governmental processes usually work in that country, the relative strength of political forces, the trustworthiness or accuracy of key sources, the validity of previous analyses on the same subject, or the presence or absence of relevant changes in the context in which the activity is occurring. It is important that such assumptions be explicitly recognized and questioned.

Indicators (chapter 6): Indicators are observable or potentially observable actions or events that are monitored to detect or evaluate change over time. For example, indicators might be used to measure changes toward an undesirable condition such as political instability, a humanitarian crisis, or an impending attack. They can also point toward a desirable condition such as economic or democratic reform. The special value of indicators is that they create an awareness that prepares an analyst's mind to recognize the earliest signs of significant change that might otherwise be overlooked. Developing an effective set of indicators is more difficult than it might seem. The Indicator Validator helps analysts assess the diagnosticity of their indicators.

Analysis of Competing Hypotheses (chapter 7): This technique requires analysts to start with a full set of plausible hypotheses rather than with a single most likely hypothesis. Analysts then take each item of evidence, one at a time, and judge its consistency or inconsistency with each hypothesis. The idea is to refute hypotheses rather than confirm them. The most likely hypothesis is the one with the least evidence against it, not the most evidence for it. This process applies a key element of scientific method to intelligence analysis. The software for the technique is available to the Intelligence Community and can be downloaded from a Web site at no cost. The software includes a tutorial for self-learning, but some training and facilitation during the initial use is recommended.[1]

Premortem Analysis and Structured Self-Critique (chapter 9): These two easy-to-use techniques enable a small team of analysts who have been working together on any type of future-oriented analysis to challenge effectively the accuracy of their own conclusions. Premortem Analysis uses a form of reframing, in which restating the question or problem from another perspective enables one to see it in a different way and come up with different answers. Imagine yourself several years in the future. You suddenly learn from an unimpeachable source that your original estimate was wrong. Then imagine what could have happened to cause your estimate to be wrong. Looking back to explain something that has happened is much easier than looking into the future to forecast what will happen.

---

1. The software is available at www.pherson.org/ACH.html and www2.parc.com/istl/projects/ach/ach.html.

With Structured Self-Critique, analysts respond to a list of questions about a variety of factors, including sources of uncertainty, analytic processes that were used, critical assumptions, diagnosticity of evidence, information gaps, and the potential for deception. Rigorous use of both of these techniques can help prevent a future need for a postmortem.

What If? Analysis (chapter 9): In conducting a What If? Analysis, one imagines that an unexpected event has happened and then, with the benefit of "hindsight," analyzes how it could have happened and considers the potential consequences. This type of exercise creates an awareness that prepares the analyst's mind to recognize early signs of a significant change, and it may enable a decision maker to plan ahead for that contingency. A What If? Analysis can be a tactful way of alerting decision makers to the possibility that they may be wrong.

3.3 COMMON ERRORS IN SELECTING TECHNIQUES

The value and accuracy of an analytic product depends in part upon selection of the most appropriate technique or combination of techniques for doing the analysis. Unfortunately, it is easy for analysts to go astray when selecting the best method. Lacking effective guidance, analysts are vulnerable to various influences:[2]

* College or graduate-school recipe: Analysts are inclined to use the tools they learned in college or graduate school whether or not those tools are the best application for the different context of intelligence analysis.

* Tool rut: Analysts are inclined to use whatever tool they already know or have readily available. Psychologist Abraham Maslow observed that "if the only tool you have is a hammer, it is tempting to treat everything as if it were a nail."[3]

* Convenience shopping: The analyst, guided by the evidence that happens to be available, uses a method appropriate for that evidence, rather than seeking out the evidence that is really needed to address the intelligence issue. In other words, the evidence may sometimes drive the technique selection instead of the analytic need driving the evidence collection.

---

2. The first three items here are from Craig S. Fleisher and Babette E. Bensoussan, *Strategic and Competitive Analysis: Methods and Techniques for Analyzing Business Competition* (Upper Saddle River, N.J.: Prentice Hall, 2003), 22–23.

3. Abraham Maslow, *Psychology of Science* (New York: Harper and Row, 1966). A similar quote is attributed to Abraham Kaplan, "Give a child a hammer and he suddenly discovers that everything he encounters needs pounding."

* Time constraints: Analysts can easily be overwhelmed by their in-boxes and the myriad tasks they have to perform in addition to their analytic workload. The temptation is to avoid techniques that would "take too much time." In reality, however, many useful techniques take very little time, even as little as a couple of hours. And the time analysts spend up front can save time in the long run by keeping them from going off on a wrong track or by substantially reducing the time required for editing and coordination—while helping them to produce higher quality and more compelling analysis than might otherwise be possible.

3.4 ONE PROJECT, MULTIPLE TECHNIQUES

Many projects require the use of multiple techniques, which is one reason this book includes fifty different techniques. Each technique may provide only one piece of a complex puzzle, and knowing how to put these pieces together for any specific project is part of the art of structured analysis. Separate techniques might be used for generating ideas, evaluating ideas, identifying assumptions, drawing conclusions, and challenging previously drawn conclusions. Chapter 12, "Practitioner's Guide to Collaboration," discusses stages in the collaborative process and the various techniques applicable at each stage.

Multiple techniques can also be used to check the accuracy and increase the confidence in an analytic conclusion. Research shows that forecasting accuracy is increased by combining "forecasts derived from methods that differ substantially and draw from different sources of information."[4] This is a particularly appropriate function for the Delphi Method (chapter 9), which is a structured process for eliciting judgments from a panel of outside experts. If a Delphi panel produces results similar to the internal analysis, one can have significantly greater confidence in those results. If the results differ, further research may be appropriate to understand why and evaluate the differences.

3.5 STRUCTURED TECHNIQUE SELECTION GUIDE

Analysts must be able, with minimal effort, to identify and learn how to use those techniques that best meet their needs and fit their styles. The guide outlined in this section consists of a list of twelve short questions about what an analyst may want or need to do. Following each question are the techniques that can help an analyst best perform a particular task. (*Note:* If only the chapter

---

4. J. Scott Armstrong, "Combining Forecasts," in *Principles of Forecasting*, ed. J. Scott Armstrong (New York: Springer Science+Business Media, 2001), 418–439.

number and title are given, all or almost all the techniques listed for that chapter are potentially relevant. If one or more techniques are shown in parentheses after the chapter number and title, only the listed techniques in that chapter are relevant.)

To find structured techniques that would be most applicable for a task, the analyst picks the statement(s) that best describes what he or she wants to do and then looks up the relevant chapter(s). Each chapter starts with a brief discussion of that category of analysis followed by a short, one-paragraph description of each technique in the chapter. The analyst should read the introductory discussion and the paragraph describing each technique before reading the full description of those techniques that seem most applicable to the specific issue. The description for each technique describes when, why, and how to use it. For many techniques, the information provided is sufficient for an analyst to use the technique. For more complex techniques, however, training in the technique or assistance by an experienced user of the technique is strongly recommended.

SELECTING THE RIGHT TECHNIQUE
Choose What You Want to Do

① Define the project?

Chapter 4: Decomposition and Visualization (Getting Started Checklist, Customer Checklist, Issue Redefinition)

Chapter 5: Idea Generation

② Get started? Generate a list, for example, of driving forces, variables to be considered, indicators, important players, historical precedents, sources of information, or questions to be answered? Organize, rank, score, or prioritize the list?

Chapter 4: Decomposition and Visualization

Chapter 5: Idea Generation

③ Examine and make sense of the data? Figure out what is going on?

Chapter 4: Decomposition and Visualization (Chronologies and Timelines, Sorting, Network Analysis, Mind Maps and Concept Maps)

Chapter 5: Idea Generation (Cross-Impact Matrix)

④ Explain a recent event; assess the most likely outcome of an evolving situation?

Chapter 7: Hypothesis Generation and Testing

Chapter 8: Assessment of Cause and Effect

Chapter 9: Challenge Analysis

⑤ Monitor a situation to gain early warning of events or changes that may affect critical interests? Avoid surprise?

Chapter 6: Scenarios and Indicators

Chapter 9: Challenge Analysis

⑥ Generate and test hypotheses?

Chapter 7: Hypothesis Generation and Testing

Chapter 8: Assessment of Cause and Effect (Key Assumptions Check)

⑦ Assess the possibility of deception?

Chapter 7: Hypothesis Generation and Testing (Analysis of Competing Hypotheses, Deception Detection)

Chapter 8: Assessment of Cause and Effect (Key Assumptions Check, Role Playing, Red Hat Analysis)

⑧ Foresee the future?

Chapter 6: Scenarios and Indicators

Chapter 7: Hypothesis Generation and Testing (Analysis of Competing Hypotheses)

Chapter 8: Assessment of Cause and Effect (Key Assumptions Check, Structured Analogies)

Chapter 9: Challenge Analysis

Chapter 11: Decision Support (Complexity Manager)

⑨ Challenge your own mental model?

Chapter 9: Challenge Analysis

Chapter 5: Idea Generation

Chapter 7: Hypothesis Generation and Testing (Diagnostic Reasoning, Analysis of Competing Hypotheses)

Chapter 8: Assessment of Cause and Effect (Key Assumptions Check)

⑩ See events from the perspective of the adversary or other players?

Chapter 8: Assessment of Cause and Effect (Key Assumptions Check, Role Playing, Red Hat Analysis)

Chapter 9: Challenge Analysis (Red Team Analysis, Delphi Method)

Chapter 10: Conflict Management

⑪ Manage conflicting mental models or opinions?

Chapter 10: Conflict Management

Chapter 7: Hypothesis Generation and Testing (Analysis of Competing Hypotheses, Argument Mapping)

Chapter 8: Assessment of Cause and Effect (Key Assumptions Check)

⑫ Support a manager, commander, action officer, planner, or policy-maker in deciding between alternative courses of action; draw actionable conclusions?

Chapter 11: Decision Support

Chapter 10: Conflict Management

Chapter 7: Hypothesis Generation and Testing (Analysis of Competing Hypotheses)

4 Decomposition and Visualization

4

Decomposition and Visualization

4.1   Getting Started Checklist   [45]

4.2   Customer Checklist   [47]

4.3   Issue Redefinition   [49]

4.4.   Chronologies and Timelines   [52]

4.5   Sorting   [56]

4.6   Ranking, Scoring, Prioritizing   [59]

4.7   Matrices   [64]

4.8   Network Analysis   [68]

4.9   Mind Maps and Concept Maps   [76]

4.10   Process Maps and Gantt Charts   [82]

CHAPTER 4

Decomposition and Visualization

O ne of the most obvious constraints that analysts face in their work is the limit on how much information most people can keep at the forefront of their minds and think about at the same time. Imagine that you have to make a difficult decision. You make a list of pros and cons. When it comes time to make the decision, however, the lists may be so long that you can't think of them all at the same time to weigh off pros against cons. This often means that when you think about the decision, you will vacillate, focusing first on the pros and then on the cons, favoring first one decision and then the other. Now imagine how much more difficult it would be to think through an intelligence problem with many interacting variables. The limitations of human thought make it difficult, if not impossible, to do error-free analysis without the support of some external representation of the parts of the problem that is being addressed.

Two common approaches for coping with this limitation of our working memory are *decomposition*—that is, breaking down the problem or issue into its component parts so that each part can be considered separately—and *visualization*—placing all the parts on paper or on a computer screen in some organized manner designed to facilitate understanding how the various parts interrelate. Actually, all structured analytic techniques employ these approaches, as the externalization of one's thinking is part of the definition of structured analysis. For some of the basic techniques, however, decomposing an issue to present the data in an organized manner is the principal contribution they make to more effective analysis. These are the basic techniques that will be described in this chapter.

Any technique that gets a complex thought process out of the analyst's head and onto paper or the computer screen can be helpful. The use of even a simple technique such as a checklist can be extremely productive. Consider, for example, the work of Dr. Peter Pronovost, who is well known for his research documenting that a simple checklist of precautions reduces infections, deaths, and costs in hospital intensive care units (ICUs). Dr. Pronovost developed a checklist of five standard precautions against infections that can occur when ICU staff use catheter lines to connect machines to a patient's body in a hospital intensive care unit. ICUs in the United States insert five million such lines into patients each year, and national statistics show that, after ten days, 4 percent of those lines become infected. Infections occur in 80,000 patients each year, and between 5 percent and 28 percent die, depending on how sick the patient is at the start. A month of observation showed that doctors skipped at least one of the precautions in more than a third of all patients.

The Michigan Health and Hospital Association decided in 2003 to require that its hospitals use three different checklists developed by Dr. Pronovost for ICUs, and it made nurses responsible for documenting compliance. Nurses were instructed to intervene if a doctor did not follow every step on a checklist. Obviously, some doctors were offended by the idea that they needed checklists and were being monitored by nurses, and none liked the additional paperwork. However, during its first eighteen months, this checklist program saved more than 1,500 lives and an estimated $75,000,000, and these gains had been sustained for almost four years at the time the referenced article was written.[1]

> *Analysis is breaking information down into its component parts. Anything that has parts also has a structure that relates these parts to each other. One of the first steps in doing analysis is to determine an appropriate structure for the analytic problem, so that one can then identify the various parts and begin assembling information on them. Because there are many different kinds of analytic problems, there are also many different ways to structure analysis.*
>
> —Richards J. Heuer Jr.,
> *The Psychology of Intelligence Analysis* (1999).

These results make one wonder about the potential value of a checklist for intelligence analysts.

Overview of Techniques

Getting Started Checklist, Customer Checklist, and Issue Redefinition are three techniques that can be combined to help analysts launch a new project. If an analyst can start off in the right direction and avoid having to change course later, a lot of time can be saved. However, analysts should still be prepared to change

---

1. Atul Gawande, "The Checklist," *New Yorker,* December 10, 2007, www.newyorker.com/reporting/2007/12/10/071210fa_fact_gawande. Also see Marshall Goldsmith, "Preparing Your Professional Checklist," *Business Week,* January 15, 2008, www.businessweek.com/managing/content/jan2008/ca20080115_768325.htm?campaign_id=rss_topStories.

course should their research so dictate. As Albert Einstein said, "If we knew what we were doing, it would not be called research."

Chronologies and Timelines are used to organize data on events or actions. They are used whenever it is important to understand the timing and sequence of relevant events or to identify key events and gaps.

Sorting is a basic technique for organizing data in a manner that often yields new insights. Sorting is effective when information elements can be broken out into categories or subcategories for comparison by using a computer program, such as a spreadsheet. It is particularly effective during initial data gathering and hypothesis generation.

Ranking, Scoring, and Prioritizing provide how-to guidance on three different ranking techniques—Ranked Voting, Paired Comparison, and Weighted Ranking. Combining an idea-generation technique such as Structured Brainstorming with a ranking technique is an effective way for an analyst to start a new project or to provide a foundation for interoffice or interagency collaboration. The idea-generation technique is used to develop lists of driving forces, variables to be considered, indicators, possible scenarios, important players, historical precedents, sources of information, questions to be answered, and so forth. Such lists are even more useful once they are ranked, scored, or prioritized to determine which items are most important, most useful, most likely, or should be at the top of the priority list.

Matrices are generic analytic tools for sorting and organizing data in a manner that facilitates comparison and analysis. They are used to analyze the relationships among any two sets of variables or the interrelationships among a single set of variables. A Matrix consists of a grid with as many cells as needed for whatever problem is being analyzed. Some analytic topics or problems that use a matrix occur so frequently that they are described in this book as separate techniques.

Network Analysis is used extensively by counterterrorism, counternarcotics, counterproliferation, law enforcement, and military analysts to identify and monitor individuals who may be involved in illegal activity. Social Network Analysis is used to map and analyze relationships among people, groups, organizations, computers, Web sites, and any other information processing entities. The terms Network Analysis, Association Analysis, Link Analysis, and Social Network Analysis are often used interchangeably.

Mind Maps and Concept Maps are visual representations of how an individual or a group thinks about a topic of interest. Such diagrams have two basic elements— the ideas that are judged relevant to whatever topic one is thinking about, and the lines that show and briefly describe the connections between these ideas. Mind Maps and Concept Maps are used for two purposes: by an individual or a group to help sort out their own thinking or to facilitate the communication of a complex set of relationships to others, as in a briefing or an intelligence report.

Process Maps and Gantt Charts were developed for use in industry and the military, but they are also useful to intelligence analysts. Process Mapping is a technique for identifying and diagramming each step in a complex process; this includes event flow charts, activity flow charts, and commodity flow charts. A Gantt Chart is a specific type of Process Map that uses a matrix to chart the progression of a multifaceted process over a specific period of time. Both techniques can be used to track the progress of plans or projects of intelligence interest being undertaken by a foreign government, a criminal or terrorist group, or any other nonstate actor—for example, tracking development of a weapons system or preparations for a military, terrorist, or criminal attack.

Other comparable techniques for organizing and presenting data include various types of graphs, diagrams, and trees. They are not discussed in this book because they are well covered in other works, and it was necessary to draw a line on the number of techniques included here.

4.1 GETTING STARTED CHECKLIST

The Getting Started Checklist is a simple tool to help analysts launch a new project. Past experience has shown that much time can be saved if an analyst takes a few moments to reflect on the task at hand before plunging in. Much analysis is done under time pressure, and this often works to the detriment of the quality of the final product as well as the efficiency of the research and drafting process.

▶ **When to Use It and Value Added**

By getting the fundamentals right at the start of a project, analysts can avoid having to change course later on. This groundwork can save a lot of time and greatly improve the quality of the final product.

▶ **The Method**

Analysts should answer several questions at the beginning of a new project. The following is our list of suggested starter questions, but there is no single best way to begin. Other lists can be equally effective.

* What has prompted the need for the analysis? For example, was it a news report, a new intelligence report, a new development, a perception of change, or a customer request?

* What is the key intelligence question that needs to be answered?

* Why is this issue important, and how can analysis make a meaningful contribution?

* Has your organization or any other organization ever answered this question or a similar question before, and, if so, what was said? To whom was this analysis delivered, and what has changed since that time?

* Who are the principal customers? Are these customers' needs well understood? If not, try to gain a better understanding of their needs and the style of reporting they like.

* Are there other stakeholders who would have an interest in the answer to this question? Who might see the issue from a different perspective and prefer that a different question be answered? Consider meeting with others who see the question from a different perspective.

* From your first impressions, what are all the possible answers to this question? For example, what alternative explanations or outcomes should be considered before making an analytic judgment on the issue?

* Depending on responses to the previous questions, consider rewording the key intelligence question. Consider adding subordinate or supplemental questions.

* Generate a list of potential sources or streams of reporting to be explored.

* Reach out and tap the experience and expertise of analysts in other offices or organizations—both within and outside the government—who are knowledgeable on this topic. For example, call a meeting or conduct a virtual meeting to brainstorm relevant evidence and to develop a list of alternative hypotheses, driving forces, key indicators, or important players.

▷ **Relationship to Other Techniques**

Other techniques that help when you are first starting a project include Customer Checklist, Issue Redefinition, Structured Brainstorming, Starbursting, Key Assumptions Check, and Multiple Hypothesis Generation.

▷ **Origins of This Technique**

This is the authors' list of suggested starter questions. There is no single best way to do this. Others lists can be equally effective.

CUSTOMER CHECKLIST

The Customer Checklist helps an analyst tailor the product to the needs of the principal customer for the analysis. When used appropriately, it ensures that the product is of maximum possible value to this customer. If the product—whether a paper, briefing, or Web posting—is intended to serve many different kinds of customers, it is important to focus on the customer or customers that constitute the main audience and meet their specific concerns or requirements.

▶ **When to Use It and Value Added**

Think about the customer when you are first starting on a project and again before you begin to write. The product will be more effective if the needs and preferences of the principal customer are kept in mind at each step in the process. Using the checklist also helps you to focus attention on what matters most and to generate a rigorous response to the tasking at hand.

▶ **The Method**

Before preparing an outline or drafting a paper, ask the following questions:

* Who is the key person for whom the product is being developed?

* Will this product answer the question the customer asked or the question the customer should be asking? If necessary, clarify this before proceeding.

* What is the most important message to give this customer?

* How is the customer expected to use this information?

* How much time does the customer have to digest this product?

* What format would convey the information most effectively?

* Is it possible to capture the essence in one or a few key graphics?

* What classification is most appropriate for this product? Is it necessary to consider publishing the paper at more than one classification level?

* What is the customer's level of tolerance for technical language? How much detail would the customer expect? Can the details be provided in appendices or backup papers, graphics, notes, or pages?

* Will any structured analytic technique be used? If so, should it be flagged in the product?

* Would the customer expect you to reach out to other experts within or outside the Intelligence Community to tap their expertise in drafting this paper? If this has been done, how has the contribution of other experts been flagged in the product? In a footnote? In a source list?

* To whom or to what source might the customer turn for other views on this topic? What data or analysis might others provide that could influence how the customer reacts to what is being prepared in this product?

▶ **Relationship to Other Techniques**

Other techniques that help an analyst get over the hump when first starting on a project include Getting Started Checklist, Issue Redefinition, Structured Brainstorming, Starbursting, and Multiple Hypotheses Generation.

▶ **Origins of This Technique**

This checklist was developed by Randy Pherson, Pherson Associates, LLC (www.pherson.org), for use in analytic training programs.

ISSUE REDEFINITION

Many analytic projects start with an issue statement. What is the issue, why is it an issue, and how will it be addressed? Issue Redefinition is a technique for experimenting with different ways to define an issue. This is important, because seemingly small differences in how an issue is defined can have significant effects on the direction of the research.

▶ When to Use It

Using Issue Redefinition at the beginning of a project can get you started off on the right foot. It may also be used at any point during the analytic process when a new hypothesis or critical new evidence is introduced. Issue Redefinition is particularly helpful in preventing "mission creep," which results when analysts unwittingly take the direction of analysis away from the core intelligence question or issue at hand, often as a result of the complexity of the problem or a perceived lack of information. Analysts have found Issue Redefinition effective when their thinking is stuck in a rut, and they need help to get out of it.

It is most effective when the definition process is collaboratively developed and tracked in an open and sharable manner, such as on a wiki. The dynamics of the wiki format—including the ability to view edits, nest information, and link to other sources of information—allow analysts to understand and explicitly share the reasoning behind the genesis of the core issue and additional questions as they arise.

▶ Value Added

Proper issue identification can save a great deal of time and effort by forestalling unnecessary research and analysis on a poorly stated issue. Issues are often poorly presented when they are

* Solution driven (Where are the weapons of mass destruction in Iraq?)

* Assumption driven (When China launches rockets into Taiwan, will the Taiwanese government collapse?)

* Too broad or ambiguous (What is the status of Russia's air defense system?)

* Too narrow or misdirected (Who is voting for President Hugo Chávez in the election?)

▶ The Method

The following tactics can be used to stimulate new or different thinking about the best way to state an issue or problem. (See Figure 4.3 for an example.) These tactics may be used in any order.

✳ **Rephrase:** Redefine the issue without losing the original meaning. Review the results to see if they provide a better foundation upon which to conduct the research and assessment to gain the best answer. Example: Rephrase the original question, "How much of a role does Aung San Suu Kyi play in the ongoing unrest in Burma?" as, "How active is the National League for Democracy, headed by Aung San Suu Kyi, in the antigovernment riots in Burma?"

✳ **Ask why?** Ask a series of "why" or "how" questions about the issue definition. After receiving the first response, ask "why" to do that or "how" to do it. Keep asking such questions until you are satisfied that the real problem has emerged. This process is especially effective in generating possible alternative answers.

✳ **Broaden the focus:** Instead of focusing on only one piece of the puzzle, step back and look at several pieces together. What is the issue connected to? Example: The original question, "How corrupt is the Pakistani president?" leads to the question, "How corrupt is the Pakistani government as a whole?"

✳ **Narrow the focus:** Can you break down the issue further? Take the question and ask about the components that make up the problem. Example: The original question, "Will the European Union ratify a new constitution?" can be broken down to, "How do individual member states view the new European Union constitution?"

✳ **Redirect the focus:** What outside forces impinge on this issue? Is deception involved? Example: The original question, "What are the terrorist threats against the U.S. homeland?" is revised to, "What opportunities are there to interdict terrorist plans?"

✳ **Turn 180 degrees:** Turn the issue on its head. Is the issue the one asked or the opposite of it? Example: The original question, "How much of the ground capability of China's People's Liberation Army would be involved in an initial assault on Taiwan?" is rephrased as, "How much of the ground capability of China's People's Liberation Army would not be involved in the initial Taiwan assault?"

▶ Relationship to Other Techniques

Issue Redefinition is often used simultaneously with the Getting Started Checklist and the Customer Checklist. The technique is also known as Issue Development, Problem Restatement, and Reframing the Question.

Figure 4.3	Issue Redefinition Example

Initial question: Is China selling ballistic missiles to Iran?

Rephrase: Is Iran buying ballistic missiles from China?

Ask "Why?": Why would China sell ballistic missiles to Iran?

Because China seeks influence with Iran.

Why does China want influence with Iran?

Because China wants to reduce U.S. influence in the Persian Gulf region.

Why does China want to reduce U.S. influence in the Persian Gulf region?

Because China wants to reduce the U.S. influence throughout the world.

Final Question: **Is China's sale of military equipment to the Middle East part of a worldwide strategy to reduce U.S. influence?**

Broaden the focus: Is there a partnership between China and Iran?

Narrow the focus: What kinds of ballistic missiles would China sell to Iran?

Redirect the focus: Why would Iran want Chinese missiles? How is Iran going to pay for any purchased missiles?

Turn 180 degrees: Is China buying ballistic missiles from Iran?

▶ **Origins of This Technique**

This is an edited version of Defense Intelligence Agency training materials. It also draws on Morgan D. Jones, "Problem Restatement," chap. 3, in *The Thinker's Toolkit* (New York: Three Rivers Press, 1998).

A chronology is a list that places events or actions in the order in which they occurred; a timeline is a graphic depiction of those events put in context of the time of the events and the time between events. Both are used to identify trends or relationships among the events or actions and, in the case of a timeline, among the events and actions as well as other developments in the context of the overarching intelligence problem.

▶ When to Use It

Chronologies and timelines aid in organizing events or actions. Whenever it is important to understand the timing and sequence of relevant events or to identify key events and gaps, these techniques can be useful. The events may or may not have a cause-and-effect relationship.

▶ Value Added

Chronologies and timelines aid in the identification of patterns and correlations among events. These techniques also allow you to relate seemingly disconnected events to the big picture to highlight or identify significant changes or to assist in the discovery of trends, developing issues, or anomalies. They can serve as a catch-all for raw data when the meaning of the data has not yet been identified. Multiple-level timelines allow analysts to track concurrent events that may have an effect on each other. Although timelines may be developed at the onset of an analytic task to ascertain the context of the activity to be analyzed, timelines and chronologies also may be used in postmortem intelligence studies to break down the intelligence reporting, find the causes for intelligence failures, and highlight significant events after an intelligence surprise.

The activities on a timeline can lead an analyst to hypothesize the existence of previously unknown events. In other words, the series of known events may make sense only if other previously unknown events had occurred. The analyst can then look for other indicators of those missing events.

Timelines and chronologies can be very useful for organizing information in a format that can be readily understood in a briefing.

▶ Potential Pitfalls

In using timelines, analysts may assume, incorrectly, that events following earlier events were *caused* by the earlier events. Also, the value of this technique may be reduced if the analyst lacks imagination in identifying contextual events that relate to the information in the chronology or timeline.

▶ The Method

Chronologies and timelines are effective yet simple ways for you to order incoming information as you go through your daily message traffic. An Excel spreadsheet or even a Word document can be used to log the results of research and marshal evidence. You can use tools such as the Excel drawing function or the Analysts' Notebook to draw the timeline. Follow these steps.

* When researching the problem, ensure that the relevant information is listed with the date or order in which it occurred. Make sure the data are properly referenced.

* Review the chronology or timeline by asking the following questions.
    - What are the temporal distances between key events? If "lengthy," what caused the delay? Are there missing pieces of data that may fill those gaps that should be collected?
    - Did the analyst overlook piece(s) of intelligence information that may have had an impact on or be related to the events?
    - Conversely, if events seem to have happened more rapidly than were expected, or if not all events appear to be related, is it possible that the analyst has information related to multiple event timelines?
    - Does the timeline have all the critical events that are necessary for the outcome to occur?
    - When did the information become known to the analyst or a key player?
    - What are the intelligence gaps?
    - Are there any points along the timeline when the target is particularly vulnerable to U.S. intelligence collection activities or countermeasures?
    - What events outside this timeline could have influenced the activities?

* If preparing a timeline, synopsize the data along a line, usually horizontal or vertical. Use the space on both sides of the line to highlight important analytic points. For example, place facts above the line and points of analysis or commentary below the line. Alternatively, contrast the activities of different groups, organizations, or streams of information by placement above or below the line. If multiple actors

are involved, you can use multiple lines, showing how and where they converge.

* Look for relationships and patterns in the data connecting persons, places, organizations, and other activities. Identify gaps or unexplained time periods, and consider the implications of the absence of evidence. Prepare a summary chart detailing key events and key analytic points in an annotated timeline.

▶ **Example**

A team of analysts working on strategic missile forces knows what steps are necessary to prepare for and launch a nuclear missile. (See Figure 4.4.) The analysts have been monitoring a country that is believed to be close to testing a new variant of its medium-range surface-to-surface ballistic missile. They have seen the initial steps of a test launch in mid-February and decide to initiate a concentrated watch of the primary and secondary test launch facilities. Observed and expected activities are placed into a timeline to gauge the potential dates of a test launch. The analysts can thus estimate when a possible missile launch may occur and make decision makers aware of indicators of possible activity.

▶ **Origins of This Technique**

Chronologies and Timelines are well-established techniques used in many fields. The information here is from Defense Intelligence Agency training materials and Jones, "Sorting, Chronologies, and Timelines," chap. 6, in *The Thinker's Toolkit*.

Figure 4.4 Timeline Estimate of Missile Launch Date

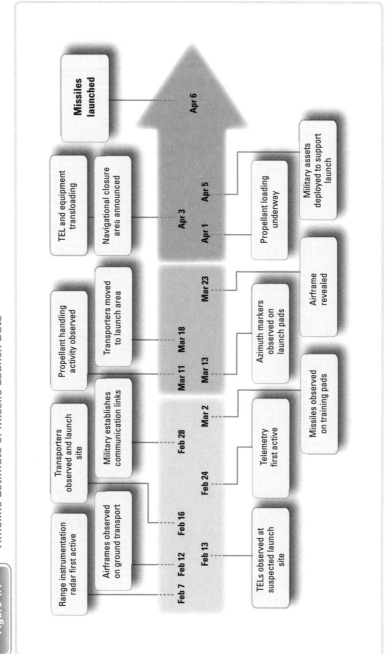

4.5   SORTING

Sorting is a basic technique for organizing a large body of data in a manner that often yields new insights.

▶ **When to Use It**

Sorting is effective when information elements can be broken out into categories or subcategories for comparison with each other, most often by using a computer program, such as a spreadsheet. This technique is particularly effective during the initial data gathering and hypothesis generation phases of analysis, but you may also find sorting useful at other times.

▶ **Value Added**

Sorting large amounts of data into relevant categories that are compared with each other can provide analysts with insights into trends, similarities, differences, or abnormalities of intelligence interest that otherwise would go unnoticed. When you are dealing with transactions data in particular (for example, communications intercepts or transfers of goods or money), it is very helpful to sort the data first.

▶ **Potential Pitfalls**

Improper sorting can hide valuable insights as easily as it can illuminate them. Standardizing the data being sorted is imperative. Working with an analyst who has experience in sorting can help you avoid this pitfall in most cases.

▶ **The Method**

Follow these steps:

    ∗ Review the categories of information to determine which category or combination of categories might show trends or an abnormality that would provide insight into the problem you are studying. Place the data into a spreadsheet or a database using as many fields (columns) as necessary to differentiate among the data types (dates, times, locations, people, activities, amounts, etc.). List each of the facts, pieces of information, or hypotheses involved in the problem that are relevant to your sorting schema. (Use paper, whiteboard, movable sticky notes, or other means for this.)

    ∗ Review the listed facts, information, or hypotheses in the database or spreadsheet to identify key fields that may allow you to uncover possible patterns or groupings. Those patterns or groupings then illustrate the schema categories and can be listed as header categories. For example, if an examination of terrorist activity shows that most attacks occur in hotels and restaurants but that the times of the attacks vary, "Location" is the main category; while "Date" and "Time" are secondary categories.

* Group those items according to the sorting schema in the categories that were defined in step 1.

* Choose a category and sort the data within that category. Look for any insights, trends, or oddities. Good analysts notice trends; great analysts notice anomalies.

* Review (or ask others to review) the sorted facts, information, or hypotheses to see if there are alternative ways to sort them. List any alternative sorting schema for your problem. One of the most useful applications for this technique is to sort according to multiple schemas and examine results for correlations between data and categories. But remember that correlation is not the same as causation.

▶ **Examples**

Example 1: Are a foreign adversary's military leaders pro-U.S., anti-U.S., or neutral on their attitudes toward U.S. policy in the Middle East? To answer this question, analysts sort the leaders by various factors determined to give insight into the issue, such as birthplace, native language, religion, level of professional education, foreign military or civilian/university exchange training (where/when), field/command assignments by parent service, political influences in life, and political decisions made. Then they review the information to see if any parallels exist among the categories.

Example 2: Analysts review the data from cell phone communications among five conspirators to determine the frequency of calls, patterns that show who is calling whom, changes in patterns of frequency of calls prior to a planned activity, dates and times of calls, subjects discussed, and so forth.

Example 3: Analysts are reviewing all information related to an adversary's Weapons of Mass Destruction (WMD) program. Electronic intelligence reporting shows more than 300,000 emitter collections over the past year alone. The analysts' sorting of the data by type of emitter, dates of emission, and location shows varying increases and decreases of emitter activity with some minor trends identifiable. The analysts filter out all collections except those related to air defense. The unfiltered information is sorted by type of air defense system, location, and dates of activity. Of note is a period when there is an unexpectedly large increase of activity in the air defense surveillance and early warning systems. The analysts review relevant external events and find that a major opposition movement outside the country held a news conference where it detailed the adversary's WMD activities, including locations of the activity within the country. The air defense emitters for all suspected locations of WMD activity, including several not included in the press conference, increased to a war level of surveillance within four hours of the press conference. The analysts reviewed all air defense activity locations that showed the increase assumed to be related to the press conference and the WMD programs and found two locations showing increased activity but not previously listed as WMD related. These new locations were added to collection planning to determine what relationship, if any, they had to the WMD program.

▶ **Origins of This Technique**

Sorting is a long-established procedure for organizing data. The description here is from Defense Intelligence Agency training materials.

4.6 RANKING, SCORING, PRIORITIZING

I n this section we will describe three techniques for ranking, scoring, or prioritizing items on any list according to the item's importance, desirability, priority, value, probability, or any other criterion.

▷ When to Use It

Use of a ranking technique is often the next step after using an idea-generation technique such as Structured Brainstorming, Virtual Brainstorming, or Nominal Group Technique (see chapter 5). A ranking technique is appropriate whenever there are too many items to rank easily just by looking at the list; the ranking has significant consequences and must be done as accurately as possible; or it is useful to aggregate the opinions of a group of analysts.

▷ Value Added

Combining an idea-generation technique with a ranking technique is an excellent way for an analyst to start a new project or to provide a foundation for inter-office or interagency collaboration. An idea-generation technique is often used to develop lists of such things as driving forces, variables to be considered, or important players. Such lists are more useful once they are ranked, scored, or prioritized. For example, you might determine which items are most important, most useful, most likely, or that need to be done first.

▷ Potential Pitfalls

When any of these techniques is used to aggregate the opinions of a group of analysts, the rankings provided by each group member are added together and averaged. This means that the opinions of the outliers, whose views are quite different from the others, are blended into the average. As a result, the ranking does not show the range of different opinions that might be present in a group. In some cases the identification of outliers with a minority opinion can be of great value. Further research might show that the outliers are correct.

▷ The Method

Of the three methods discussed here, Ranked Voting is the easiest and quickest to use and it is often sufficient. However, it is not as accurate after you get past the top two or three ranked items, because the group usually has not thought as much (and may not care as much) about the lower-ranked items. Ranked Voting also provides less information than either Paired Comparison or Weighted Ranking. Ranked Voting shows only that one item is ranked higher or lower than another; it does not show how much higher or lower. Paired Comparison does provide this information, and Weighted Ranking provides even more information. It specifies the criteria that are used in making the ranking, and weights are assigned to those criteria for each of the items in the list.

Ranked Voting

In a Ranked Voting exercise, members of the group individually rank each item in order according to the member's preference or what the member regards as the item's importance. Depending upon the number of items or the specific analytic needs, the group can decide to rank all the items or only the top three to five. The group leader or facilitator passes out simple ballots listing all the items to be voted on. Each member votes his or her order of preference. If a member views two items as being of equal preference, the votes can be split between them. For example, if two items are tied for second place, each receives a 2.5 ranking. Any items that are not voted on are considered to be tied for last place. After members of the group have voted, the votes are added up. The item with the lowest number is ranked number 1. Kendall's W statistic is a simple procedure for calculating the degree of consensus, if that information is needed.

Paired Comparison

Paired Comparison compares each item against every other item, and the analyst can assign a score to show how much more important or more preferable or more probable one item is than the others. This technique provides more than a simple ranking, as it shows the degree of importance or preference for each item. The list of items can then be ordered along a dimension, such as importance or preference, using an interval-type scale.

Follow these steps to use the technique:

* List the items to be compared. Assign a letter to each item.

* Create a table with the letters across the top and down the left side as in Figure 4.6a. The results of the comparison of each pair of items are marked in the cells of this table. Note the diagonal line of darker-colored cells. These cells are not used, as each item is never compared with itself. The cells below this diagonal line are not used because they would duplicate a comparison in the cells above the diagonal line. If you are working in a group, distribute a blank copy of this table to each participant.

* Looking at the cells above the diagonal row of gray cells, compare the item in the row with the one in the column. For each cell, decide which of the two items is more important (or more preferable or more probable). Write the letter of

Figure 4.6a

Paired Comparison Matrix

	A	B	C	D	E	F	Score	%
A		**B, 3**	C, 1	A, 1	A, 1	F, 2	2	10
B			**B, 1**	D, 1	**B, 2**	**B, 1**	7	35
C				D, 1	E, 1	F, 1	1	5
D					D, 2	D, 1	5	25
E						F, 1	1	5
F							4	20

the winner of this comparison in the cell, and score the degree of difference on a scale from 0 (no difference) to 3 (major difference) as in Figure 4.6a.

∗ Consolidate the results by adding up the total of all the values for each of the items and put this number in the "Score" column. For example, in Figure 4.6a item B has one 3 in the first row plus one 2, and two 1s in the second row, for a score of 7.

∗ Finally, it may be desirable to convert these values into a percentage of the total score. To do this, divide the total number of scores (20 in the example) by the score for each individual item. Item B, with a score of 7, is ranked most important or most preferred. Item B received a score of 35 percent (7 divided by 20) as compared with 25 percent for item D and only 5 percent each for items C and E, which received only one vote each. This example shows how Paired Comparison captures the degree of difference between each ranking.

∗ To aggregate rankings received from a group of analysts, simply add the individual scores for each analyst.

Weighted Ranking

In Weighted Ranking, a specified set of criteria are used to rank items. The analyst creates a table with items to be ranked listed across the top row and criteria for ranking these items listed down the far left column (see Figure 4.6b). There are a variety of valid ways to proceed with this ranking. A simple version of Weighted

Ranking has been selected for presentation here because intelligence analysts are normally making subjective judgments rather than dealing with hard numbers. As you read the following steps, refer to Figure 4.6b:

* Create a table with one column for each item. At the head of each column, write the name of an item or assign it a letter to save space.

* Add two more blank columns on the left side of this table. Count the number of selection criteria, and then adjust the table so that it has that number of rows plus three more, one at the top to list the items and two at the bottom to show the raw scores and percentages for each item. In the first column on the left side, starting with the second row, write in all the selection criteria down the left side of the table. There is some value in listing the criteria roughly in order of importance, but that is not critical. Leave the bottom two rows blank for the scores and percentages.

* Now work down the far left hand column assigning weights to the selection criteria based on their relative importance for judging the ranking of the items. Depending upon how many criteria there are, take either 10 points or 100 points and divide these points between the selection criteria based on what is believed to be their relative importance in ranking the items. In other words, ask what percentage of the decision should be based on each of these criteria? Be sure that the weights for all the selection criteria combined add up to either 10 or 100, whichever is selected. Also be sure that all the criteria are phrased in such a way that a higher weight is more desirable.

* Work across the rows to write the criterion weight in the left side of each cell.

* Next, work across the matrix one row (selection criterion) at a time to evaluate the relative ability of each of the items to satisfy that selection criteria. Use a ten-point rating scale, where 1 = low and 10 = high, to rate each item separately. (Do not spread the ten points proportionately across all the items as was done to assign weights to the criteria.) Write this rating number after the criterion weight in the cell for each item.

* Again, work across the matrix one row at a time to multiply the criterion weight by the item rating for that criterion, and enter this number for each cell as shown in Figure 4.6b.

* Now add the columns for all the items. The result will be a ranking of the items from highest to lowest score. To gain a better understanding of the relative ranking of one item as compared with another, convert these raw scores to percentages. To do this, first add together all the scores in the "Totals" row to get a total number. Then divide the score for each item by this total score to get a percentage ranking for each item. All the percentages together must add up to

Figure 4.6b   Weighted Ranking Matrix

Criteria	Weight	A	B	C	D	E	F
				Items			
1	3	3 x 7 = 21	3 x 8 = 24	3 x 8 = 24	3 x 5 = 15	3 x 6 = 18	3 x 7 = 21
2	3	3 x 5 = 15	3 x 8 = 24	3 x 9 = 27	3 x 7 = 21	3 x 4 = 12	3 x 5 = 15
3	2	2 x 8 = 16	2 x 9 = 18	2 x 3 = 6	2 x 2 = 4	2 x 3 = 6	2 x 7 = 14
4	1	1 x 6 = 6	1 x 3 = 3	1 x 8 = 8	1 x 6 = 6	1 x 9 = 9	1 x 7 = 7
5	1	1 x 7 = 7	1 x 9 = 9	1 x 7 = 7	1 x 8 = 8	1 x 6 = 6	1 x 8 = 8
Totals	10	65	78	72	54	51	65
%	100	16.9%	20.3%	18.7%	14%	13.2%	16.9%

100 percent. In Figure 4.6b it is apparent that item B has the number one ranking (with 20.3 percent), while item E has the lowest (with 13.2 percent).

▷ **Relationship to Other Techniques**

Some form of ranking, scoring, or prioritizing is commonly used with Structured Brainstorming, Virtual Brainstorming, or Nominal Group Technique, all of which generate ideas that should be evaluated or prioritized. Applications of the Delphi Method may also generate ideas from outside experts that need to be evaluated or prioritized.

▷ **Origins of This Technique**

Ranking, Scoring, and Prioritizing are common analytic processes in many fields. All three forms of ranking described here are based largely on Internet sources. For Ranked Voting, we referred to http://en.wikipedia.org/wiki/Voting_system; for Paired Comparison, www.mindtools.com; and for Weighted Ranking, www.ifm.eng.cam.ac.uk/dstools/choosing/criter.html. We also reviewed the Weighted Ranking process described in Morgan Jones's *The Thinker's Toolkit*. This method is taught at some government agencies, but we found it to be more complicated than necessary for intelligence applications that typically use fuzzy expert-generated data rather than hard numbers.

4.7 **MATRICES**

A matrix is an analytic tool for sorting and organizing data in a manner that facilitates comparison and analysis. It consists of a simple grid with as many cells as needed for whatever problem is being analyzed.

Some analytic topics or problems that use a matrix occur so frequently that they are handled in this book as separate techniques. For example:

*   Analysis of Competing Hypotheses (chapter 7) uses a matrix to analyze the relationships between evidence and hypotheses.

*   Cross-Impact Matrix (chapter 5) uses a matrix to analyze the interactions among variables or driving forces that will determine an outcome. Such a Cross-Impact Matrix is part of Complexity Manager (chapter 11).

*   Gantt Charts (chapter 5) use a matrix to analyze the relationship between tasks to be accomplished and the time period for those tasks.

*   Decision Matrix (chapter 11) uses a matrix to analyze the relationships between goals or preferences and decision options.

*   Ranking, Scoring, Prioritizing (this chapter) uses a matrix to record the relationships between pairs of items in a matrix, and Weighted Ranking uses a matrix to analyze the relationships between items and criteria for judging those items.

▶ **When to Use It**

Matrices are used to analyze the relationship between any two sets of variables or the interrelationships between a single set of variables. Among other things, they enable analysts to

*   Compare one type of information with another.
*   Compare pieces of information of the same type.
*   Categorize information by type.
*   Identify patterns in the information.
*   Separate elements of a problem.

A matrix is such an easy and flexible tool to use that it should be one of the first tools analysts think of when dealing with a large body of data. One limiting factor in the use of matrices is that information must be organized along only two dimensions.

▶ Value Added

Matrices provide a visual representation of a complex set of data. By presenting information visually, a matrix enables analysts to deal effectively with more data than they could manage by juggling various pieces of information in their head. The analytic problem is broken down to component parts so that each part (that is, each cell in the matrix) can be analyzed separately, while ideally maintaining the context of the problem as a whole.

A matrix can also be used to establish an analytic framework for understanding a problem, to suggest a more rigorous structure for explaining a phenomenon, or to generate a more comprehensive set of alternatives.

▶ The Method

A matrix is a tool that can be used in many different ways and for many different purposes. What matrices have in common is that each has a grid with sufficient columns and rows for you to enter two sets of data that you want to compare. Organize the category headings for each set of data in some logical sequence before entering the headings for one set of data in the top row and the headings for the other set in the far left column. Then enter the data in the appropriate cells.

Figure 4.7, "Rethinking the Concept of National Security: A New Ecology" is an example of a complex matrix that not only organizes data but also tells its own analytic story. It shows how the concept of national security has evolved over recent decades—and suggests that the way we define national security will continue to expand in the coming years. In this matrix, threats to national security are arrayed along the vertical axis, beginning at the top with the most traditional actor, the nation-state. At the bottom end of the spectrum are systemic threats, such as infectious diseases or threats that "have no face." The top row of the matrix presents the three primary mechanisms for dealing with threats: military force, policing and monitoring, and collaboration. The cells in the matrix provide historic examples of how the three different mechanisms of engagement have been used to deal with the five different sources of threats. The top left cell (dark gray) presents the classic case of using military force to resolve nation-state differences. In contrast, at the bottom right corner various actors are strongly motivated to collaborate with each other in dealing with systemic threats, such as the outbreak of a pandemic disease.

Classic definitions of national security focus on the potential for conflicts involving nation-states. This is represented by the top left cell which lists three

Figure 4.7

Rethinking the Concept of National Security: A New Ecology

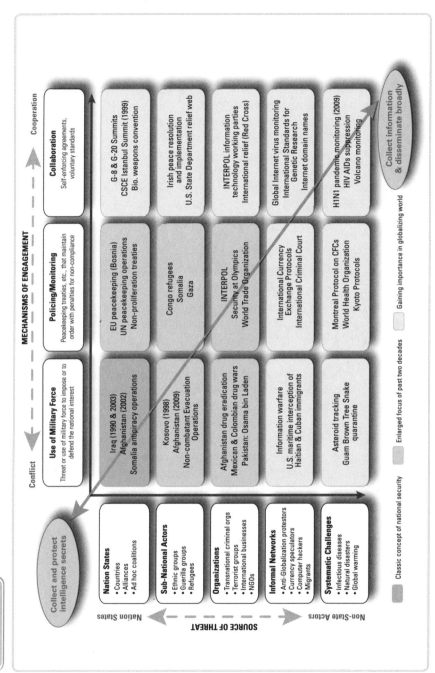

Source: 2009 Pherson Associates, LLC.

military operations. In recent decades the threat has expanded to include threats posed by subnational actors as well as terrorist and other criminal organizations. Similarly, the use of peacekeeping and international policing has become more common than in the past. This shift to a broader use of the term "national security" is represented by the other five cells (medium blue) in the top left of the matrix. The remaining cells (light blue) to the right and at the bottom of the matrix represent how the concept of national security is continuing to expand as the world becomes increasingly globalized.

By using a matrix to present the expanding concept of national security in this way, one sees that patterns relating to how key players collect intelligence and share information vary along the two primary dimensions. In the upper left of Figure 4.7, the practice of nation-states is to seek intelligence on their adversaries, classify it, and protect it. As one moves diagonally across the matrix to the lower right, however, this practice reverses. In the lower right of this figure, information is usually available from unclassified sources and the imperative is to disseminate it to everyone as soon as possible. This dynamic can create serious tensions at the midpoint, for example, when those working in the homeland security arena must find ways to share sensitive national security information with state and local law enforcement officers.

▶ **Origins of This Technique**

The description of this basic and widely used technique is from Pherson Associates, LLC, training materials. The National Security matrix was developed by Randy Pherson.

4.8   NETWORK ANALYSIS

Network Analysis is the review, compilation, and interpretation of data to determine the presence of associations among individuals, groups, businesses, or other entities; the meaning of those associations to the people involved; and the degrees and ways in which those associations can be strengthened or weakened.[2] It is the best method available to help analysts understand and identify opportunities to influence the behavior of a set of actors about whom information is sparse. In the fields of law enforcement and national security, information used in Network Analysis usually comes from informants or from physical or technical surveillance. These networks are most often clandestine and therefore not visible to open source collectors. Although software has been developed to help collect, sort, and map data, it is not essential to many of these analytic tasks. Social Network Analysis, which involves measuring associations, does require software.

Analysis of networks is broken down into three stages, and analysts can stop at the stage that answers their questions.

✳ Network Charting is the process of and associated techniques for identifying people, groups, things, places, and events of interest (nodes) and drawing connecting lines (links) between them on the basis of various types of association. The product is often referred to as a Link Chart.

✳ Network Analysis is the process and techniques that take the chart and strive to make sense of the data represented by the chart by grouping associations (sorting) and identifying patterns in and among those groups.

✳ Social Network Analysis (SNA) is the mathematical measuring of variables related to the distance between nodes and the types of associations in order to derive even more meaning from the chart, especially about the degree and type of influence one node has on another.

▶ **When to Use It**

Network Analysis is used extensively in law enforcement, counterterrorism analysis, and analysis of transnational issues such as narcotics and weapons proliferation to identify and monitor individuals who may be involved in illegal activity. Network Charting (or Link Charting) is used to literally "connect the dots" between people, groups, or other entities of intelligence or criminal interest. Network

---

2. "Association Analysis," undated draft provided to the authors by Marilyn B. Peterson, Defense Intelligence Agency.

Analysis puts these dots in context, and Social Network Analysis helps identify hidden associations and degrees of influence between the dots.

▶ Value Added

Network Analysis has proved to be highly effective in helping analysts identify and understand patterns of organization, authority, communication, travel, financial transactions, or other interactions between people or groups that are not apparent from isolated pieces of information. It often identifies key leaders, information brokers, or sources of funding. It can identify additional individuals or groups who need to be investigated. If done over time, it can help spot change within the network. Indicators monitored over time may signal preparations for offensive action by the network or may reveal opportunities for disrupting the network.

SNA software helps analysts do these tasks by facilitating the retrieval, charting, and storage of large amounts of information. Software is not necessary for this task, but is enormously helpful. The SNA software included in many network analysis packages is essential for measuring associations.

▶ Potential Pitfalls

This method is extremely dependent upon having at least one good source of information. It is hard to know when information may be missing, and the boundaries of the network may be fuzzy and constantly changing, in which case it is difficult to determine whom to include. The constantly changing nature of networks over time can cause information to become outdated. You can be misled if you do not constantly question the data being entered, update the chart regularly, and look for gaps and consider their potential significance.

You should never rely blindly on the SNA software but strive to understand how the application being used works. As with any software, different applications measure different things in different ways, and the devil is always in the details.

▶ The Method

Analysis of networks attempts to answer the question "Who is related to whom and what is the nature of their relationship and role in the network?" The basic network analysis software identifies key nodes and shows the links between them. SNA software measures the frequency of flow between links and explores the significance of key attributes of the nodes. We know of no software that does the intermediate task of grouping nodes into meaningful clusters, though algorithms do exist and are used by individual analysts. In all cases, however, you must interpret what is represented, looking at the chart to see how it reflects organizational structure, modes of operation, and patterns of behavior.

Network Charting: The key to good network analysis is to begin with a good chart. An example of such a chart is Figure 4.8a, which shows the terrorist network

Figure 4.8a

Social Network Analysis: The September 11 Hijackers

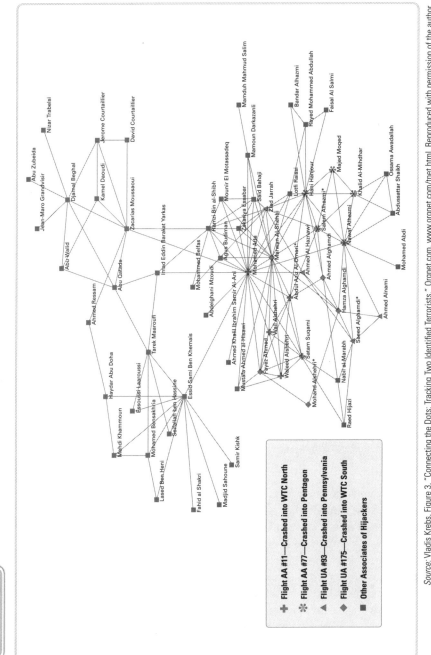

Flight AA #11—Crashed into WTC North

Flight AA #77—Crashed into Pentagon

Flight UA #93—Crashed into Pennsylvania

Flight UA #175—Crashed into WTC South

Other Associates of Hijackers

Source: Vladis Krebs, Figure 3, "Connecting the Dots: Tracking Two Identified Terrorists," Orgnet.com. www.orgnet.com/tnet.html. Reproduced with permission of the author.

behind the attacks of September 11, 2001. It was compiled by networks researcher Valdis E. Krebs using data available from news sources on the Internet in early 2002.

There are tried and true methods for making good charts that allow the analyst to save time, avoid unnecessary confusion, and arrive more quickly at insights. Network charting usually involves the following steps.

* Identify at least one reliable source or stream of data to serve as a beginning point.
* Identify, combine, or separate nodes within this reporting.
* List each node in a database, association matrix, or software program.
* Identify interactions among individuals or groups.
* List interactions by type in a database, association matrix, or software program.
* Identify each node and interaction by some criterion that is meaningful to your analysis. These criteria often include frequency of contact, type of contact, type of activity, and source of information.
* Draw the connections between nodes—connect the dots—on a chart by hand, using a computer drawing tool, or using Network Analysis software. If you are not using software, begin with the nodes that are central to your intelligence question. Make the map more informative by presenting each criterion in a different color or style or by using icons or pictures. A very complex chart may use all of these elements on the same link or node. The need for additional elements often happens when the intelligence question is murky (for example, when "I know something bad is going on, but I don't know what"); when the chart is being used to answer multiple questions; or when a chart is maintained over a long period of time.
* Work out from the central nodes, adding links and nodes until you run out of information from the good sources.
* Add nodes and links from other sources, constantly checking them against the information you already have. Follow all leads, whether they are people, groups, things, or events, and regardless of source. Make note of the sources.
* Stop in these cases: when you run out of information, when all of the new links are dead ends, when all of the new links begin to turn in on each other like a spider web, or when you run out of time.
* Update the chart and supporting documents regularly as new information becomes available, or as you have time. Just a few minutes a day will pay enormous dividends.

* Rearrange the nodes and links so that the links cross over each other as little as possible. This is easier to accomplish if you are using software. Many software packages can rearrange the nodes and links in various ways.

* Cluster the nodes. Do this by looking for "dense" areas of the chart and relatively "empty" areas. Draw shapes around the dense areas. Use a variety of shapes, colors, and line styles to denote different types of clusters, your relative confidence in the cluster, or any other criterion you deem important.

* Cluster the clusters, if you can, using the same method.

* Label each cluster according to the common denominator among the nodes it contains. In doing this you will identify groups, events, activities, and/or key locations. If you have in mind a model for groups or activities, you may be able to identify gaps in the chart by what is or is not present that relates to the model.

* Look for "cliques"—a group of nodes in which every node is connected to every other node, though not to many nodes outside the group. These groupings often look like stars or pentagons. In the intelligence world, they often turn out to be clandestine cells.

* Look in the empty spaces for nodes or links that connect two clusters. Highlight these nodes with shapes or colors. These nodes are brokers, facilitators, leaders, advisers, media, or some other key connection that bears watching. They are also points where the network is susceptible to disruption.

* Chart the flow of activities between nodes and clusters. You may want to use arrows and time stamps. Some software applications will allow you to display dynamically how the chart has changed over time.

* Analyze this flow. Does it always go in one direction or in multiple directions? Are the same or different nodes involved? How many different flows are there? What are the pathways? By asking these questions, you can often identify activities, including indications of preparation for offensive action and lines of authority. You can also use this knowledge to assess the resiliency of the network. If one node or pathway were removed, would there be alternatives already built in?

* Continually update and revise as nodes or links change.

Figure 4.8b is a modified version of the 9/11 hijacker network depicted in Figure 4.8a. It has been marked to identify the different types of clusters and nodes discussed under Network Analysis. Cells are seen as stars or pentagons, potential cells are circled, and the large diamond surrounds the cluster of cells. Brokers are

Figure 4.8b

Social Network Analysis: September 11 Hijacker Key Nodes

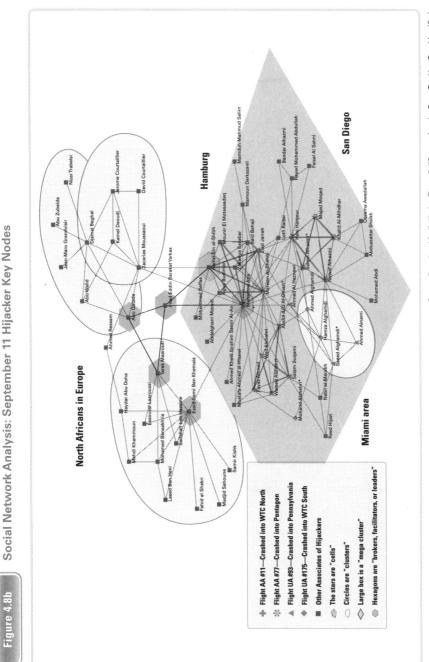

North Africans in Europe

Hamburg

San Diego

Miami area

Legend:
- ✚ Flight AA #11—Crashed into WTC North
- ✳ Flight AA #77—Crashed into Pentagon
- ▲ Flight UA #93—Crashed into Pennsylvania
- ◆ Flight UA #175—Crashed into WTC South
- ■ Other Associates of Hijackers
- ✦ The stars are "cells"
- ◯ Circles are "clusters"
- ◇ Large box is a "mega cluster"
- ⬡ Hexagons are "brokers, facilitators, or leaders"

Source: Based on Vladis Krebs, Figure 3, "Connecting the Dots: Tracking Two Identified Terrorists," Orgnet.com. www.orgnet.com/tnet.html. Reproduced with permission of the author. With changes by Cynthia Storer.

shown as nodes surrounded by small pentagons. Note the broker in the center. This node has connections to all of the other brokers. This is a senior leader: Al-Qaeda's former head of operations in Europe, Imad Eddin Barakat Yarkas.

Figure 4.8c   Social Network Analysis

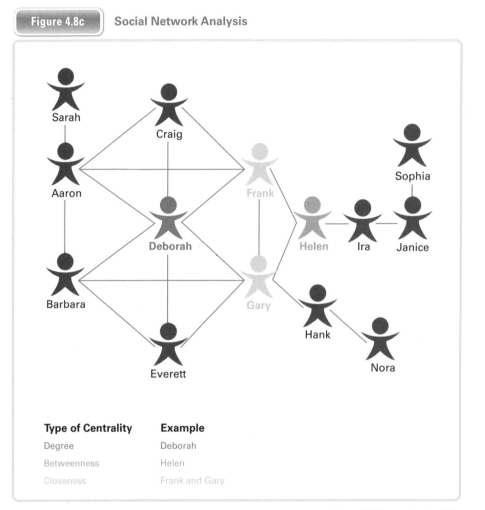

Type of Centrality	Example
Degree	Deborah
Betweenness	Helen
Closeness	Frank and Gary

Source: 2009 Pherson Associates, LLC.

Social Network Analysis requires a specialized software application. It is important, however, for analysts to familiarize themselves with the basic process and measures and the specialized vocabulary used to describe position and function within the network. The following three types of centrality are illustrated in Figure 4.8c:

* Degree centrality: This is measured by the number of direct connections that a node has with other nodes. In the network depicted in Figure 4.8c, Deborah has the most direct connections. She is a "connector" or a "hub" in this network.

* Betweenness centrality: Helen has fewer direct connections than does Deborah, but she plays a vital role as a "broker" in the network. Without her, Ira and Janice would be cut off from the rest of the network. A node with high betweenness has great influence over what flows—or does not flow—through the network.

* Closeness centrality: Frank and Gary have fewer connections than does Deborah, yet the pattern of their direct and indirect ties allows them to access all the nodes in the network more quickly than anyone else. They are in the best position to monitor all the information that flows through the network.

▷ **Origins of This Technique**

This is an old technique that has been transformed by the development of sophisticated software programs for organizing and analyzing large databases. Each of the following sources has made significant contributions to the description of this technique: Valdis E. Krebs, "Social Network Analysis, A Brief Introduction," www.orgnet.com/sna.html; Krebs, "Uncloaking Terrorist Networks," *First Monday*, 7, no. 4 (April 1, 2002), http://firstmonday.org/htbin/cgiwrap/bin/ojs/index.php/fm/article/view/941/863; Robert A. Hanneman, "Introduction to Social Network Methods," Department of Sociology, University of California Riverside, http://faculty.ucr.edu/~hanneman/nettext/C1_Social_Network_Data.html#Populations; Marilyn B. Peterson, Defense Intelligence Agency, "Association Analysis," undated draft, used with permission of the author; Cynthia Storer and Averill Farrelly, Pherson Associates, LLC; Pherson Associates training materials.

4.9 MIND MAPS AND CONCEPT MAPS

Mind Maps and Concept Maps are visual representations of how an individual or a group thinks about a topic of interest. Such a diagram has two basic elements: the ideas that are judged relevant to whatever topic one is thinking about, and the lines that show and briefly describe the connections between these ideas. The two dominant approaches to creating such diagrams are Mind Mapping and Concept Mapping (see Figures 4.9a and 4.9b). Other approaches include cognitive, causal, and influence mapping as well as idea mapping. There are many commercial and freely available software products that support this mapping function and that are known by many different names.[3] Diverse groups within the intelligence community are using various methods for creating meaningful diagrams.

▷ When to Use It

Whenever you think about a problem, develop a plan, or consider making even a very simple decision, you are putting a series of thoughts together. That series of thoughts can be represented visually with words or images connected by lines that represent the nature of the relationship between them. Any thinking for any purpose, whether about a personal decision or analysis of an intelligence issue, can be diagrammed in this manner. Such mapping is usually done for either of two purposes:

✳ By an individual or a group to help sort out their own thinking and achieve a shared understanding of key concepts. By getting the ideas out of their heads and down on paper or a computer screen, the individual or group is better able to remember, critique, and modify the ideas.

✳ To facilitate the communication to others of a complex set of relationships. Examples are an intelligence report, a briefing, a school classroom, or a graphic prepared by an analyst for prosecutors to use in a jury trial.

▷ Value Added

Mapping facilitates the presentation or discussion of a complex body of information. It is useful because it presents a considerable amount of information that can generally be seen at a glance. Creating a visual picture of the basic structure of a

---

3. See www.mind-mapping.org for a comprehensive compendium of information on all types of software that supports knowledge management and information organization in graphic form. Many of these software products are available at no cost.

Figure 4.9a   Concept Map of Concept Mapping

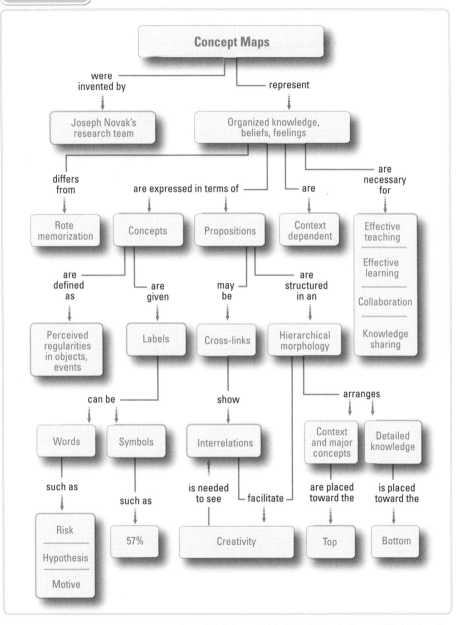

Source: R. R. Hoffman and J. D. Novak, Institute for Human and Machine Cognition, Pensacola, Fla. Reproduced with permission of the author.

Figure 4.9b

Mind Map of Mind Mapping

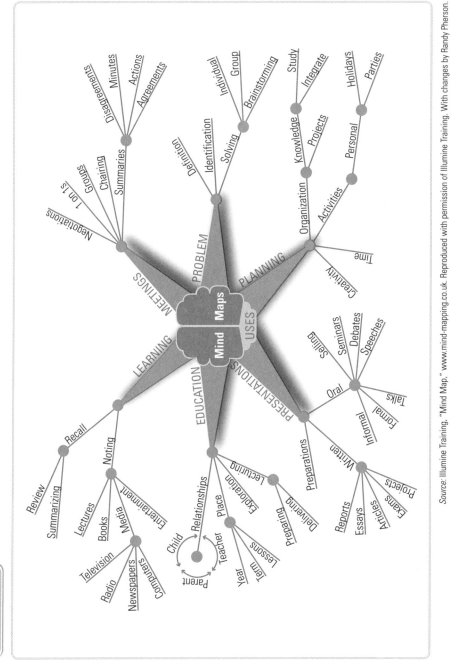

Source: Illumine Training, "Mind Map," www.mind-mapping.co.uk. Reproduced with permission of Illumine Training. With changes by Randy Pherson.

complex problem helps analysts be as clear as possible in stating precisely what they want to express. Diagramming skills enable analysts to stretch their analytic capabilities.

Mind Maps and Concept Maps vary greatly in size and complexity depending on how and why they are being used. When used for structured analysis, a Mind Map or a Concept Map is typically larger, sometimes much larger, than the examples shown in this chapter. Many are of modest size and complexity. Like any model, such a map is a simplification of reality. It does not necessarily try to capture all the nuances of a complex system of relationships. Instead, it provides, for example, an outline picture of the overall structure of a system of variables, showing which variables are relevant to a given problem or issue and how they are related to each other. Once you have this information, you are well along toward knowing what further research needs to be done and perhaps even how to organize the written report. For some projects, the diagram can be the analytical product or a key part of it.

When a Mind Map or Concept Map is created as a group project, its principal value may be the process the group goes through in constructing the map, not the map itself. When a group gets together to identify all the parts of a complex system and figure out how they relate to each other, the process often elicits new ideas, clarifies concepts, identifies relevant bodies of knowledge, and brings to the surface—and often resolves—differences of opinion at an early stage of a project before anything is put in writing. Although such a map may be a bare skeleton, the discussion will have revealed a great deal more information than can be shown in a single map. The process also gives the group a shared experience and a common basis for further discussion. It ensures that this initial effort is truly a group effort at defining the problem, not something done by one member of the group and then presented after the fact for coordination by the others. Some mapping software supports virtual collaboration so that analysts at different locations can work on a map simultaneously and see each other's work as it is done.[4]

After having participated in this group process to define the problem, the group should be better able to identify what further research needs to be done and able to parcel out additional work among the best qualified members of the group. The group should also be better able to prepare a report that represents as fully as possible the collective wisdom of the group as a whole.

Analysts and students also find that Mind Map and Concept Map software products are useful tools for taking notes during an oral briefing or lecture.

---

4. Tanja Keller, Sigmar-Olaf Tergan, and John Coffey, "Concept Maps Used as a 'Knowledge and Information Awareness' Tool for Supporting Collaborative Problem Solving in Distributed Groups," Proceedings of the Second International Conference on Concept Mapping, San Jose, Costa Rica, September 5-8, 2006.

By developing a map as the lecture proceeds, the analyst or student can chart the train of logic and capture all the data presented in a coherent map that includes all the key elements of the subject.

▶ The Method

Start a Mind Map or Concept Map with a focal question that defines what is to be included. Then follow these steps:

* Make a list of concepts that relate in some way to the focal question.

* Starting with the first dozen or so concepts, sort them into groupings within the diagram space in some logical manner. These groups may be based on things they have in common or on their status as either direct or indirect causes of the matter being analyzed.

* Begin making links between related concepts, starting with the most general concepts. Use lines with arrows to show the direction of the relationship. The arrows may go in either direction or in both directions.

* Choose the most appropriate words for describing the nature of each relationship. The lines might be labeled with words such as "causes," "influences," "leads to," "results in," "is required by," or "contributes to." Selecting good linking phrases is often the most difficult step.

* While building all the links between the concepts and the focal question, look for and enter crosslinks between concepts.

* Don't be surprised if, as the map develops, you discover that you are now diagramming on a different focus question from the one you started with. This can be a good thing. The purpose of a focus question is not to lock down the topic but to get the process going.

* Finally, reposition, refine, and expand the map structure as appropriate.

Mind Mapping and Concept Mapping can be done manually, but mapping software is strongly recommended; it is much easier and faster to move concepts and links around on a computer screen than it is to do so manually. There are many different software programs for various types of mapping, and each has strengths and weaknesses. These products are usually variations of the main contenders, Mind Mapping and Concept Mapping. The two leading techniques differ in the following ways:

* Mind Mapping has only one main or central idea, and all other ideas branch off from it radially in all directions. The central idea is preferably shown as an image rather than in words, and images are used throughout the map.

"Around the central word you draw the 5 or 10 main ideas that relate to that word. You then take each of those child words and again draw the 5 or 10 main ideas that relate to each of those words."[5] A Concept Map has a more flexible form. It can have multiple hubs and clusters. It can also be designed around a central idea, but it does not have to be and often is not designed that way. It does not normally use images. A Concept Map is usually shown as a network, although it too can be shown as a hierarchical structure like Mind Mapping when that is appropriate. Concept Maps can be very complex and are often meant to be viewed on a large-format screen.

﹡ Mind Mapping was originally developed as a fast and efficient way to take notes during briefings and lectures. Concept Mapping was originally developed as a means of mapping students' emerging knowledge about science; it has a foundation in the constructivist theory of learning, which emphasizes that "meaningful learning involves the assimilation of new concepts and propositions into existing cognitive structures."[6] Concept Maps are frequently used as teaching tools. Most recently, they have come to be used to develop "knowledge models," in which large sets of complex Concept Maps are created and hyperlinked together to represent analyses of complex domains or problems.

▷ **Relationship to Other Techniques**

Mind and Concept Mapping can be used to present visually the results generated by a number of other techniques, especially the various types of brainstorming and/or Cross-Impact Analysis, both described in chapter 5.

▷ **Origins of This Technique**

Mapping is an old technique that has been given new life by the development of software that makes it both more useful and easier to use. Information on Concept Mapping is available at http://cmap.ihmc.us/conceptmap.html. For information on Mind Mapping, see Tony and Barry Buzan, *The Mind Map Book* (Essex, England: BBC Active, 2006). For information on mapping in general, see Eric Hanson, "A Survey of Concept Mapping Tools," http://datalab.cs.pdx.edu/sidewalk/pub/survey.of.concept.maps; and Banxia Software, "What's in a Name? Cognitive Mapping, Mind Mapping, Concept Mapping," www.banxia.com/dexplore/whatsiname.html.

---

5. Tony Buzan, *The Mind Map Book*, 2nd ed. (London: BBC Books, 1995).

6. Joseph D. Novak and Alberto J. Canas, *The Theory Underlying Concept Maps and How to Construct and Use Them,* Technical Report IHMC Cmap Tools 2006–01 (Penascola: Florida Institute for Human and Machine Cognition, 2006), http://cmap.ihmc.us/Publications/ResearchPapers/TheoryUnderlyingConcept Maps.pdf.

4.10 PROCESS MAPS AND GANTT CHARTS

Process Mapping is an umbrella term that covers a variety of procedures for identifying and depicting visually each step in a complex procedure. It includes flow charts of various types (Activity Flow Charts, Commodity Flow Charts, Causal Flow Charts), Relationship Maps, and Value Stream Maps commonly used to assess and plan improvements for business and industrial processes. A Gantt Chart is a specific type of Process Map that was developed to facilitate the planning, scheduling, and management of complex industrial projects.

▶ **When to Use It**

Process Maps, including Gantt Charts, are used by intelligence analysts to track, understand, and monitor the progress of activities of intelligence interest being undertaken by a foreign government, a criminal or terrorist group, or any other nonstate actor. For example, a Process Map can be used to monitor progress in developing a new weapons system, preparations for a major military action, or the execution of any other major plan that involves a sequence of observable steps. It is often used to identify and describe the *modus operandi* of a criminal or terrorist group, including the preparatory steps that such a group typically takes prior to a major action. It has been used to describe and monitor the process of radicalization by which a normal youth may be transformed over time into a terrorist.

▶ **Value Added**

The process of constructing a Process Map or a Gantt Chart helps analysts think clearly about what someone else needs to do to complete a complex project. When a complex plan or process is understood well enough to be diagrammed or charted, analysts can then answer questions such as the following: What are they doing? How far along are they? What do they still need to do? What resources will they need to do it? How much time do we have before they have this capability? Is there any vulnerable point in this process where they can be stopped or slowed down?

The Process Map or Gantt Chart is a visual aid for communicating this information to the customer. If sufficient information can be obtained, the analyst's understanding of the process will lead to a set of indicators that can be used to monitor the status of an ongoing plan or project.

▶ The Method

There is a substantial difference in appearance between a Process Map and a Gantt Chart. In a Process Map, the steps in the process are diagrammed sequentially with various symbols representing starting and end points, decisions, and actions connected with arrows. Diagrams can be created with readily available software such as Microsoft Visio.

A Gantt Chart is a matrix that lists tasks in a project or steps in a process down the far left column, with the estimated time period for accomplishing these tasks or steps in weeks, months, or years across the top row. For each task or step, a horizontal line or bar shows the beginning and ending of the time period for that task or step. Professionals working with Gantt Charts use tools such as Microsoft Project to draw the chart. Gantt Charts can also be made with Microsoft Excel or by hand on graph paper.

Detailed guidance on creating a Process Map or Gantt Chart is readily available from the sources described under Origins of This Technique.

▶ Example

The Intelligence Community has considerable experience monitoring terrorist groups. This example describes how an analyst would go about creating a Gantt Chart of a generic terrorist attack-planning process (see Figure 4.10). The analyst starts by making a list of all the tasks that terrorists must complete, estimating the schedule for when each task will be started and finished, and determining what resources are needed for each task. Some tasks need to be completed in a sequence, with each task being more-or-less completed before the next activity can begin. These are called sequential, or linear, activities. Other activities are not dependent upon completion of any other tasks. These may be done at any time before or after a particular stage is reached. These are called nondependent, or parallel, tasks.

Note whether each terrorist task to be performed is sequential or parallel. It is this sequencing of dependent and nondependent activities that is critical in determining how long any particular project or process will take. The more activities that can be worked in parallel, the greater the chances of a project being completed on time. The more tasks that must be done sequentially, the greater the chances of a single bottleneck delaying the entire project.

When entering tasks into the Gantt Chart, enter the sequential tasks first in the required sequence. Ensure that they don't start until the tasks they depend upon have been completed. Then enter the parallel tasks in an appropriate time frame toward the bottom of the matrix so that they do not interfere with the sequential tasks on the critical path to completion of the project.

Figure 4.10

Gantt Chart of Terrorist Attack Planning

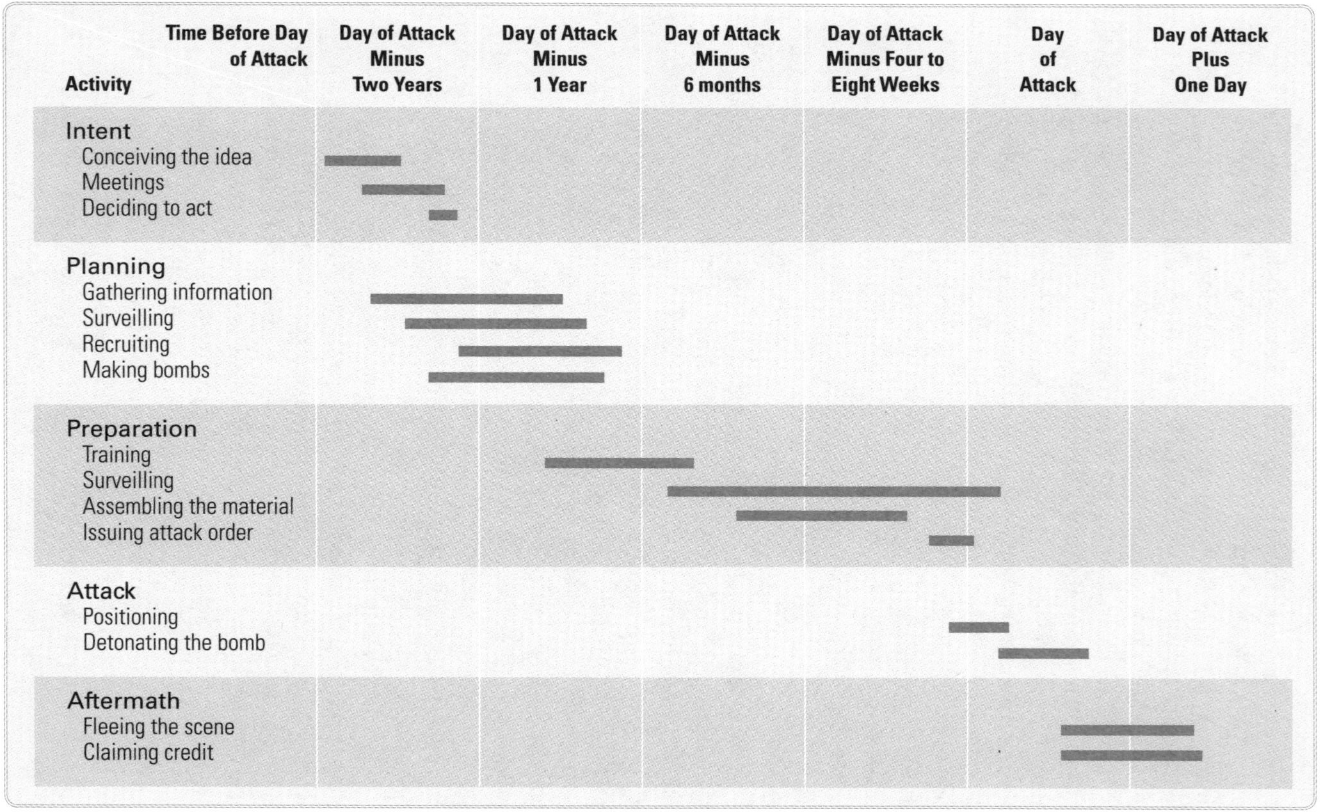

Activity	Time Before Day of Attack	Day of Attack Minus Two Years	Day of Attack Minus 1 Year	Day of Attack Minus 6 months	Day of Attack Minus Four to Eight Weeks	Day of Attack	Day of Attack Plus One Day
Intent							
Conceiving the idea		▮					
Meetings		▮					
Deciding to act		▮					
Planning							
Gathering information			▮				
Surveilling			▮				
Recruiting			▮				
Making bombs			▮				
Preparation							
Training			▮	▮			
Surveilling				▮			
Assembling the material					▮		
Issuing attack order					▮		
Attack							
Positioning					▮		
Detonating the bomb						▮	
Aftermath							
Fleeing the scene							▮
Claiming credit							▮

Source: Based on Gantt Chart by Richard Damelio, *The Basics of Process Mapping* (Florence, Ky.: Productivity Press, 2006). www.ganttchart.com.

Gantt Charts that map a generic process can also be used to track data about a more specific process as it is received. For example, the Gantt Chart depicted in Figure 4.10 can be used as a template over which new information about a specific group's activities could be layered by using a different color or line type. Layering in the specific data allows an analyst to compare what is expected with the actual data. The chart can then be used to identify and narrow gaps or anomalies in the data and even to identify and challenge assumptions about what is expected or what is happening. The analytic significance of considering such possibilities can mean the difference between anticipating an attack and wrongly assuming that a lack of activity means a lack of intent. The matrix illuminates the gap and prompts the analyst to consider various explanations.

▶ **Origin of This Technique**
Development of Gantt Charts was considered a revolutionary advance in the early 1900s. During the period of industrial development, Gantt charts were used to plan industrial processes, and they are still in common use. Information on how to create and use Gantt Charts is readily available at www.ganttchart.com. Information on how to use other types of Process Mapping is available in Richard Damelio, *The Basics of Process Mapping* (Florence, Ky.: Productivity Press, 2006).

5

Idea
Generation

5

Idea Generation

5.1   Structured Brainstorming   [92]

5.2   Virtual Brainstorming   [97]

5.3   Nominal Group Technique   [99]

5.4.   Starbursting   [102]

5.5   Cross-Impact Matrix   [104]

5.6   Morphological Analysis   [108]

5.7   Quadrant Crunching   [111]

CHAPTER 5

Idea Generation

New ideas, and the combination of old ideas in new ways, are essential elements of effective intelligence analysis. Some structured techniques are specifically intended for the purpose of eliciting or generating ideas at the very early stage of a project, and they are the topic of this chapter.

In one sense, all structured analytic techniques are idea-generation techniques when they are used in a collaborative group process. A group or team using a structured analytic technique is usually more effective than a single individual in generating new ideas and in synthesizing divergent ideas. The structured process helps identify differences in perspective and different assumptions among team or group members, and thus stimulates learning and new ideas.

> *Imagination is more important than knowledge. For while knowledge defines all we currently know and understand, imagination points to all we might yet discover and create.*
>
> —Albert Einstein

Overview of Techniques

Structured Brainstorming is not a group of colleagues just sitting around talking about a problem. Rather, it is a group process that follows specific rules and procedures. It is often used at the beginning of a project to identify a list of relevant variables, driving forces, a full range of hypotheses, key players or stakeholders, available evidence or sources of information, potential solutions to a problem, potential outcomes or scenarios, or, in law enforcement, potential suspects or avenues of investigation. It requires little training, and is one of the most frequently used structured techniques in the Intelligence Community. It is most helpful when paired with a mechanism such as a wiki that allows analysts to capture and record the results of their brainstorming. The wiki also allows participants to refine or make additions to the brainstorming results even after the face-to-face session has ended.

Virtual Brainstorming is a way to use Structured Brainstorming when participants are in different geographic locations. The absence of face-to-face contact has disadvantages, but it also has advantages. The remote process can help relieve some of the pressure analysts may feel from bosses or peers in a face-to-face format. It can also increase productivity, because participants can make their inputs on a wiki at their convenience without having to read others' ideas quickly while thinking about their own ideas and waiting for their turn to speak. The wiki format—including the ability to upload documents and even hand-drawn graphics or photos—allows analysts to capture and track brainstorming ideas and return to them at a later date.

Nominal Group Technique, often abbreviated NGT, serves much the same function as Structured Brainstorming, but it uses a quite different approach. It is the preferred technique when there is a concern that a senior member or outspoken member of the group may dominate the meeting, that junior members may be reluctant to speak up, or that the meeting may lead to heated debate. Nominal Group Technique encourages equal participation by requiring participants to present ideas one at a time in round-robin fashion until all participants feel that they have run out of ideas.

Starbursting is a form of brainstorming that focuses on generating questions rather than answers. To help in defining the parameters of a research project, use Starbursting to identify the questions that need to be answered. Questions start with the words Who, What, When, Where, Why, and How. Brainstorm each of these words, one at a time, to generate as many questions as possible about the research topic.

Cross-Impact Matrix is a technique that can be used after any form of brainstorming session that identifies a list of variables relevant to a particular analytic project. The results of the brainstorming session are put into a matrix, which is used to guide a group discussion that systematically examines how each variable influences all other variables to which it is judged to be related in a particular problem context. The group discussion is often a valuable learning experience that provides a foundation for further collaboration. Results of cross-impact discussions can be maintained in a wiki for continuing reference.

Morphological Analysis is useful for dealing with complex, nonquantifiable problems for which little data are available and the chances for surprise are significant. It is a generic method for systematically identifying and considering all possible relationships in a multidimensional, highly complex, usually nonquantifiable problem space. It helps prevent surprises in intelligence analysis by generating a large number of outcomes for any complex situation, thus reducing the chance that events will play out in a way that the analyst has not previously imagined and has not at least considered. Training and practice are required before this method is used, and a facilitator experienced in Morphological Analysis may be necessary.

Quadrant Crunching is an application of Morphological Analysis that uses key assumptions and their opposites as a starting point for systematically generating a large number of alternative outcomes. For example, an analyst might use Quadrant Crunching to identify the many different ways that a terrorist might attack a water supply. The technique forces analysts to rethink an issue from a broad range of perspectives and systematically question all the assumptions that underlie their lead hypothesis. It is most useful for ambiguous situations for which little information is available.

5.1 STRUCTURED BRAINSTORMING

Structured Brainstorming is one of several different forms of brainstorming described in this chapter. People sometimes say they are brainstorming when they sit with a few colleagues or even by themselves and try to come up with relevant ideas. That is not what Structured Brainstorming is about. It is a group process that follows specific rules and procedures designed for maximum productivity. The advent of collaborative tools such as wikis has helped bring structure to the brainstorming process. Whether brainstorming begins with a face-to-face session or is done entirely online, the collaborative features of wikis can facilitate the analytic process by obliging analysts to capture results in a sharable format that can be posted, understood by others, and refined for future use. In addition, wikis amplify and extend the brainstorming process—potentially improving the results—because each edit and the reasoning for it is tracked, and disagreements or refinements can be openly discussed and explicitly summarized on the wiki.

▶ **When to Use It**

Structured Brainstorming is one of the most widely used analytic techniques. It is often used at the beginning of a project to identify a list of relevant variables, driving forces, a full range of hypotheses, key players or stakeholders, available evidence or sources of information, potential solutions to a problem, potential outcomes or scenarios, or, for law enforcement, potential suspects or avenues of investigation.

It is often appropriate to follow a brainstorming session with Cross-Impact Analysis to examine the relationship between each of the variables, players, or other factors identified by the brainstorming. Later in the analytic process, brainstorming can be used again, if needed, to pull the team out of an analytic rut or to stimulate new investigative leads.

▶ **Value Added**

The stimulus for creativity comes from two or more analysts bouncing ideas off each other. A brainstorming session usually exposes an analyst to a greater range of ideas and perspectives than the analyst could generate alone, and this broadening of views typically results in a better analytic product.

▶ **The Method**

There are seven general rules to follow, and then a twelve-step process for Structured Brainstorming. Here are the rules:

* Be specific about the purpose and the topic of the brainstorming session. Announce the topic beforehand, and ask participants to come to the session with some ideas or to forward them to the facilitator before the session.

* New ideas are always encouraged. Never criticize an idea during the divergent (creative) phase of the process no matter how weird or unconventional or improbable it might sound. Instead, try to figure out how the idea might be applied to the task at hand.

* Allow only one conversation at a time, and ensure that everyone has an opportunity to speak.

* Allocate enough time to do the brainstorming correctly. It often takes one hour to set the rules of the game, get the group comfortable, and exhaust the conventional wisdom on the topic. Only then do truly creative ideas begin to emerge.

* To avoid groupthink and stimulate divergent thinking, include one or more "outsiders" in the group—that is, astute thinkers who do not share the same body of knowledge or perspective as the other group members but do have some familiarity with the topic.

* Write it down! Track the discussion by using a whiteboard, an easel, or sticky notes (see Figure 5.1).

* Summarize the key findings at the end of the session. Ask the participants to write down the most important thing they learned on a 3 x 5 card as they depart the session. Then prepare a short summary and distribute the list to the participants (who may add items to the list) and to others interested in the topic (including supervisors and those who could not attend). Capture these findings and disseminate them to attendees and other interested parties either by e-mail or, preferably, a wiki. If there is a need to capture the initial brainstorming results as a "snapshot in time," simply upload the results as a .pdf or other word processing document, but still allow the brainstorming discussion to continue on the wiki.

The facilitator or group leader should present the focal question, explain and enforce the ground rules, keep the meeting on track, stimulate discussion by asking questions, record the ideas, and summarize the key findings. Participants should be encouraged to express every idea that pops into their heads. Even ideas that are outside the realm of the possible may stimulate other ideas that are more feasible. The group should have at least four and no more than twelve participants. Five to seven is an optimal number; if there are more than twelve people, divide into two groups.

Figure 5.1   **Picture of Brainstorming**

Source: 2009 Pherson Associates, LLC.

There are several different forms of brainstorming. The following twelve-step process was developed for the CIA's Sherman Kent School for Intelligence Analysis and has worked well for a number of years. The process is divided into two phases: a divergent thinking (creative) phase when ideas are presented and a convergent thinking phase when these ideas are evaluated.

* Pass out Post-it or "sticky" notes and Sharpie-type pens or markers to all participants.

* Pose the problem or topic in terms of a "focal question." Display this question in one sentence for all to see on a large easel or whiteboard.

* Ask the group to write down responses to the question with a few key words that will fit on a Post-it. When a response is written down, the participant is asked to read it out loud or to give it to the facilitator who will read it out loud. Sharpie-type pens are used so that people can easily see what is written on the Post-it notes later in the exercise.

* Stick all the Post-its on a wall in the order in which they are called out. Treat all ideas the same. Encourage participants to build on one another's ideas.

* Usually there is an initial spurt of ideas followed by pauses as participants contemplate the question. After five or ten minutes there is often a long pause of a minute or so. This slowing down suggests that the group has "emptied the barrel of the obvious" and is now on the verge of coming up with some fresh insights and ideas. Do not talk during this pause even if the silence is uncomfortable.

* After two or three long pauses, conclude this divergent thinking phase of the brainstorming session.

* Ask all participants as a group to go up to the wall and rearrange the Post-its in some organized manner. This arrangement might be by affinity groups (groups that have some common characteristic), scenarios, a pre-determined priority scale, or a time sequence. Participants are not allowed to talk during this process. Some Post-its may be moved several times, but they will gradually be clustered into logical groupings. Post-its may be copied if necessary to fit one idea into more than one group.

* When all Post-its have been arranged, ask the group to select a word or phrase that best describes each grouping.

* Look for Post-its that do not fit neatly into any of the groups. Consider whether such an outlier is useless noise or the germ of an idea that deserves further attention.

* Assess what the group has accomplished. Have new ideas or concepts been identified, have key issues emerged, or are there areas that need more work or further brainstorming?

* To identify the potentially most useful ideas, the facilitator or group leader should establish up to five criteria for judging the value or importance of the ideas. If so desired, then use the Ranking, Scoring, Prioritizing technique, described in chapter 4, for voting on or ranking or prioritizing ideas.

* Set the analytic priorities accordingly, and decide on a work plan for the next steps in the analysis.

▶ Relationship to Other Techniques

As discussed under "When to Use It," some form of brainstorming is commonly combined with a wide variety of other techniques. It is often an early step in many analytic projects used to identify ideas, variables, evidence, possible outcomes, suspects, or hypotheses that are then processed by using other structured techniques.

Structured Brainstorming is also called Divergent/Convergent Thinking. Other forms of brainstorming described in this chapter include Nominal Group Technique and Virtual Brainstorming. If there is any concern that a brainstorming session may be dominated by a senior officer or that junior personnel may be reluctant to speak up, Nominal Group Technique may be the best choice.

▷ **Origins of This Technique**

Brainstorming was a creativity technique used by advertising agencies in the 1940s. It was popularized in a book by advertising manager Alex Osborn, *Applied Imagination: Principles and Procedures of Creative Problem Solving* (New York: Scribner's, 1953). There are many versions of brainstorming. The description here is a combination of information from Randy Pherson, "Structured Brainstorming," in *Handbook of Analytic Tools and Techniques* (Reston, Va.: Pherson Associates, LLC, 2008), and training materials from the CIA's Sherman Kent School for Intelligence Analysis.

VIRTUAL BRAINSTORMING

Virtual Brainstorming is the same as Structured Brainstorming except that it is done online with participants who are geographically dispersed or unable to meet in person. The advantages and disadvantages of Virtual Brainstorming as compared with Structured Brainstorming are discussed in the "Value Added" section.

▶ **When to Use It**

Virtual Brainstorming is an appropriate technique to use for a panel of outside experts or a group of personnel from the same organization who are working in different locations. It is also appropriate for a group of analysts working at several locations within a large metropolitan area, such as Washington, D.C., where distances and traffic can cause a two-hour meeting to consume most of the day for some participants.

▶ **Value Added**

Virtual Brainstorming can be as productive as face-to-face Structured Brainstorming. The productivity of face-to-face brainstorming is constrained by what researchers on the subject call "production blocking." Participants have to wait their turn to speak. And they have to think about what they want to say while trying to pay attention to what others are saying. Something always suffers. What suffers depends upon how the brainstorming session is organized. Often, it is the synergy that can be gained when participants react to one another's ideas. Synergy occurs when an idea from one participant triggers a new idea in another participant, an idea that otherwise may not have arisen. For intelligence analysts, synergistic thinking may be the most fundamental source of gains from brainstorming.

In synchronous Virtual Brainstorming, all participants are engaged at the same time. In asynchronous Virtual Brainstorming, participants can make their inputs and read the inputs of others at their convenience. This means that nothing is competing for a participant's attention when he or she is suggesting ideas or when reading the input of others. If the brainstorming session is spread over two or three days, participants can occasionally revisit their inputs and the inputs of others with a fresh mind; this process usually generates further ideas.

Another benefit of Virtual Brainstorming, whether synchronous or asynchronous, is that participants can provide their inputs anonymously if the software needed to support that feature is available. This is particularly useful in an environment where status or hierarchy influence people's behavior. Anonymity is sometimes necessary to elicit original ideas rather than "politically correct" ideas.

Of course, face-to-face meetings have significant benefits. There is often a downside to online communication as compared with face-to-face communication. (Guidance for facilitators of Virtual Brainstorming is available in the article by Nancy Settle-Murphy and Julia Young listed under "Origins of This Technique.")

▷ **The Method**

Virtual Brainstorming is usually a two-phase process. It usually begins with the divergent process of creating as many relevant ideas as possible. The second phase is a process of convergence when the ideas are sorted into categories, weeded out, prioritized, or combined and molded into a conclusion or plan of action. Software is available for performing these common functions online. The nature of this second step will vary depending on the specific topic and the goal of the brainstorming session.

▷ **Relationship to Other Techniques**

See the discussions of Structured Brainstorming and Nominal Group Technique and compare the relative advantages and possible weaknesses of each.

▷ **Origins of This Technique**

Virtual Brainstorming is the application of conventional brainstorming to the computer age. The discussion here combines information from several sources: Alan R. Dennis and Mike L. Williams, "Electronic Brainstorming: Theory, Research and Future Directions," Indiana University, Information Systems Technical Reports and Working Papers, TR116-1, April 2002, www.bus.indiana.edu/ardennis/wp; Alan R. Dennis and Joseph S. Valacich, "Computer Brainstorming: More Heads Are Better than One," *Journal of Applied Psychology* 78 (August1993): 531–537; Nancy Settle-Murphy and Julia Young, "Virtual Brainstorming: A New Approach to Creative Thinking," *Communique,* 2009, www.facilitate.com/Resources_Communique.html.

ominal Group Technique (NGT) is a process for generating and evaluating ideas. It is a form of brainstorming, but NGT has always had its own identity as a separate technique. The goals of Nominal Group Technique and Structured Brainstorming are the same—the generation of good, innovative, and viable ideas. NGT differs from Structured Brainstorming in several important ways. Most important, ideas are presented one at a time in round-robin fashion.

▶ When to Use It

NGT prevents the domination of a discussion by a single person. Use it whenever there is concern that a senior officer or executive or an outspoken member of the group will control the direction of the meeting by speaking before anyone else. It is also appropriate to use NGT rather than Structured Brainstorming if there is concern that some members may not speak up or if the issue under discussion is controversial and may provoke a heated debate. NGT can be used to coordinate the initial conceptualization of a problem before the research and writing stages begin. Like brainstorming, NGT is commonly used to identify ideas (assumptions, hypotheses, drivers, causes, variables, important players) that can then be incorporated into other methods.

▶ Value Added

NGT can be used both to generate ideas and to provide backup support in a decision-making process where all participants are asked to rank or prioritize the ideas that are generated. If it seems desirable, all ideas and votes can be kept anonymous. Compared with Structured Brainstorming, which usually seeks to generate the greatest possible number of ideas—no matter how far out they may be—NGT may focus on a limited list of carefully considered opinions.

The technique allows participants to focus on each idea as it is presented, rather than having to think simultaneously about preparing their own ideas and listening to what others are proposing—a situation that often happens with Structured Brainstorming. NGT encourages piggybacking on ideas that have already been presented—in other words, combining, modifying, and expanding others' ideas.

▶ The Method

An NGT session starts with the facilitator asking an open-ended question, such as, "What factors will influence . . . ?" "How can we learn if . . . ?" "In what circumstances might . . . happen?" "What should be included or not included in this research project?" The facilitator answers any questions about what is expected of participants and then gives participants five to ten minutes to work privately to jot down on note cards their initial ideas in response to the focal question. This part of the process is followed by these steps:

＊ The facilitator calls on one person at a time to present one idea. As each idea is presented, the facilitator writes a summary description on a flip chart or whiteboard. This process continues in a round-robin fashion until all ideas have been exhausted. If individuals have run out of ideas, they pass when called upon for an idea, but they can participate again later if they have another idea when their turn comes up again. The facilitator can also be an active participant, writing down his or her own ideas. There is no discussion until all ideas have been presented; however, the facilitator can clarify ideas to avoid duplication.

＊ When no new ideas are forthcoming, the facilitator initiates a group discussion to ensure that there is a common understanding of what each idea means. The facilitator asks about each idea, one at a time, in the order presented, but no argument for or against any idea is allowed. It is possible at this time to expand or combine ideas, but no change can be made to any idea without the approval of the original presenter of the idea.

＊ Voting to rank or prioritize the ideas as discussed in chapter 4 is optional, depending upon the purpose of the meeting. When voting is done, it is usually by secret ballot, although various voting procedures may be used depending in part on the number of ideas and the number of participants. It usually works best to employ a ratio of one vote for every three ideas presented. For example, if the facilitator lists twelve ideas, each participant is allowed to cast four votes. The group can also decide to let participants give an idea more than one vote. In this case, someone could give one idea three votes and another idea only one vote. An alternative procedure is for each participant to write what he or she considers the five best ideas on a 3 × 5 card. One might rank the ideas on a scale of 1 to 5, with five points for the best idea, four points for the next best, down to one point for the least favored idea. The cards are then passed to the facilitator for tabulation and announcement of the scores. It may then be desirable to have a second round of voting to rank the top three or five ideas.

▶ Relationship to Other Techniques

Analysts should consider Structured Brainstorming and Virtual Brainstorming as well as Nominal Group Technique and determine which technique is most appropriate for the conditions in which it will be used.

▶ Origins of This Technique

Nominal Group Technique was developed by A. L. Delbecq and A. H. Van de Ven and first described in "A Group Process Model for Problem Identification and Program Planning," *Journal of Applied Behavioral Science* VII (July-August, 1971): 466-491. The discussion of NGT here is a synthesis of several sources: James M. Higgins, *101 Creative Problem Solving Techniques: The Handbook of New Ideas for Business,* rev. ed. (Winter Park, Fla.: New Management Publishing Company, 2006); www.asq.org/learn-about-quality/idea-creation-tools/overview/nominal-group. html; http://syque.com/quality_tools/toolbook/NGT/ngt.htm; and www.mycoted .com/Nominal_Group_Technique.

5.4   STARBURSTING

Starbursting is a form of brainstorming that focuses on generating questions rather than eliciting ideas or answers. It uses the six questions commonly asked by journalists: Who? What? When? Where? Why? and How?

▶ **When to Use It**

Use Starbursting to help define your research project. After deciding on the idea, topic, or issue to be analyzed, brainstorm to identify the questions that need to be answered by the research. Asking the right questions is a common prerequisite to finding the right answer.

▶ **The Method**

The term "Starbursting" comes from the image of a six-pointed star. To create a Starburst diagram, begin by writing one of the following six words at each point of the star: Who, What, When, Where, Why, and How. Then start the brainstorming session, using one of these words at a time to generate questions about the topic. Don't try to answer the questions as they are identified; just focus on developing as many questions as possible. After generating questions that start with each of the six words, ask the group either to prioritize the questions to be answered or to sort the questions into logical categories. Figure 5.4 is an example of a Starbursting diagram. It identifies questions to be asked about a biological attack in a subway.

▶ **Relationship to Other Techniques**

This Who, What, When, Where, Why, and How approach can be combined very effectively with the Getting Started Checklist and Issue Redefinition tools in chapter 4. Ranking, Scoring, Prioritizing (chapter 4) can be used to prioritize the questions to be worked on. Starbursting is also directly related to the analysis of cause and effect as discussed in chapter 8.

▶ **Origin of This Technique**

Starbursting is one of many techniques developed to stimulate creativity. The basic idea for Figure 5.4 comes from the MindTools Web site at www.mindtools.com/pages/article/newCT_91.htm.

Figure 5.4

Starbursting Diagram of a Lethal Biological Event at a Subway Station

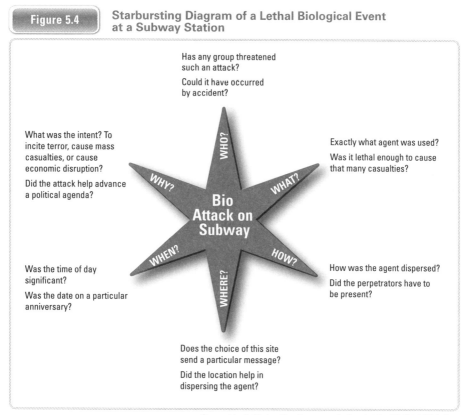

Has any group threatened such an attack?

Could it have occurred by accident?

What was the intent? To incite terror, cause mass casualties, or cause economic disruption?

Did the attack help advance a political agenda?

Exactly what agent was used?

Was it lethal enough to cause that many casualties?

Was the time of day significant?

Was the date on a particular anniversary?

How was the agent dispersed?

Did the perpetrators have to be present?

Does the choice of this site send a particular message?

Did the location help in dispersing the agent?

Source: A basic Starbursting diagram can be found at the MindTools Web site: www.mindtools.com/pages/article/worksheets/Starbursting.pdf. This version was created by the authors.

5.5 CROSS-IMPACT MATRIX

The Cross-Impact Matrix helps analysts deal with complex problems when "everything is related to everything else." By using this technique, analysts and decision makers can systematically examine how each factor in a particular context influences all other factors to which it appears to be related.

▶ When to Use It

The Cross-Impact Matrix is useful early in a project when a group is still in a learning mode trying to sort out a complex situation. Whenever a brainstorming session or other meeting is held to identify all the variables, drivers, or players that may influence the outcome of a situation, the next logical step is to use a Cross-Impact Matrix to examine the interrelationships among each of these variables. A group discussion of how each pair of variables interacts can be an enlightening learning experience and a good basis on which to build ongoing collaboration. How far one goes in actually filling in the matrix and writing up a description of the impacts associated with each variable may vary depending upon the nature and significance of the project. At times, just the discussion is sufficient. Writing up the interactions with the summary for each pair of variables can be done effectively in a wiki.

Analysis of cross-impacts is also useful when:

* A situation is in flux, and there is a need to understand all the factors that might influence the outcome. This also requires understanding how all the factors relate to each other, and how they might influence each other.

* A situation is stable, and there is a need to identify and monitor all the factors that could upset that stability. This, too, requires understanding how the various factors might interact to influence each other.

* A significant event has just occurred, and there is a need to understand the implications of the event. What other significant forces are influenced by the event, and what are the implications of this influence?

▶ Value Added

When analysts are estimating or forecasting future events, they consider the dominant forces and potential future events that might influence an outcome. They then weigh the relative influence or likelihood of these forces or events, often considering them individually without regard to sometimes significant interactions that might occur. The Cross-Impact Matrix provides a context for the discussion of these interactions. This discussion often reveals that variables or issues once believed to be simple and independent are, in reality, interrelated. The information sharing that occurs during a small-group discussion of each potential cross-impact can be an invaluable learning experience. For this reason alone, the Cross-Impact Matrix is a useful tool that can be applied at some point in almost any study that seeks to explain current events or forecast future outcomes.

The Cross-Impact Matrix provides a structure for managing the complexity that makes intelligence analysis so difficult. It requires that all assumptions about the relationships between variables be clearly articulated. Thus, any conclusions reached through this technique can be defended or critiqued by tracing the analytical argument back through a path of underlying premises.

▶ **The Method**

Assemble a group of analysts knowledgeable on various aspects of the subject. The group brainstorms a list of variables or events that would likely have some effect on the issue being studied. The project coordinator then creates a matrix and puts the list of variables or events down the left side of the matrix and the same variables or events across the top.

The matrix is then used to consider and record the relationship between each variable or event and every other variable or event. For example, does the presence of Variable 1 increase or diminish the influence of Variables 2, 3, 4, etc.? Or does the occurrence of Event 1 increase or decrease the likelihood of Events 2, 3, 4, etc.? If one variable does affect the other, the positive or negative magnitude of this effect can be recorded in the matrix by entering a large or small + or a large or small – in the appropriate cell (or by making no marking at all if there is no significant effect). The terminology used to describe each relationship between a pair of variables or events is that it is "enhancing," "inhibiting," or "unrelated."

The matrix shown in Figure 5.5 has six variables, with thirty possible interactions. Note that the relationship between each pair of variables is assessed twice, as the relationship may not be symmetric. That is, the influence of Variable 1 on Variable 2 may not be the same as the impact of Variable 2 on Variable 1. It is not unusual for a Cross-Impact Matrix to have substantially more than thirty possible interactions, in which case careful consideration of each interaction can be time consuming.

Analysts should use the Cross-Impact technique to focus on significant interactions between variables or events that may have been overlooked, or combinations of variables that might reinforce each other. Combinations of variables that

Figure 5.5

Cross-Impact Matrix

	Variable 1	Variable 2	Variable 3	Variable 4	Variable 5	Variable 6
Variable 1			+		▬	
Variable 2			-	**+**	+	+
Variable 3	+	-		+		-
Variable 4		**+**			+	-
Variable 5	▬	+		+		
Variable 6	-	+	▬	-	-	

Variables 2 and 4 in the cross impact matrix above have the greatest effect on the other variables, while variable 6 has the most negative effect.

Direction and magnitude of the effect:
+ strong positive
+ positive
  neutral
- negative
▬ strong negative

reinforce each other can lead to surprisingly rapid changes in a predictable direction. On the other hand, for some problems it may be sufficient simply to recognize that there is a relationship and the direction of that relationship.

The depth of discussion and the method used for recording the results are discretionary. Each depends upon how much you are learning from the discussion, and that will vary from one application of this matrix to another. If the group discussion of the likelihood of these variables or events and their relationships to each other is a productive learning experience, keep it going. If key relationships are identified that are likely to influence the analytic judgment, fill in all cells in the matrix and take good notes. If the group does not seem to be learning much, cut the discussion short.

As a collaborative effort, team members can conduct their discussion online with input recorded in a wiki. Set up a wiki with space to enter information about each cross-impact. Analysts can then, as time permits, enter new information or edit previously entered information about the interaction between each pair of variables. This record will serve as a point of reference or a memory jogger throughout the project.

▶ Relationship to Other Techniques

Matrices as a generic technique with many types of applications are discussed in chapter 4. The use of a Cross-Impact Matrix as described here frequently follows some form of brainstorming at the start of an analytic project to elicit the further assistance of other knowledgeable analysts in exploring all the relationships among the relevant factors identified by the brainstorming. It can be a good idea to build on the discussion of the Cross-Impact Matrix by developing a visual Mind Map or Concept Map of all the relationships.

See also Complexity Manager (chapter 11). An integral part of the Complexity Manager technique is a form of Cross-Impact Analysis that takes the analysis a step further toward an informed conclusion.

▶ Origins of This Technique

The Cross-Impact Matrix technique was developed in the 1960s as one element of a quantitative futures analysis methodology called Cross-Impact Analysis. Richards Heuer became familiar with it when the CIA was testing the Cross-Impact Analysis methodology. He started using it as an intelligence analysis technique, as described here, more than thirty years ago.

MORPHOLOGICAL ANALYSIS

Morphological Analysis is a method for systematically structuring and examining all the possible relationships in a multidimensional, highly complex, usually nonquantifiable problem space. The basic idea is to identify a set of variables and then look at all the possible combinations of these variables.

Morphological Analysis is a generic method used in a variety of disciplines. For intelligence analysis, it helps prevent surprise by generating a large number of feasible outcomes for any complex situation. This exercise reduces the chance that events will play out in a way that the analyst has not previously imagined and considered. Specific applications of this method are Quadrant Crunching (discussed later in this chapter), Multiple Scenarios Generation (chapter 6), and Quadrant Hypothesis Generation (chapter 7). Training and practice are required before using this method, and the availability of a facilitator experienced in morphological analysis is highly desirable.

▶ **When to Use It**

Morphological Analysis is most useful for dealing with complex, nonquantifiable problems for which little information is available and the chances for surprise are great. It can be used, for example, to identify possible variations of a threat, possible ways a crisis might occur between two countries, possible ways a set of driving forces might interact, or the full range of potential outcomes in any ambiguous situation. Morphological Analysis is generally used early in an analytic project, as it is intended to identify all the possibilities, not to drill deeply into any specific possibility.

Although Morphological Analysis is typically used for looking ahead, it can also be used in an investigative context to identify the full set of possible explanations for some event.

▶ **Value Added**

By generating a comprehensive list of possible outcomes, analysts are in a better position to identify and select those outcomes that seem most credible or that most deserve attention. This list helps analysts and decision makers focus on what actions need to be undertaken today to prepare for events that could occur in the future. They can then take the actions necessary to prevent or mitigate the effect of bad outcomes and help foster better outcomes. The technique can also sensitize analysts to low probability/high impact developments, or "nightmare scenarios," which could have significant adverse implications for influencing policy or allocation of resources.

The product of Morphological Analysis is often a set of potential noteworthy scenarios, with indicators of each, plus the intelligence collection requirements for each scenario. Another benefit is that morphological analysis leaves a clear audit trail about how the judgments were reached.

▶ The Method

Morphological analysis works through two common principles of creativity techniques: decomposition and forced association. Start by defining a set of key parameters or dimensions of the problem, and then break down each of those dimensions further into relevant forms or states or values that the dimension can assume—as in the example described later in this section. Two dimensions can be visualized as a matrix and three dimensions as a cube. In more complicated cases, multiple linked matrices or cubes may be needed to break the problem down into all its parts.

The principle of forced association then requires that every element be paired with and considered in connection with every other element in the morphological space. How that is done depends upon the complexity of the case. In a simple case, each combination may be viewed as a potential scenario or problem solution and examined from the point of view of its possibility, practicability, effectiveness, or other criteria. In complex cases, there may be thousands of possible combinations and computer assistance is required. With or without computer assistance, it is often possible to quickly eliminate about 90 percent of the combinations as not physically possible, impracticable, or undeserving of attention. This narrowing-down process allows the analyst to concentrate only on those combinations that are within the realm of the possible and most worthy of attention.

▶ Example

The Intelligence Community is asked to consider how a terrorist attack on the water supply might unfold. In the absence of direct information about specific terrorist planning for such an attack, a group of analysts uses structured brainstorming to identify the following key dimensions of the problem: group, type of attack, target, and intended impact. For each dimension, the analysts identify as many elements as possible. For example, the group could be an outsider, an insider, or a visitor to a facility, while the location could be an attack on drinking water, wastewater, or storm sewer runoff. The analysts then array this data into a matrix, illustrated in Figure 5.6, and begin to create as many permutations as possible using different combinations of the matrix boxes. These permutations allow the analysts to identify and consider multiple combinations for further exploration.

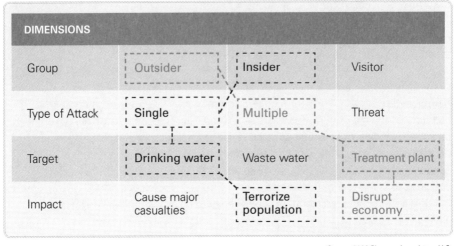

Figure 5.6 | **Morphological Analysis: Terrorist Attack Options**

DIMENSIONS			
Group	Outsider	Insider	Visitor
Type of Attack	Single	Multiple	Threat
Target	Drinking water	Waste water	Treatment plant
Impact	Cause major casualties	Terrorize population	Disrupt economy

Source: 2009 Pherson Associates, LLC.

One possible scenario, shown in the matrix, is an outsider who carries out multiple attacks on a treatment plant to cause economic disruption. Another possible scenario is an insider who carries out a single attack on drinking water to terrorize the population.

Analysts who might be interested in using a computerized version of Morphology Analysis are referred to the Swedish Morphology Society (www.swemorph.com). This Web site has detailed guidance and examples of the use of Morphological Analysis for futures research, disaster risk management, complex socio-technical problems, policy research, and other problems comparable to those faced by intelligence analysts.

▶ **Origins of This Technique**

The current form of Morphology Analysis was developed by astronomer Fritz Zwicky and described in his book *Discovery, Invention, Research Through the Morphological Approach* (Toronto: Macmillan, 1969). Basic information about this method is available from two well-known Web sites that provide information on creativity tools: http://creatingminds.org and www.mindtools.com. For more advanced information, see *General Morphological Analysis: A General Method for Non-Quantified Modeling* (1998); *Wicked Problems: Structuring Social Messes with Morphological Analysis* (2008); and *Futures Studies Using Morphological Analysis* (2009), all downloadable from the Swedish Morphology Society's Web site, www.swemorph.com.

5.7   QUADRANT CRUNCHING

Quadrant Crunching is an application of Morphological Analysis methodology, a systematic procedure for identifying all the potentially feasible combinations between several sets of variables. Quadrant Crunching helps analysts avoid surprise by examining multiple possible combinations of selected key variables. It also helps analysts to identify and systematically challenge assumptions, explore the implications of contrary assumptions, and discover "unknown unknowns." By generating multiple possible outcomes for any situation, Quadrant Crunching reduces the chance that events could play out in a way that has not previously been at least imagined and considered. Training and practice are required before an analyst should use this technique, and an experienced facilitator is recommended.

▶ When to Use It

Quadrant Crunching is most useful for dealing with highly ambiguous situations for which few data are available and the chances for surprise are great. It was developed by Pherson Associates, LLC, in 2006, to help counterterrorism analysts and decision makers identify the many different ways radical extremists might mount a terrorist attack. But analysts can apply it more broadly to generate a wide range of potential outcomes of any type—many of which have not previously been contemplated. The technique forces analysts to rethink an issue from many perspectives and systematically question assumptions that underlie their lead hypothesis. As a result, analysts can be more confident that they have considered a broad range of possible permutations for a particularly complex and ambiguous situation. In so doing, analysts are more likely to anticipate most of the ways a situation can develop (or terrorists might launch an attack) and to spot indicators that signal a specific scenario is starting to develop.

▶ Value Added

Quadrant Crunching combines the methodology of a Key Assumptions Check (chapter 8) with Multiple Scenarios Generation (chapter 6). It reduces the potential for surprise by providing a structured framework with which the analyst can generate an array of alternative scenarios or stories. The technique requires analysts to identify and systematically challenge all their key assumptions about how a terrorist attack might be launched or any other specific situation might evolve. By critically examining each assumption and how a contrary assumption might play out, analysts can better assess their level of confidence in their predictions, the strength of their lead hypothesis, and the likelihood of their lead scenario.

The process is a useful platform for developing indicator lists and for generating collection requirements. It also helps decision makers focus on what actions need to be undertaken today to best prepare for events that could transpire in the future. By reviewing an extensive list of potential scenarios, decision makers are in a better position to select those that seem most credible or that most deserve attention. They can then take the necessary actions to avoid or mitigate the impact of bad scenarios and help foster more desirable ones. The technique also can be used to sensitize decision makers to potential "wild cards" (low probability/high impact developments) or "nightmare scenarios," both of which could have significant policy or resource implications.

▶ The Method

Quadrant Crunching is sometimes described as a Key Assumptions Check on steroids. It is most useful when there is a well-established lead hypothesis that can be articulated clearly. Quadrant Crunching calls on the analyst to break down the lead hypothesis into its component parts, identifying the key assumptions that underlie the lead hypothesis, or dimensions that focus on Who, What, When, Where, Why, and How. Once the key dimensions of the lead hypothesis are articulated, the analyst generates at least two examples of contrary dimensions. For example, two contrary dimensions for a single attack would be simultaneous attacks and cascading attacks. The various contrary dimensions are then arrayed in sets of 2 × 2 matrices. If four dimensions are identified for a particular topic, the technique would generate six different 2 × 2 combinations of these four dimensions (AB, AC, AD, BC, BD, and CD). Each of these pairs would be presented as a 2 × 2 matrix with four quadrants. Different scenarios would be generated for each quadrant in each matrix. If two stories are imagined for each quadrant in each of these 2 × 2 matrices, a total of 48 different ways the situation could evolve will have been generated. Similarly, if six drivers are identified, the technique will generate as many as 120 different stories to consider (see Figure 5.7a).

Once a rich array of potential scenarios has been generated, the analyst's task is to identify which of the various scenarios are the most deserving of attention.

> *The best way to have a good idea is to have a lot of ideas.*
>
> Louis Pasteur

| Figure 5.7a | Quadrant Crunching: Creating a Set of Stories |

# of Dimensions	# of Matrices Generated	# of "Scenario Categories" (4 per Matrix)	# of Scenarios (Up to 2 per Quadrant)
3	3	12	24
4	6	24	48
5	10	40	80
6	15	60	120

Source: 2009 Pherson Associates, LLC.

The last step in the process is to develop lists of indicators for each scenario in order to track whether a particular scenario is beginning to emerge.

The Quadrant Crunching technique can be illustrated by exploring the question "How might terrorists attack our domestic water system?"

* State the conventional wisdom for the most likely way this terrorist attack might be launched. For example, "Al-Qaeda or its affiliates will contaminate the domestic water supply causing mass casualties."

* Break down this statement into its component parts or key assumptions. For example, the statement makes four key assumptions: (a) a single attack, (b) involving drinking water, (c) conducted by an outside attacker, (d) that causes large numbers of casualties.

* Posit a contrary assumption for each key assumption. For example, what if there are multiple attacks instead of a single attack?

* Identify at least two dimensions of that contrary assumption. For example, what are different ways a multiple attack could be launched? Two possibilities would be simultaneous attacks (as in the September 2001 attacks on the World Trade Center and the Pentagon) or cascading attacks (as in the sniper killings in the Washington, D.C., area in October 2002).

* Repeat this process for each of the key dimensions. Try to develop two contrary dimensions for each contrary assumption. (See Figure 5.7b.)

Figure 5.7b

Terrorist Attacks on Water Systems: Flipping Assumptions

Key Assumption	Contrary Assumption	Contrary Dimensions
Single attack	Multiple attacks	• Simultaneous • Cascading
Contamination	Other strategies	• Denial of service • Water as a weapon
Drinking water	Waste water	• Treatment plants • Sewage pipes
Outsider	Insider	• Staff employees • Contractors/visitors
Major casualties	Minor casualties	• Terrorize population • Disrupt economy

Source: 2009 Pherson Associates, LLC.

＊ Array pairs of contrary dimensions into sets of 2 × 2 matrices. In this case, ten different 2 × 2 matrices would be created. Two of the ten matrices are shown in Figure 5.7c.

＊ For each cell in each matrix generate one to three examples of how terrorists might launch an attack. In some cases, such a scenario might already

Figure 5.7c

Terrorist Attacks on Water Systems: Sample Matrices

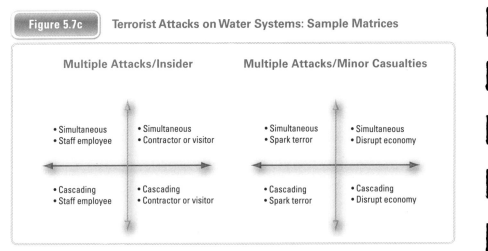

Multiple Attacks/Insider

• Simultaneous • Staff employee	• Simultaneous • Contractor or visitor
• Cascading • Staff employee	• Cascading • Contractor or visitor

Multiple Attacks/Minor Casualties

• Simultaneous • Spark terror	• Simultaneous • Disrupt economy
• Cascading • Spark terror	• Cascading • Disrupt economy

Source: 2009 Pherson Associates, LLC.

have been imagined. In other quadrants there may be no credible scenario. But several of the quadrants will usually stretch the analysts' thinking, pushing them to think about the dynamic in new and different ways.

* Review all the scenarios generated; using a pre-established set of criteria, select those most deserving of attention. In this example, possible criteria might be those scenarios that are most likely to:
  - Cause the most damage; have the most impact.
  - Be the hardest to detect or prevent.
  - Pose the greatest challenge for consequence management.

* This process is illustrated in Figure 5.7d. In this case, three stories were selected as the most likely scenarios. Story 1 became Scenario A, Stories 4

Figure 5.7d   **Selecting Scenarios**

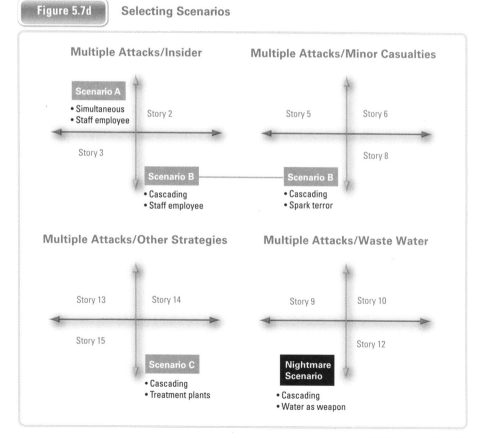

Source: 2009 Pherson Associates, LLC.

and 7 were combined to form Scenario B, and Story 16 became Scenario C. It may also be desirable to select one or two additional scenarios that might be described as "wild cards" or "nightmare scenarios." These are scenarios that have a low probability of occurring but are worthy of attention because their impact would be so great if they did occur. The figure shows Story 11 as a nightmare scenario.

＊ Consider what decision makers might do to prevent bad scenarios from happening, mitigate their impact, and deal with their consequences.

＊ Generate a list of key indicators to help assess which, if any, of these scenarios is beginning to emerge.

▶ Relationship to Other Techniques
Quadrant Crunching is a specific application of a generic method called Morphological Analysis (described in this chapter). It draws on the results of the Key Assumptions Check and can contribute to Multiple Scenarios Generation. It can also be used to identify Indicators.

▶ Origins of This Technique
The Quadrant Crunching technique was developed by Randy Pherson and Alan Schwartz to meet a specific analytic need. It was first published in Randy Pherson, *Handbook of Analytic Tools and Techniques* (Reston, Va.: Pherson Associates, LLC, 2008).

6 Scenarios and Indicators

6

Scenarios and Indicators

6.1   Scenarios Analysis   [122]

6.2   Indicators   [132]

6.3   Indicators Validator   [140]

CHAPTER 6

Scenarios and Indicators

I n the complex, evolving, uncertain situations that intelligence analysts and decision makers must deal with, the future is not easily predicable. Some events are intrinsically of low predictability. The best the analyst can do is to identify the driving forces that may determine future outcomes and monitor those forces as they interact to become the future. Scenarios are a principal vehicle for doing this. Scenarios are plausible and provocative stories about how the future might unfold. When alternative futures have been clearly outlined, decision makers can mentally rehearse these futures and ask themselves, "What should I be doing now to prepare for these futures?"

Scenarios Analysis provides a framework for considering multiple plausible futures. As Peter Schwartz, author of *The Art of the Long View,* has argued, "The future is plural."[1] Trying to divine or predict a single outcome typically is a disservice to senior intelligence officials, decision makers, and other clients. Generating several scenarios (for example, those that are most likely, least likely, and most dangerous) helps focus attention on the key underlying forces and factors most likely to influence how a situation develops. Analysts can also use scenarios to examine assumptions and deliver useful warning messages when high impact/low probability scenarios are included in the exercise.

> *The central mission of intelligence analysis is to warn US officials about dangers to national security interests and to alert them to perceived openings to advance US policy objectives. Thus the bulk of analysts' written and oral deliverables points directly or indirectly to the existence, characteristics, and implications of threats to and opportunities for US national security.*
>
> —Jack Davis, "Strategic Warning," Sherman Kent School for Intelligence Analysis, September 2001.

Identification and monitoring of indicators or signposts can provide early warning of the direction in which the future is heading, but these early signs are

---

1. Peter Schwartz, *The Art of the Long View: Planning for the Future in an Uncertain World* (New York: Doubleday, 1996).

not obvious. The human mind tends to see what it expects to see and to overlook the unexpected. These indicators take on meaning only in the context of a specific scenario with which they have been identified. The prior identification of a scenario and associated indicators can create an awareness that prepares the mind to recognize early signs of significant change.

Change sometimes happens so gradually that analysts don't notice it, or they rationalize it as not being of fundamental importance until it is too obvious to ignore. Once analysts take a position on an issue, they typically are slow to change their minds in response to new evidence. By going on the record in advance to specify what actions or events would be significant and might change their minds, analysts can avert this type of rationalization.

Another benefit of scenarios is that they provide an efficient mechanism for communicating complex ideas. A scenario is a set of complex ideas that can be described with a short label. These labels provide a lexicon for thinking and communicating with other analysts and decision makers about how a situation or a country is evolving.

Overview of Techniques

Scenarios Analysis identifies the multiple ways in which a situation might evolve. This form of analysis can help decision makers develop plans to exploit whatever opportunities might arise or avoid whatever risks the future may hold. Three different techniques for generating scenarios are described along with guidance on when and how to use each technique. Simple Scenarios is a quick and easy way for either an individual analyst or a small group of analysts to generate scenarios. It starts with the current analytic line and then explores other alternatives. Alternative Futures Analysis is a more systematic and imaginative procedure that uses a group of experts, often including decision makers and a trained facilitator. With some additional effort, Multiple Scenarios Generation can handle a much larger number of scenarios than Alternative Futures Analysis can handle. It also requires a facilitator, but the use of this technique can greatly reduce the chance that events could play out in a way that was not at least foreseen as a possibility.

Indicators are a classic technique used to seek early warning of some undesirable event. Indicators are often paired with scenarios to identify which of several possible scenarios is developing. They are also used to measure change toward an undesirable condition, such as political instability or a desirable condition, such as economic reform. Use indicators whenever you need to track a specific situation to monitor, detect, or evaluate change over time. The indicator list becomes the basis for directing collection efforts and for routing relevant information to all interested parties. It can also serve as the basis for your filing system to keep track of indicators.

Indicators Validator is a new tool that is useful for assessing the diagnostic power of an indicator. An indicator is most diagnostic when it clearly points to the likelihood of only one scenario or hypothesis and suggests that the others are unlikely. Too frequently indicators are of limited value, because they may be consistent with several different outcomes or hypotheses.

6.1 SCENARIOS ANALYSIS

Identification and analysis of scenarios helps to reduce uncertainties and manage risk. By postulating different scenarios analysts can identify the multiple ways in which a situation might evolve. This process can help decision makers develop plans to exploit whatever opportunities the future may hold or, conversely, to avoid risks. Monitoring of indicators keyed to various scenarios can provide early warnings of the direction in which the future may be heading.

Several techniques are available for developing and analyzing scenarios. The first part of this section discusses when and why to use any form of Scenarios Analysis. The subsections then discuss when and how to use each of the three Scenario Analysis techniques: Simple Scenarios, Alternative Futures Analysis, and Multiple Scenarios Generation.

> *It is important that we think deeply and creatively about the future, or else we run the risk of being surprised and unprepared. At the same time, the future is uncertain, so we must prepare for multiple plausible futures, not just the one we expect to happen. Scenarios contain the stories of these multiple futures, from the expected to the wildcard, in forms that are analytically coherent and imaginatively engaging. A good scenario grabs us by the collar and says, 'Take a good look at this future. This could be your future. Are you going to be ready?'*
>
> —Andy Hines, "The Current State of Scenario Development," *Foresight* (March 2007).

▶ **When to Use It**

Scenarios Analysis is most useful when a situation is complex or when the outcomes are too uncertain to trust a single prediction. When decision makers and analysts first come to grips with a new situation or challenge, there usually is a degree of uncertainty about how events will unfold. It is at this point, when national policies are in the initial stages of formulation, that Scenarios Analysis can have a strong impact on decision makers' thinking. Scenarios do not predict the future, but a good set of scenarios bounds the range of possible futures for which a decision maker may need to be prepared. Scenarios Analysis can also be used as a strategic planning tool that brings decision makers and stakeholders together with experts to envisage the alternative futures for which they must plan.[2]

---

2. See, for example, Brian Nichiporuk, *Alternative Futures and Army Force Planning: Implications for the Future Force Era* (Santa Monica, Calif.: RAND, 2005).

The amount of time and effort required depends upon the specific technique used. Simple Scenarios can be used by an analyst working alone without any technical or methodological support, although a group effort is preferred for most structured techniques. The time required for Alternative Futures Analysis and Multiple Scenarios Generation varies, but it can require a team of experts spending several days working together on a project. A facilitator knowledgeable about scenarios analysis is recommended, as this will definitely save time and produce better results.

▶ **Value Added**

When analysts are thinking about scenarios, they are rehearsing the future so that decision makers can be prepared for whatever direction that future takes. Instead of trying to estimate the most likely outcome (and being wrong more often than not), scenarios provide a framework for considering multiple plausible futures. Trying to divine or predict a single outcome can be a disservice to senior intelligence officials, decision makers, and other valued clients. Generating several scenarios helps to focus attention on the key underlying forces and factors most likely to influence how a situation will develop. Scenarios also can be used to examine assumptions and deliver useful warning messages when high impact/low probability scenarios are included in the exercise.

Analysts have learned, from past experience, that involving decision makers in a scenarios exercise is an effective way to communicate the results of this technique and to sensitize them to important uncertainties. Most participants find the process of developing scenarios as useful as any written report or formal briefing. Those involved in the process often benefit in several ways. Analysis of scenarios can:

* Suggest indicators to monitor for signs that a particular future is becoming more or less likely.

* Help analysts and decision makers anticipate what would otherwise be surprising developments by forcing them to challenge assumptions and consider plausible "wild card" scenarios or discontinuous events.

* Produce an analytic framework for calculating the costs, risks, and opportunities represented by different outcomes.

* Provide a means of weighing multiple unknown or unknowable factors and presenting a set of plausible outcomes.

* Bound a problem by identifying plausible combinations of uncertain factors.

When decision makers or analysts from different intelligence disciplines or organizational cultures are included on the team, new insights invariably emerge as new information and perspectives are introduced. Analysts from outside the organizational culture of a particular analytic unit or team are likely to see a problem in different ways and are likely to challenge the working assumptions and established mental models of the analytic unit. By changing the "analytic lens" through which a problem is seen, analysts are forced to reevaluate their assumptions about the priority order of key factors driving the issue. By engaging in a multifaceted and systematic examination of an issue, analysts also gain greater confidence in their assessments.

▶ 6.1.1 The Method: Simple Scenarios

Of the three scenario techniques described here, Simple Scenarios is the easiest one to use. It is the only one of the three that can be implemented by an analyst working alone rather than in a group or a team, and it is the only one for which a coach or a facilitator is not needed. On the other hand, it is less systematic than the others, and the results may be less than optimal, especially if the work is done by an individual rather than a group. Here are the steps for using this technique:

* Clearly define the focal issue and the specific goals of the futures exercise.

* Make a list of forces, factors, and events that are likely to influence the future.

* Organize the forces, factors, and events that are related to each other into five to ten affinity groups that are expected to be the driving forces in how the focal issue will evolve.

* Label each of these drivers and write a brief description of each. For example, one training exercise for this technique is to forecast the future of the fictional country of Caldonia by identifying and describing six drivers. Generate a matrix, as shown in Figure 6.1.1, with a list of drivers down the left side. The columns of the matrix are used to describe scenarios. Each scenario is assigned a value for each driver. The values are strong or positive (+), weak or negative (−), and blank if neutral or no change.
    − Government effectiveness: To what extent does the government exert control over all populated regions of the country and effectively deliver services?
    − Economy: Does the economy sustain a positive growth rate?
    − Civil society: Can nongovernmental and local institutions provide appropriate services and security to the population?

Figure 6.1.1

Simple Scenarios

	Best Case *An imperfect peace*	Worst Case *Fragmentation*	Mainline *Descent into order*	Additional Scenario *Pockets of civility*
Government effectiveness	+	–	–	–
Economy	+	–	–	+
Civil society		–	+	+
Insurgency	–	+	+	
Drug trade		+		+
Foreign influence	+			

Source: 2009 Pherson Associates, LLC.

- Insurgency: Does the insurgency pose a viable threat to the government? Is it able to extend its dominion over greater portions of the country?
- Drug trade: Is there a robust drug-trafficking economy?
- Foreign influence: Do foreign governments, international financial organizations, or nongovernmental organizations provide military or economic assistance to the government?

* Generate at least four different scenarios—a best case, worst case, mainline, and at least one other by assigning different values (+, 0, –) to each driver.

* This is a good time to reconsider both drivers and scenarios. Is there a better way to conceptualize and describe the drivers? Are there important forces that have not been included? Look across the matrix to see the extent to which each driver discriminates among the scenarios. If a driver has the same value across all scenarios, it is not discriminating and should be deleted. To stimulate thinking about other possible scenarios, consider the key assumptions that were made in deciding on the most likely scenario. What if some of these

assumptions turn out to be invalid? If they are invalid, how might that affect the outcome, and are such outcomes included within the available set of scenarios?

* For each scenario, write a one-page story to describe what that future looks like and/or how it might come about. The story should illustrate the interplay of the drivers.

* For each scenario, describe the implications for the decision maker.

* Generate a list of indicators, or "observables," for each scenario that would help you discover that events are starting to play out in a way envisioned by that scenario.

* Monitor the list of indicators on a regular basis.

▶ **6.1.2 The Method: Alternative Futures Analysis**

Alternative Futures Analysis and Multiple Scenarios Generation differ from Simple Scenarios in that they are usually larger projects that rely on a group of experts, often including academics and decision makers. They use a more systematic process, and the assistance of a knowledgeable facilitator is very helpful.

Alternative Futures Analysis differs from Multiple Scenarios Generation only in the number of scenarios that are analyzed. For reasons noted below, Alternative Futures Analysis is limited to two driving forces. Each driving force is a spectrum with two extremes, and these drivers combine to make four possible scenarios. Multiple Scenarios Generation has no such limitation other than the practical limitations of time and complexity.

The steps in the Alternative Futures Analysis process are:

* Clearly define the focal issue and the specific goals of the futures exercise.

* Brainstorm to identify the key forces, factors, or events that are most likely to influence how the issue will develop over a specified time period.

* If possible, group these various forces, factors, or events to form two critical drivers that are expected to determine the future outcome. In the example on the future of Cuba (Figure 6.1.2), the two key drivers are Effectiveness of Government and Strength of Civil Society. If there are more than two critical drivers, do not use this technique. Use the Multiple Scenarios Generation technique, which can handle a larger number of scenarios.

* As in the Cuba example, define the two ends of the spectrum for each driver.

* Draw a 2 × 2 matrix. Label the two ends of the spectrum for each driver.

* Note that the square is now divided into four quadrants. Each quadrant represents a scenario generated by a combination of the two drivers. Now give a name to each scenario, and write it in the relevant quadrant.

* Generate a narrative story of how each hypothetical scenario might come into existence. Include a hypothetical chronology of key dates and events for each of the scenarios.

* Describe the implications of each scenario should it be what actually develops.

* Generate a list of indicators, or "observables," for each scenario that would help determine whether events are starting to play out in a way envisioned by that scenario.

* Monitor the list of indicators on a regular basis.

Figure 6.1.2 **Alternative Futures Analysis: Cuba**

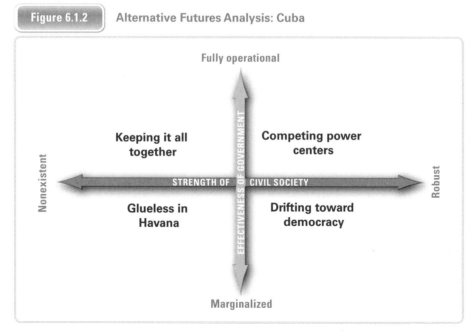

Source: 2009 Pherson Associates, LLC.

▶ 6.1.3 The Method: Multiple Scenarios Generation

Multiple Scenarios Generation is similar to Alternative Futures Analysis except that with this technique, you are not limited to two critical drivers generating four scenarios. By using multiple 2 × 2 matrices pairing every possible combination of multiple driving forces, you can create a very large number of possible scenarios. This is sometimes desirable to make sure nothing has been overlooked. Once generated, the scenarios can be screened quickly without detailed analysis of each one. Once sensitized to these different scenarios, analysts are more likely to pay attention to outlying data that would suggest that events are playing out in a way not previously imagined.

Training and an experienced facilitator are needed to use this technique. Here are the basic steps:

* Clearly define the focal issue and the specific goals of the futures exercise.

* Brainstorm to identify the key forces, factors, or events that are most likely to influence how the issue will develop over a specified time period.

* Define the two ends of the spectrum for each driver.

* Pair the drivers in a series of 2 × 2 matrices.

* Develop a story or two for each quadrant of each 2 × 2 matrix.

* From all the scenarios generated, select those most deserving of attention because they illustrate compelling and challenging futures not yet being considered.

* Develop indicators for each scenario that could be tracked to determine whether or not the scenario is developing.

The technique can be illustrated by exploring the focal question "What is the future of the insurgency in Iraq?" (See Figure 6.1.3a.) Here are the steps:

* Convene a group of experts (including some creative thinkers who can challenge the group's mental model) to brainstorm the forces and factors that are likely to determine the future of the insurgency in Iraq.

* Select from this list those factors or drivers whose outcome is the hardest to predict or for which analysts cannot confidently assess how the driver will influence future events. In the Iraq example, three drivers meet these criteria:
   – The role of neighboring states (Iran, Syria)
   – The capability of Iraq's security services (police and military)
   – The political environment in Iraq

Figure 6.1.3a **Multiple Scenarios Generation: Future of the Iraq Insurgency**

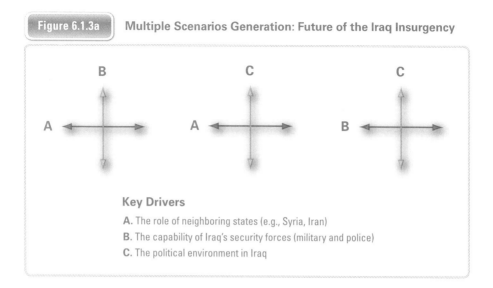

Key Drivers

A. The role of neighboring states (e.g., Syria, Iran)
B. The capability of Iraq's security forces (military and police)
C. The political environment in Iraq

* Define the ends of the spectrum for each driver. For example, the neighboring state could be stable and supportive at one end and unstable and disruptive at the other end of the spectrum.

* Pair the drivers in a series of 2 × 2 matrices as shown in Figure 6.1.3a.

* Develop a story or a couple of stories describing how events might unfold for each quadrant of each 2 × 2 matrix. For example, in the 2 × 2 matrix that is defined by the role of neighboring states and the capability of Iraq's security forces, analysts would be tasked with describing how the insurgency would function in each quadrant on the basis of the criteria defined at the far end of each spectrum. In the upper left hand quadrant, the criteria would be stable and supportive neighboring states but ineffective internal security capabilities. (See Figure 6.1.3b.) In this "world," one might imagine a regional defense umbrella that would help to secure the borders. Another possibility is that the neighboring states would have the Shiites and Kurds under control, with the only remaining insurgents Sunnis, who continue to harass the Shia-led central government.

* Review all the stories generated, and select those most deserving of attention. For example, which scenario
    - Presents the greatest challenges to Iraqi and U.S. decision makers?
    - Raises particular concerns that have not been anticipated?

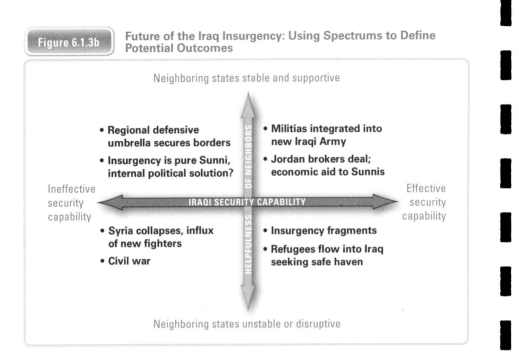

Figure 6.1.3b Future of the Iraq Insurgency: Using Spectrums to Define Potential Outcomes

Neighboring states stable and supportive

HELPFULNESS OF NEIGHBORS

Ineffective security capability

IRAQI SECURITY CAPABILITY

Effective security capability

- Regional defensive umbrella secures borders
- Insurgency is pure Sunni, internal political solution?

- Militias integrated into new Iraqi Army
- Jordan brokers deal; economic aid to Sunnis

- Syria collapses, influx of new fighters
- Civil war

- Insurgency fragments
- Refugees flow into Iraq seeking safe haven

Neighboring states unstable or disruptive

- Surfaces new dynamics that should be addressed?
- Suggests new collection needs?

* Select a few scenarios that might be described as "wild cards" (low probability/high impact developments) or "nightmare scenarios" (see Figure 6.1.3c).

* Consider what decision makers might do to prevent bad scenarios from occurring or enable good scenarios to develop.

* Generate a list of key indicators to help monitor which scenario story best describes how events are beginning to play out.

▶ **Relationship to Other Techniques**

Any scenario analysis might be followed by constructing a Cross-Impact Matrix to identify and analyze potential interactions or feedback loops between the various driving forces in each scenario.

Multiple Scenarios Generation is a specific application of Morphological Analysis, described in chapter 5.

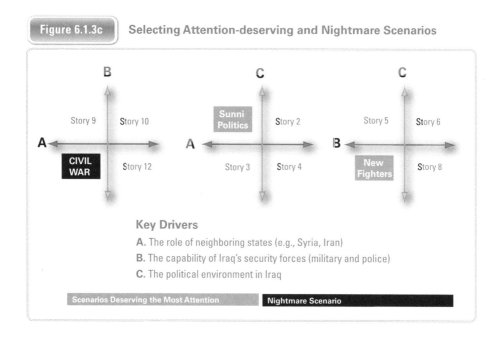

Figure 6.1.3c Selecting Attention-deserving and Nightmare Scenarios

Key Drivers

A. The role of neighboring states (e.g., Syria, Iran)
B. The capability of Iraq's security forces (military and police)
C. The political environment in Iraq

Scenarios Deserving the Most Attention   Nightmare Scenario

▷ **Origins of This Technique**

Scenarios Analysis is a broad concept that can be implemented in various ways for a variety of purposes. Three variations of Scenarios Analysis that seem most useful for intelligence analysis were selected for description here. The model of Simple Scenarios was developed by Pherson Associates, LLC. Alternative Futures Analysis and Multiple Scenarios Generation were previously described in Randy Pherson, *Handbook of Analytic Tools and Techniques* (Reston, Va.: Pherson Associates, LLC, 2008). For information on other approaches to Scenarios Analysis, see Andy Hines, "The Current State of Scenario Development: An Overview of Techniques," *Foresight* 9, no. 1 (March 2007). The Multiple Scenarios Generation illustrations are drawn from a report prepared by Alan Schwartz (PolicyFutures, LLC), "Scenarios for the Insurgency in Iraq," Special Report 174 (Washington, D.C.: United States Institute of Peace, October 2006).

6.2 INDICATORS

ndictors are observable phenomena that can be periodically reviewed to help track events, spot emerging trends, and warn of unanticipated changes. An indicators list is a pre-established set of observable or potentially observable actions, conditions, facts, or events whose simultaneous occurrence would argue strongly that a phenomenon is present or is very likely to occur. Indicators can be monitored to obtain tactical, operational, or strategic warnings of some future development that, if it were to occur, would have a major impact.

The identification and monitoring of indicators are fundamental tasks of intelligence analysis, as they are the principal means of avoiding surprise. They are often described as forward-looking or predictive indicators. In the law enforcement community indicators are also used to assess whether a target's activities or behavior is consistent with an established pattern. These are often described as backward-looking or descriptive indicators.

▶ When to Use It

Indicators provide an objective baseline for tracking events, instilling rigor into the analytic process, and enhancing the credibility of the final product. Descriptive indicators are best used to help the analyst assess whether there are sufficient grounds to believe that a specific action is taking place. They provide a systematic way to validate a hypothesis or help substantiate an emerging viewpoint. Figure 6.2a is an example of a list of descriptive indicators, in this case pointing to a clandestine drug laboratory.

A classic application of forward-looking indicators is to seek early warning of some undesirable event, such as a military attack or a nuclear test by a foreign country. Today indicators are often paired with scenarios to identify which of several possible scenarios is developing. They are also used to measure change that points toward an undesirable condition, such as political instability or a humanitarian crisis, or toward a desirable condition, such as economic reform or democratization. Analysts can use this technique whenever they need to track a specific situation to monitor, detect, or evaluate change over time. In the private sector, indicators are used to track whether a new business strategy is working or whether a low-probability scenario is developing that offers new commercial opportunities.

▶ Value Added

The human mind sometimes sees what it expects to see and can overlook the unexpected. Identification of indicators creates an awareness that prepares the

Figure 6.2a   Descriptive Indicators of a Clandestine Drug Laboratory

- Noxious odors associated with chemical/industrial use—ammonia, ether, solvents; strong or prolonged odor.
- Exhaust fans on house or outbuilding constantly running or running in cold weather.
- All windows darkened or covered.
- Windows sealed and/or painted.
- Abnormal use of electricity and water.
- High electric and/or water bills.
- Purchase of large quantities of chemicals from hardware and other stores such as:
  - Acetone in multi-gallon lots.
  - Sodium hydroxide products (e.g., "Drano") by the case.
- Purchase of lab supplies or equipment.
- Purchase of key chemicals (ether, etc.) or glassware from or through local companies.
- Delivery frequently being made by parcel services of glassware, chemicals, etc.

Source: Pamphlet from ALERT Unit, New Jersey State Police, 1990; republished in *The Community Model*, Counterdrug Intelligence Coordinating Group, 2003.

mind to recognize early signs of significant change. Change often happens so gradually that analysts don't see it, or they rationalize it as not being of fundamental importance until it is too obvious to ignore. Once analysts take a position on an issue, they can be reluctant to change their minds in response to new evidence. By specifying in advance the threshold for what actions or events would be significant and might cause them to change their minds, analysts can seek to avoid this type of rationalization.

Defining explicit criteria for tracking and judging the course of events makes the analytic process more visible and available for scrutiny by others, thus enhancing the credibility of analytic judgments. Including an indicators list in the finished product helps decision makers track future developments and builds a more concrete case for the analytic conclusions.

Preparation of a detailed indicator list by a group of knowledgeable analysts is usually a good learning experience for all participants. It can be a useful medium for an exchange of knowledge between analysts from different organizations or those with different types of expertise—for example, analysts who specialize in a particular country and those who are knowledgeable about a particular field, such as military mobilization, political instability, or economic development.

The indicator list becomes the basis for directing collection efforts and for routing relevant information to all interested parties. It can also serve as the basis for the analyst's filing system to keep track of these indicators.

When analysts or decision makers are sharply divided over the interpretation of events (for example, how the war in Iraq or Afghanistan is progressing), of the guilt or innocence of a "person of interest," or the culpability of a counterintelligence suspect, indicators can help depersonalize the debate by shifting attention away from personal viewpoints to more objective criteria. Emotions often can be diffused and substantive disagreements clarified if all parties agree in advance on a set of criteria that would demonstrate that developments are—or are not—moving in a particular direction or that a person's behavior suggests that he or she is guilty as suspected or is indeed a spy.

▷ **Potential Pitfalls**

The quality of indicators is critical, as poor indicators lead to analytic failure. For these reasons, analysts must periodically review the validity and relevance of an indicators list. Narrowly conceived or outdated indicators can reinforce analytic bias, encourage analysts to discard new evidence, and lull consumers of information inappropriately. Indicators can also prove to be invalid over time, or they may turn out to be poor "pointers" to what they were supposed to show. By regularly checking the validity of the indicators, analysts may also discover that their original assumptions were flawed. Finally, if an opponent learns what indicators are on your list, the opponent may make operational changes to conceal what you are looking for or arrange for you to see contrary indicators.

▷ **The Method**

The first step in using this technique is to create a list of indicators. (See Figure 6.2b for a sample indicators list.) The second step is to monitor these indicators regularly to detect signs of change. Developing the indicator list can range from a simple process to a sophisticated team effort. For example, with minimum effort you could jot down a list of things you would expect to see if a particular situation were to develop as feared or foreseen. Or you could join with others to define multiple variables that would influence a situation and then rank the value of each variable based on incoming information about relevant events, activities, or official statements. In both cases, some form of brainstorming, hypothesis generation, or scenario development is often used to identify the indicators.

Figure 6.2b Using Indicators to Track Emerging Scenarios in Zambria

The following developments would signal that a particular scenario is unfolding.

Scenario One: Treading Water

- A prime minister with weak reform credentials takes office as part of a compromise between the president and the political opposition.
- A full but divided Parliament is seated but incapable of passing major legislation.
- The government meets basic International Monetary Fund standards but fails to qualify for budget aid.
- The president maintains some rhetorical support for modernization but declines to take forceful action.
- The police demonstrate the ability to cope with sporadic demonstrations but make slow progress in developing their overall capabilities.

Scenario Two: The Unraveling of Democracy

- The president publicly retreats from his commitment to structural reforms.
- The government violates its agreement with the IMF, leading to a significant decrease in aid pledged by other major international donors.
- Public demonstrations draw thousands of participants and persist for several days.
- Extremist groups resurface, or revolutionary groups call for alternative approaches to government.
- Police step up repressive tactics or, conversely, abandon their posts en masse.
- Successive prime ministers and their cabinets are forced to resign.
- Upcoming legislative elections are cancelled or postponed indefinitely.

Scenario Three: Turning the Corner

- Parliament accepts a pro-reform prime minister and passes legislation on a regular basis.
- Some state-owned industries are privatized, and the government work force is scaled back, leading to the disbursement of large portions of international aid.
- The benefits of modernization and accompanying aid become more apparent, and leading opposition politicians tone down their antireform rhetoric.
- Legislative elections occur as planned with little violence and are pronounced free and fair by international experts.
- Business leaders announce new private investments capable of generating permanent jobs numbering in the tens of thousands.
- Instances of human rights violations by the police decrease dramatically.

Source: 2009 Pherson Associates, LLC.

A good indicator must meet several criteria, including the following:

* Observable and collectible. There must be some reasonable expectation that, if present, the indicator will be observed and reported by a reliable source. If an indicator is to monitor change over time, it must be collectable over time.

* Valid. An indicator must be clearly relevant to the end state the analyst is trying to predict or assess, and it must be inconsistent with all or at least some of the alternative explanations or outcomes. It must accurately measure the concept or phenomenon at issue.

* Reliable. Data collection must be consistent when comparable methods are used. Those observing and collecting data must observe the same things. Reliability requires precise definition of the indicators.

* Stable. An indicator must be useful over time to allow comparisons and to track events. Ideally, the indicator should be observable early in the evolution of a development so that analysts and decision makers have time to react accordingly.

* Unique. An indicator should measure only one thing and, in combination with other indicators, should point only to the phenomenon being studied. Valuable indicators are those that are not only consistent with a specified scenario or hypothesis but are also inconsistent with alternative scenarios or hypotheses. The Indicators Validator tool, described later in this chapter, can be used to check the diagnosticity of indicators.

Any indicator list used to monitor whether something has happened, is happening, or will happen implies at least one alternative scenario or hypothesis—that it has not happened, is not happening, or will not happen. Many indicators that a scenario or hypothesis is happening are just the opposite of indicators that it is not happening, but some are not. Some are consistent with two or more scenarios or hypotheses. Therefore, an analyst should prepare separate lists of indicators for each scenario or hypothesis. For example, consider indicators of an opponent's preparations for a military attack where there may be three hypotheses—no attack, attack, and feigned intent to attack with the goal of forcing a favorable negotiated solution. Almost all indicators of an imminent attack are also consistent with the hypothesis of a feigned attack. The analyst must identify indicators capable of diagnosing the difference between true intent to attack and feigned intent to attack. The mobilization of reserves is such a diagnostic indicator. It is so costly that it is not usually undertaken unless there is a strong presumption that the reserves will be needed.

Maintaining separate indicator lists for alternative scenarios or hypotheses is particularly useful when making a case that a certain event is unlikely to happen, as in What If? Analysis or High Impact/Low Probability Analysis.

After creating the indicator list or lists, you or the analytic team should regularly review incoming reporting and note any changes in the indicators. To the extent possible, you or the team should decide well in advance which critical indicators, if observed, will serve as early-warning decision points. In other words, if a certain indicator or set of indicators is observed, it will trigger a report advising of some modification in the intelligence appraisal of the situation.

Techniques for increasing the sophistication and credibility of an indicator list include the following:

* Establishing a scale for rating each indicator

* Providing specific definitions of each indicator

* Rating the indicators on a scheduled basis (e.g., monthly, quarterly, or annually)

* Assigning a level of confidence to each rating

* Providing a narrative description for each point on the rating scale, describing what one would expect to observe at that level

* Listing the sources of information used in generating the rating

Figure 6.2c on the next page is an example of a complex indicators chart that incorporates the first three techniques listed above.

▶ **Relationship to Other Techniques**

Indicators are closely related to a number of other techniques. Some form of brainstorming is commonly used to draw upon the expertise in creating indicators of multiple analysts with different perspectives and different specialties. The development of alternative scenarios should always involve the development and monitoring of indicators that point toward which scenario is evolving. What If? Analysis and High Impact/Low Probability Analysis depend upon the development and use of indicators. Indicators are often entered as items of evidence in Analysis of Competing Hypotheses.

The Indicators Validator, which is discussed in the next section, is a tool used to test the diagnosticity of indicators.

Figure 6.2c   Zambria Political Instability Indicators

		2008				2009				2010	
		I	II	III	IV	I	II	III	IV	I	II
Social change/conflict	Ethnic/religious discontent	•	•	•	•	•	•	•	•	•	•
	Demonstrations, riots, strikes	•	•	•	○	○	◑	■	■	■	●
Economic factors	General deterioration	○	○	○	●	◑	○	○	○	●	○
	Decreased access to foreign funds	○	◑	○	◑	●	○	○	○	○	○
	Capital flight	○	○	○	●	●	■	■	■	■	■
	Unpopular changes in economic policies	○	○	○	○	■	■	■	■	■	■
	Food/energy shortages	○	○	○	○	◑	●	■	■	■	■
	Inflation	○	○	◑	●	○	◑	■	○	○	■
Opposition activities	Organizational capabilities	○	○	○	○	○	○	•	○	○	○
	Opposition/conspiracy planning	○	○	○	○	○	○	○	○	○	○
	Terrorism and sabotage	○	○	○	○	○	○	○	○	○	○
	Insurgent armed attacks	○	○	○	○	○	○	○	○	○	○
	Public support	•	•	•	•	•	•	•	•	•	•
Military attitudes/activities	Threat to corporate military interests/dignity	•	•	•	•	•	•	•	•	•	•
	Discontent over career loss, pay, or benefits	○	○	○	◑	○	○	○	○	○	○
	Discontent over government action/policies	○	○	○	●	○	○	○	○	○	○
	Reports/rumors of coup plotting	○	○	○	○	○	○	○	○	○	○
	External support for government	○	○	○	○	○	○	○	○	○	○
	External support for opposition	○	○	○	○	○	○	○	○	○	○
	Threat of military conflict	•	•	•	•	•	•	•	•	•	•
Regime actions/capabilities	Repression/brutality	◑	◑	◑	◑	◑	◑	◑	◑	◑	◑
	Security capabilities	•	•	•	•	•	•	•	•	•	•
	Political disunity/loss of confidence	○	○	◑	◑	◑	◑	○	○	○	◑
	Loss of legitimacy	●	◑	◑	◑	◑	○	○	○	○	◑

Legend: • Negligible concern   ○ Low concern   ◑ Moderate   ● Substantial   ■ Strong

▷ Origins of This Technique

The identification and monitoring of indicators of military attack is one of the oldest forms of intelligence analysis. The discussion here is based on Randy Pherson, "Indicators," in *Handbook of Analytic Tools and Techniques* (Reston, Va.: Pherson Associates, LLC, 2008); Pherson, *The Indicators Handbook* (Reston, Va.: Pherson Associates, LLC, 2008); and the CIA's Sherman Kent School for Intelligence Analysis training materials. Cynthia M. Grabo's book, *Anticipating Surprise: Analysis for Strategic Warning* (Lanham, Md.: University Press of America, 2004), is a classic text on the development and use of Indicators.

INDICATORS VALIDATOR

T he Indicators Validator is a simple tool for assessing the diagnostic power of indicators.

▶ When to Use It

The Indicators Validator is an essential tool to use when developing indicators for competing hypotheses or alternative scenarios. (See Figure 6.3a.) Once an analyst has developed a set of alternative scenarios or future worlds, the next step is to generate indicators for each scenario (or world) that would appear if that particular world were beginning to emerge. A critical question that is not often asked is whether a given indicator would appear only in the scenario to which it is assigned or also in one or more alternative scenarios. Indicators that could appear in several scenarios are not considered diagnostic, suggesting that they are

---

Figure 6.3a   **Indicators Validator Model**

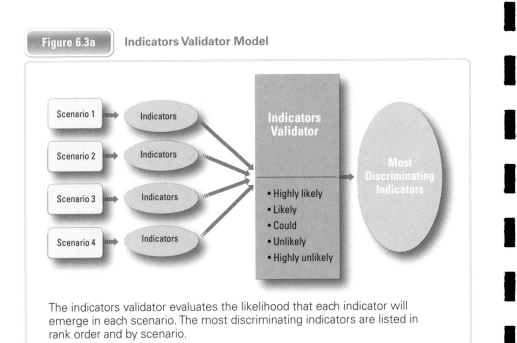

The indicators validator evaluates the likelihood that each indicator will emerge in each scenario. The most discriminating indicators are listed in rank order and by scenario.

Source: 2008 Pherson Associates, LLC.

not particularly useful in determining whether a specific scenario is emerging. The ideal indicator is highly consistent for the world to which it is assigned and highly inconsistent for all other worlds.

▶ Value Added

Employing the Indicators Validator to identify and dismiss nondiagnostic indicators can significantly increase the credibility of an analysis. By applying the tool, analysts can rank order their indicators from most to least diagnostic and decide how far up the list they want to draw the line in selecting the indicators that will be used in the analysis. In some circumstances, analysts might discover that most or all the indicators for a given scenario have been eliminated because they are also consistent with other scenarios, forcing them to brainstorm a new and better set of indicators. If analysts find it difficult to generate independent lists of diagnostic indicators for two scenarios, it may be that the scenarios are not sufficiently dissimilar, suggesting that they should be combined.

▶ The Method

* The first step is to populate a matrix similar to that used for Analysis of Competing Hypotheses. This can be done manually or by using the Indicators Validator software. The matrix should list:
   - Alternative scenarios or worlds (or competing hypotheses) along the top of the matrix (as is done for hypotheses in Analysis of Competing Hypotheses)
   - Indicators that have already been generated for all the scenarios down the left side of the matrix (as is done with evidence in Analysis of Competing Hypotheses)

* In each cell of the matrix, assess whether the indicator for that particular scenario is
   - Highly likely to appear
   - Likely to appear
   - Could appear
   - Unlikely to appear
   - Highly unlikely to appear

* Once this process is complete, re-sort the indicators so that the most discriminating indicators are displayed at the top of the matrix and the least discriminating indicators at the bottom.
   - The most discriminating indicator is "Highly Likely" to emerge in one scenario and "Highly Unlikely" to emerge in all other scenarios.

- The least discriminating indicator is "Highly Likely" to appear in all scenarios.
- Most indicators will fall somewhere in between.

* The Indicators with the most "Highly Unlikely" and "Unlikely" ratings are the most discriminating and should be retained.

* Indicators with few or no "Highly Unlikely" or "Unlikely" ratings should be eliminated.

* Once nondiscriminating indicators have been eliminated, regroup the indicators under their assigned scenario. If most indicators for a particular scenario have been eliminated, develop new—and more diagnostic—indicators for that scenario.

* Recheck the diagnostic value of any new indicators by applying the Indicators Validator to them as well.

Figure 6.3b illustrates the Indicators Validator process.

Figure 6.3b   **Indicators Validator Process**

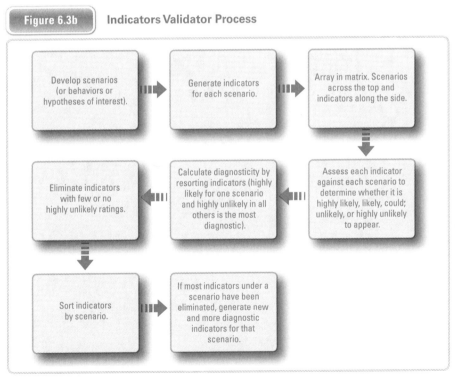

Source: 2009 Pherson Associates, LLC.

▷ Origins of This Technique

This technique was developed by Randy Pherson, Grace Scarborough, Alan Schwartz, and Sarah Beebe, Pherson Associates, LLC. It was first published in Randy Pherson, *Handbook of Analytic Tools and Techniques* (Reston, Va.: Pherson Associates, LLC, 2008). For information on other approaches to Scenarios Analysis, see Andy Hines, "The Current State of Scenario Development: An Overview of Techniques," *Foresight* 9, no. 1 (March 2007).

7

Hypothesis Generation and Testing

7

Hypothesis Generation and Testing

7.1   Hypothesis Generation   [150]

7.2   Diagnostic Reasoning   [158]

7.3   Analysis of Competing Hypotheses   [160]

7.4   Argument Mapping   [170]

7.5   Deception Detection   [173]

CHAPTER 7

Hypothesis Generation and Testing

Intelligence analysis will never achieve the accuracy and predictability of a true science, because the information with which analysts must work is typically incomplete, ambiguous, and potentially deceptive. Intelligence analysis can, however, benefit from some of the lessons of science and adapt some of the elements of scientific reasoning.

The scientific process involves observing, categorizing, formulating hypotheses, and then testing those hypotheses. Generating and testing hypotheses is a core function of intelligence analysis. A possible explanation of the past or a judgment about the future is a hypothesis that needs to be tested by collecting and presenting evidence. The first part of this chapter describes techniques for generating hypotheses. These and other similar techniques allow analysts to imagine new and alternative explanations for their subject matter, explanations that then need to be tested against the available evidence. The second part of this chapter describes techniques for testing hypotheses.

The generation and testing of hypotheses is a skill, and its subtleties do not come naturally. It is a form of reasoning that people can learn to use for dealing with high-stakes situations. What does come naturally is drawing on our existing body of knowledge and experience (mental model) to make an intuitive judgment. In most circumstances in our daily lives, this is an efficient approach that works most of the time. For intelligence analysis, however, it is not sufficient, because intelligence issues are generally so complex, and the risk and cost of error are too great. Also, the situations are often novel, so the intuitive judgment shaped by past knowledge and experience may well be wrong.

When one is facing a complex choice of options, the reliance on intuitive judgment risks following a practice called "satisficing," a term coined by Nobel Prize winner Herbert Simon by combining the words *satisfy* and *suffice*.[1] It means being satisfied with the first answer that seems adequate, as distinct

---

1. Herbert A. Simon, "A Behavioral Model of Rational Choice," *Quarterly Journal of Economics* LXIX (February 1955): 99–101.

from assessing multiple options to find the optimal or best answer. The "satisficer" who does seek out additional information may look only for information that supports this initial answer rather than looking more broadly at all the possibilities.

Good intelligence analysis of a complex issue must start with a set of alternative hypotheses. Another practice that the experienced intelligence analyst borrows from the scientist's toolkit involves the testing of alternative hypotheses. The truth of a hypothesis can never be proven beyond doubt by citing only evidence that is *consistent* with the hypothesis, because the same evidence may be and often is consistent with one or more other hypotheses. Science often proceeds by refuting or disconfirming hypotheses. A hypothesis that cannot be refuted should be taken just as seriously as a hypothesis that seems to have a lot of evidence in favor of it. A single item of evidence that is shown to be inconsistent with a hypothesis can be sufficient grounds for rejecting that hypothesis. The most tenable hypothesis is often the one with the least evidence against it.

Analysts often test hypotheses by using a form of reasoning known as abduction, which differs from the two better known forms of reasoning, deduction and induction. Abductive reasoning starts with a set of facts. One then develops hypotheses that, if true, would provide the best explanation for these facts. The most tenable hypothesis is the one that best explains the facts. Because of the uncertainties inherent to intelligence analysis, conclusive proof or refutation of hypotheses is the exception rather than the rule.

This chapter discusses four techniques for testing hypotheses. One of these, the Analysis of Competing Hypotheses (ACH) technique, was developed by Richards Heuer specifically for use in intelligence analysis. It is the application to intelligence analysis of Karl Popper's theory of science.[2] Popper was one of the most influential philosophers of science of the twentieth century. He is known for, among other things, his position that scientific reasoning should start with multiple hypotheses and proceed by rejecting or eliminating hypotheses, while tentatively accepting only those hypotheses that cannot be refuted.

This chapter describes techniques that are intended to be used specifically for hypothesis generation. Other chapters include some techniques that can be used to generate hypotheses but also have a variety of other purposes. These include Structured Brainstorming, Nominal Group Technique, and Quadrant Crunching (chapter 5), Scenarios Analysis (chapter 6), and the Delphi Method (chapter 9).

---

2. Karl Popper, *The Logic of Science* (New York: Basic Books, 1959).

Overview of Techniques

Hypothesis Generation is a category that includes three specific techniques—Simple Hypotheses, Multiple Hypotheses Generator, and Quadrant Hypothesis Generation. Simple Hypotheses is the easiest of the three, but it is not always the best selection. Use Multiple Hypotheses Generator to identify a large set of all possible hypotheses. Quadrant Hypothesis Generation is used to identify a set of hypotheses when there are just two driving forces that are expected to determine the outcome.

Diagnostic Reasoning applies hypothesis testing to the evaluation of significant new information. Such information is evaluated in the context of all plausible explanations of that information, not just in the context of the analyst's well-established mental model. The use of Diagnostic Reasoning reduces the risk of surprise, as it ensures that an analyst will have given at least some consideration to alternative conclusions. Diagnostic Reasoning differs from the Analysis of Competing Hypotheses (ACH) technique in that it is used to evaluate a single item of evidence, while ACH deals with an entire issue involving multiple pieces of evidence and a more complex analytic process.

Analysis of Competing Hypotheses is the application of Karl Popper's philosophy of science to the field of intelligence analysis. The requirement to identify and then refute all reasonably possible hypotheses forces an analyst to recognize the full uncertainty inherent in most analytic situations. At the same time, the ACH software helps the analyst sort and manage evidence to identify paths for reducing that uncertainty.

Argument Mapping is a method that can be used to put a single hypothesis to a rigorous logical test. The structured visual representation of the arguments and evidence makes it easier to evaluate any analytic judgment. Argument Mapping is a logical follow on to an ACH analysis. It is a detailed presentation of the arguments for and against a single hypothesis, while ACH is a more general analysis of multiple hypotheses. The successful application of Argument Mapping to the hypothesis favored by the ACH analysis would increase confidence in the results of both analyses.

Deception Detection is discussed in this chapter because the possibility of deception by a foreign intelligence service or other adversary organization is a distinctive type of hypothesis that analysts must frequently consider. The possibility of deception can be included as a hypothesis in any ACH analysis. Information identified through the Deception Detection technique can then be entered as evidence in the ACH matrix.

7.1   HYPOTHESIS GENERATION

I n broad terms, a hypothesis is a potential explanation or conclusion that is to be tested by collecting and presenting evidence. It is a declarative statement that has not been established as true—an "educated guess" based on observation that needs to be supported or refuted by more observation or through experimentation.

A good hypothesis:

* Is written as a definite statement, not as a question.

* Is based on observations and knowledge.

* Is testable and falsifiable.

* Predicts the anticipated results clearly.

* Contains a dependent and an independent variable. The dependent variable is the phenomenon being explained. The independent variable does the explaining.

There are many techniques that can be used to generate hypotheses, including several techniques discussed elsewhere in this book, such as Structured Brainstorming, Scenarios Analysis, Quadrant Crunching, Starbursting, and the Delphi Method. This section discusses techniques developed specifically for hypothesis generation and then presents the method for three different techniques—Simple Hypotheses, Multiple Hypotheses Generator, and Quadrant Hypothesis Generation.

▶ **When to Use It**
Analysts should use some structured procedure to develop multiple hypotheses at the start of a project when:

* The importance of the subject matter is such as to require systematic analysis of all alternatives.

* Many variables are involved in the analysis.

* There is uncertainty about the outcome.

* Analysts or decision makers hold competing views.

▷ **Value Added**

Generating multiple hypotheses at the start of a project can help analysts avoid common analytic pitfalls such as these:

* Coming to premature closure.

* Being overly influenced by first impressions.

* Selecting the first answer that appears "good enough."

* Focusing on a narrow range of alternatives representing marginal, not radical, change.

* Opting for what elicits the most agreement or is desired by the boss.

* Selecting a hypothesis only because it avoids a previous error or replicates a past success.

▷ **7.1.1 The Method: Simple Hypotheses**

To use the Simple Hypotheses method, define the problem and determine how the hypotheses are expected to be used at the beginning of the project. Will hypotheses be used in an Analysis of Competing Hypotheses, in some other hypothesis-testing project, as a basis for developing scenarios, or as a means to select from a wide range of alternative outcomes those that need most careful attention? Figure 7.1.1 illustrates the process.

Gather together a diverse group to review the available evidence and explanations for the issue, activity, or behavior that you want to evaluate. In forming this diverse group, consider that you will need different types of expertise for different aspects of the problem, cultural expertise about the geographic area involved, different perspectives from various stakeholders, and different styles of thinking (left brain/right brain, male/female). Then:

* Ask each member of the group to write down on a 3 × 5 card up to three alternative explanations or hypotheses. Prompt creative thinking by using the following:
  - Situational logic: Take into account all the known facts and an understanding of the underlying forces at work at that particular time and place.
  - Historical analogies: Consider examples of the same type of phenomenon.
  - Theory: Consider theories based on many examples of how a particular type of situation generally plays out.

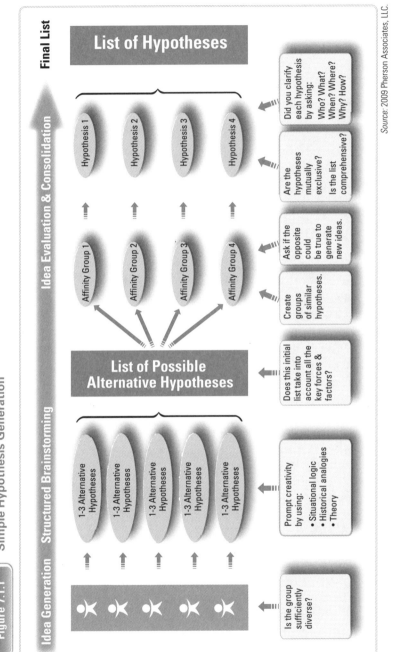

Figure 7.1.1   Simple Hypothesis Generation

Idea Generation   **Structured Brainstorming**   **Idea Evaluation & Consolidation**   **Final List**

List of Hypotheses

- Hypothesis 1
- Hypothesis 2
- Hypothesis 3
- Hypothesis 4

Did you clarify each hypothesis by asking: Who? What? When? Where? Why? How?

Are the hypotheses mutually exclusive? Is the list comprehensive?

- Affinity Group 1
- Affinity Group 2
- Affinity Group 3
- Affinity Group 4

Ask if the opposite could be true to generate new ideas.

Create groups of similar hypotheses.

List of Possible Alternative Hypotheses

Does this initial list take into account all the key forces & factors?

- 1-3 Alternative Hypotheses
- 1-3 Alternative Hypotheses
- 1-3 Alternative Hypotheses
- 1-3 Alternative Hypotheses
- 1-3 Alternative Hypotheses

Prompt creativity by using:
- Situational logic
- Historical analogies
- Theory

Is the group sufficiently diverse?

Source: 2009 Pherson Associates, LLC.

* Collect the cards and display the results on a whiteboard. Consolidate the list to avoid any duplication.

* Employ additional group and individual brainstorming techniques to identify key forces and factors.

* Aggregate the hypotheses into affinity groups and label each group.

* Use problem restatement and consideration of the opposite to develop new ideas.

* Update the list of alternative hypotheses. If the hypotheses will be used in ACH, strive to keep them mutually exclusive—that is, if one hypothesis is true all others must be false.

* Have the group clarify each hypothesis by asking the journalist's classic list of questions: Who, What, When, Where, Why, and How?

* Select the most promising hypotheses for further exploration.

▷ 7.1.2 The Method: Multiple Hypotheses Generator

The Multiple Hypotheses Generator provides a structured mechanism for generating a wide array of hypotheses. Analysts often can brainstorm a useful set of hypotheses without such a tool, but the Hypotheses Generator may give greater confidence than other techniques that a critical alternative or an outlier has not been overlooked. To use this method:

* Define the issue, activity, or behavior that is subject to examination. Do so by using the journalist's classic list of Who, What, When, Where, Why, and How for explaining this issue, activity, or behavior. Some of these questions may not be appropriate or they may be givens for the particular issue, activity, or behavior you are examining.
    - In a case in which you are seeking to challenge a favored hypothesis, identify the Who, What, When, Where, Why, and How for the given hypothesis. Then generate plausible alternatives for each key component.

* Once this process has been completed, you should have lists of alternatives for each of the Who, What, When elements.

* Strive to keep the alternatives on each list mutually exclusive.

* Generate a list of all possible permutations, as shown in Figure 7.1.2.

* Discard any permutation that simply makes no sense.

Figure 7.1.2   Hypothesis Generator: Generating Permutations

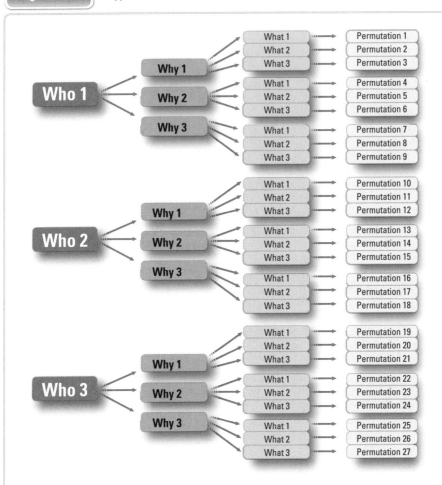

In this example, twenty-seven permutations can be generated using three questions from the journalist's list of Who, What, When, Where, Why, and How. Some of these elements may not be appropriate for a particular issue, activity, or behavior you are examining. In this case, the permutations have been created using three alternatives each for Who, Why, and What.

Source: 2009 Pherson Associates, LLC.

* Evaluate the credibility of the remaining permutations by challenging the key assumptions of each component. Some of these assumptions may be testable themselves. Assign a "credibility score" to each permutation using a 1 to 5 point scale.

* Resort the remaining permutations, listing them from most credible to least credible.

* Restate the permutations as hypotheses, ensuring that each meets the criteria of a good hypothesis.

* Select from the top of the list those hypotheses most deserving of attention.

▶ 7.1.3 The Method: Quadrant Hypothesis Generation

Use the quadrant technique to identify a basic set of hypotheses when there are two easily identified key driving forces that will determine the outcome of an issue. The technique identifies four potential scenarios that represent the extreme conditions for each of the two major drivers. It spans the logical possibilities inherent in the relationship and interaction of the two driving forces, thereby generating options that analysts otherwise may overlook.

Quadrant Hypothesis Generation is easier and quicker to use than Multiple Hypotheses Generation, but it is limited to cases in which the outcome of a situation will be determined by two major driving forces, and it depends upon the correct identification of these forces. It is less effective when there are more than two major drivers or when there are analytic differences about which forces are the major drivers.

These are the steps for Quadrant Hypothesis Generation:

* Identify the two main drivers by using techniques such as Structured Brainstorming or by surveying subject matter experts. A discussion to identify the two main drivers can be a useful exercise in itself.

* Construct a 2 × 2 matrix using the two drivers.

* Think of each driver as a continuum from one extreme to the other. Write the extremes of each of the drivers at the end of the vertical and horizontal axes.

* Fill in each quadrant with the details of what the end state would be as shaped by the two drivers.

* Develop signposts that show whether events are moving toward one of the hypotheses. Use the signposts or indicators of change to develop intelligence collection strategies to determine the direction in which events are moving.

Figure 7.1.3 **Quadrant Hypothesis Generation: Four Hypotheses on the Future of Iraq**

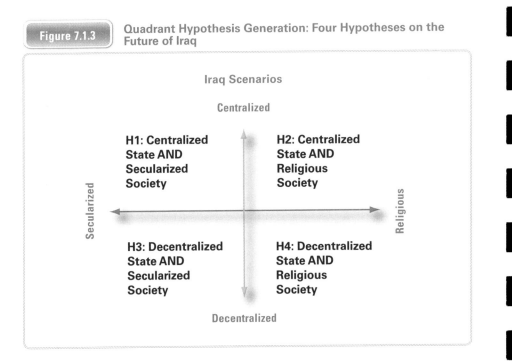

Figure 7.1.3 shows an example of a quadrant chart. In this case analysts have been tasked with developing a paper on the possible future of Iraq, focusing on the potential end state of the government. The analysts have identified and agreed upon the two key drivers in the future of the government: the level of centralization of the federal government and the degree of religious control of that government. They develop their quadrant chart and lay out the four logical hypotheses based on their decisions.

The four hypotheses derived from the quad chart can be stated as follows:

1. The final state of the Iraq government will be a centralized state and a secularized society.

2. The final state of the Iraq government will be a centralized state and a religious society.

3. The final state of the Iraq government will be a decentralized state and a secularized society

4. The final state of the Iraq government will be a decentralized state and a religious society.

▶ Relationship to Other Techniques

The product of any Scenarios Analysis can be thought of as a set of alternative hypotheses. Quadrant Hypothesis Generation is a specific application of the generic method called Morphological Analysis, described in chapter 5. Alternative Futures Analysis uses a similar quadrant chart approach to define four potential outcomes.

▶ Origins of This Technique

The generation and testing of hypotheses is a key element of scientific reasoning. The Simple Hypotheses approach was developed by Randy Pherson. The Multiple Hypotheses Generator technique was also developed by Randy Pherson, and the description is from his *Handbook of Analytic Tools and Techniques* (Reston, Va.: Pherson Associates, LLC, 2008). The description of Quadrant Hypothesis Generation is from Defense Intelligence Agency training materials.

DIAGNOSTIC REASONING

Diagnostic Reasoning applies hypothesis testing to the evaluation of a new development, the assessment of a new item of intelligence, or the reliability of a source. It is different from the Analysis of Competing Hypotheses (ACH) technique in that Diagnostic Reasoning is used to evaluate a single item of evidence, while ACH deals with an entire issue involving multiple pieces of evidence and a more complex analytic process.

▶ When to Use It

Analysts should use Diagnostic Reasoning instead of making a snap intuitive judgment when assessing the meaning of a new development in their area of interest, or the significance or reliability of a new intelligence report. The use of this technique is especially important when the analyst's intuitive interpretation of a new piece of evidence is that the new information confirms what the analyst was already thinking. Diagnostic Reasoning requires that the analyst assess whether this same information is also consistent with other reasonable conclusions, that is, with alternative hypotheses.

▶ Value Added

Diagnostic Reasoning helps balance people's natural tendency to interpret new information as consistent with their existing understanding of what is happening—that is, the analyst's mental model. It is a common experience to discover that much of the evidence supporting what one believes is the most likely conclusion is really of limited value in confirming one's existing view, because that same evidence is also consistent with alternative conclusions. One needs to evaluate new information in the context of all possible explanations of that information, not just in the context of a well-established mental model. The use of Diagnostic Reasoning reduces the element of surprise by ensuring that at least some consideration has been given to alternative conclusions.

▶ The Method

Diagnostic Reasoning is a process by which you try to refute alternative judgments rather than confirm what you already believe to be true. Here are the steps to follow:

＊ When you receive a potentially significant item of information, make a mental note of what it seems to mean (i.e., an explanation of why something happened or what it portends for the future). Make a quick intuitive judgment based on your current mental model.

＊ Brainstorm, either alone or in a small group, the alternative judgments that another analyst with a different perspective might reasonably deem to have a chance of being accurate. Make a list of these alternatives.

＊ For each alternative, ask the following question: If this alternative were true or accurate, how likely is it that I would see this new information?

＊ Make a tentative judgment based on consideration of these alternatives. If the new information is equally likely with each of the alternatives, the information has no diagnostic value and can be ignored. If the information is clearly inconsistent with one or more alternatives, those alternatives might be ruled out. Following this mode of thinking for each of the alternatives, decide which alternatives need further attention and which can be dropped from consideration.

＊ Proceed further by seeking evidence to refute the remaining alternatives rather than confirm them.

▶ **Relationship to Other Techniques**
Diagnostic Reasoning is an integral part of two other techniques: Analysis of Competing Hypotheses and Indicators Validator (chapter 6). It is presented here as a separate technique to show that its use is not limited to those two techniques. It is a fundamental form of critical reasoning that should be widely used in intelligence analysis.

▶ **Origins of This Technique**
Diagnostic Reasoning has been the principal method for medical problem solving for many years. For information on the role of Diagnostic Reasoning in the medical world, see the following recent publications: Albert S. Elstein, "Thinking About Diagnostic Thinking: A Thirty-Year Perspective," *Advances in Health Science Education,* published online by Springer Science+Business Media, August 11, 2009; and Pat Croskerry, "A Universal Model of Diagnostic Reasoning," *Academic Medicine* 84, no. 8 (August 2009). The description of Diagnostic Reasoning in this book was written by Richards Heuer.

ANALYSIS OF COMPETING HYPOTHESES

Analysis of Competing Hypotheses (ACH) is a technique that assists analysts in making judgments on issues that require careful weighing of alternative explanations or estimates. ACH involves identifying a set of mutually exclusive alternative explanations or outcomes (presented as hypotheses), assessing the consistency or inconsistency of each item of evidence with each hypothesis, and selecting the hypothesis that best fits the evidence. The idea behind this technique is to refute rather than to confirm each of the hypotheses. The most likely hypothesis is the one with the least evidence against it, as well as evidence for it, not the one with the most evidence for it.[3]

ACH can be done with pen and paper, but the use of the ACH software is strongly recommended. The software greatly reduces the time required to enter data and makes it possible to sort evidence by its diagnosticity, by the type of source, or by date or time. ACH software is available on major Intelligence Community agency systems and may be downloaded at no cost at the Pherson Associates Web site (www.pherson.org) or from the Palo Alto Research Center (www2.parc.com/istl/projects/ach/ach.html).

Enhanced, Web-based versions of ACH are now under development. They provide a common Web-based platform for analysts in different locations to collaborate on a single ACH analysis. Analysts can work either synchronously or asynchronously. They are particularly useful when analysts want to compare how they have each rated the evidence in their ACH matrix and discuss areas of disagreement. One technique, collaborative ACH, is undergoing testing for inclusion on the Intelligence Community's A-Space network. Information on the status of these Web-based, collaborative versions of ACH is available from Pherson Associates at www.pherson.org.

▶ **When to Use It**

ACH is appropriate for almost any analysis where there are alternative explanations for what has happened, is happening, or is likely to happen. Use it when the judgment or decision is so important that you cannot afford to be wrong. Use it when your gut feelings are not good enough, and when you need a systematic approach to prevent being surprised by an unforeseen outcome. Use it on

---

3. Analysis of Competing Hypotheses applies to intelligence analysis the scientific principles advocated by Karl Popper, one of the most influential philosophers of science of the twentieth century. See Karl Popper, *The Logic of Science* (New York: Basic Books, 1959).

controversial issues when it is desirable to identify precise areas of disagreement and to leave an audit trail to show what evidence was considered and how different analysts arrived at their judgments.

ACH is particularly effective when there is a robust flow of data to absorb and evaluate. For example, it is well-suited for addressing questions about technical issues in the chemical, biological, radiological, and nuclear arena. For example, "For which weapons system is this part most likely being imported?" or "Which type of missile system is Country X importing or developing?" ACH also is particularly helpful when an analyst must deal with the potential for denial and deception, as it was initially developed for that purpose.

The technique can be used by a single analyst, but it is most effective with a small team that can challenge one another's evaluation of the evidence. It structures and facilitates the exchange of evidence and ideas with colleagues in other offices or agencies. An ACH analysis requires a modest commitment of time; it usually takes at least a day to load the matrix once all the evidence has been collected and another day to work through all the stages of the analytic process before writing up any conclusions. A facilitator or a colleague previously schooled in the use of the technique is often needed to help guide analysts through the process, especially if it is the first time they have used the methodology.

▶ **Value Added**

There are a number of different ways by which ACH helps analysts produce a better analytic product. These include the following:

    ∗ It prompts analysts to start by developing a full set of alternative hypotheses. This process reduces the risk of what is called "satisficing"—going with the first answer that comes to mind that seems to meet the need. It ensures that all reasonable alternatives are considered before the analyst gets locked into a preferred conclusion.

    ∗ It requires analysts to try to refute hypotheses rather than support a single hypothesis. The technique helps analysts overcome the tendency to search for or interpret new information in a way that confirms their preconceptions and avoids information and interpretations that contradict prior beliefs. A word of caution, however. ACH works this way only when the analyst approaches an issue with a relatively open mind. An analyst who is already committed to a belief in what the right answer is will often find a way to interpret the evidence as consistent with that belief. In other words, as an antidote to confirmation bias, ACH is similar to a flu shot. Taking the flu shot will usually keep you from getting the flu, but it won't make you well if you already have the flu.

∗ It helps analysts to manage and sort evidence in analytically useful ways. It helps maintain a record of relevant evidence and tracks how that evidence relates to each hypothesis. It also enables analysts to sort data by type, date, and diagnosticity of the evidence.

∗ It spurs analysts to present conclusions in a way that is better organized and more transparent as to how these conclusions were reached than would otherwise be possible.

∗ It provides a foundation for identifying indicators that can be monitored to determine the direction in which events are heading.

∗ It leaves a clear audit trail as to how the analysis was done.

As a tool for interoffice or interagency collaboration, ACH ensures that all analysts are working from the same database of evidence, arguments, and assumptions and ensures that each member of the team has had an opportunity to express his or her view on how that information relates to the likelihood of each hypothesis. Users of ACH report that:

∗ The technique helps them gain a better understanding of the differences of opinion with other analysts or between analytic offices.

∗ Review of the ACH matrix provides a systematic basis for identification and discussion of differences between two or more analysts.

∗ Reference to the matrix helps depersonalize the argumentation when there are differences of opinion.

▶ **The Method**
Simultaneous evaluation of multiple, competing hypotheses is difficult to do without some type of analytic aid. To retain three or five or seven hypotheses in working memory and note how each item of information fits into each hypothesis is beyond the capabilities of most people. It takes far greater mental agility than the common practice of seeking evidence to support a single hypothesis that is already believed to be the most likely answer. ACH can be accomplished, however, with the help of the following eight-step process:

∗ First, identify the hypotheses to be considered. Hypotheses should be mutually exclusive; that is, if one hypothesis is true, all others must be false. The list of hypotheses should include all reasonable possibilities. Include a deception hypothesis if that is appropriate. For each hypothesis, develop a brief scenario or "story" that explains how it might be true.

* Make a list of significant "evidence," which for ACH means everything that is relevant to evaluating the hypotheses—including evidence, arguments, assumptions, and the absence of things one would expect to see if a hypothesis were true. It is important to include assumptions as well as factual evidence, because the matrix is intended to be an accurate reflection of the analyst's thinking about the topic. If the analyst's thinking is driven by assumptions rather than hard facts, this needs to become apparent so that the assumptions can be challenged. A classic example of absence of evidence is the Sherlock Holmes story of the dog barking in the night. The failure of the dog to bark was persuasive evidence that the guilty party was not an outsider but an insider who was known to the dog.

* Analyze the diagnosticity of the evidence, arguments, and assumptions to identify which inputs are most influential in judging the relative likelihood of the hypotheses. Assess each input by working across the matrix. For each hypothesis, ask, "Is this input consistent with the hypothesis, inconsistent with the hypothesis, or is it not relevant?" If it is consistent, place a "C" in the box; if it is inconsistent, place an "I"; if it is not relevant to that hypothesis leave the box blank. If a specific item of evidence, argument, or assumption is particularly compelling, place two "CCs" in the box; if it strongly undercuts the hypothesis, place two "IIs." When you are asking if an input is consistent or inconsistent with a specific hypothesis, a common response is, "It all depends on. . . ." That means the rating for the hypothesis will be based on an assumption—whatever assumption the rating "depends on." You should write down all such assumptions. After completing the matrix, look for any pattern in those assumptions—that is, the same assumption being made when ranking multiple items of evidence. After sorting the evidence for diagnosticity, note how many of the highly diagnostic inconsistency ratings are based on assumptions. Consider how much confidence you should have in those assumptions and then adjust the confidence in the ACH Inconsistency Scores accordingly. See Figure 7.3a for an example.

* Refine the matrix by reconsidering the hypotheses. Does it make sense to combine two hypotheses into one or to add a new hypothesis that was not considered at the start? If a new hypothesis is added, go back and evaluate all the evidence for this hypothesis. Additional evidence can be added at any time.

* Draw tentative conclusions about the relative likelihood of each hypothesis, basing your conclusions on an analysis of the diagnosticity of each item of evidence. The software calculates an inconsistency score based on the number of "I" or "II" ratings or a weighted inconsistency score that also includes consideration of the weight assigned to each item of evidence. The hypothesis with the lowest

Figure 7.3a   ACH: Entering and Coding Evidence

Figure 7.3a ACH: Entering and Coding Evidence

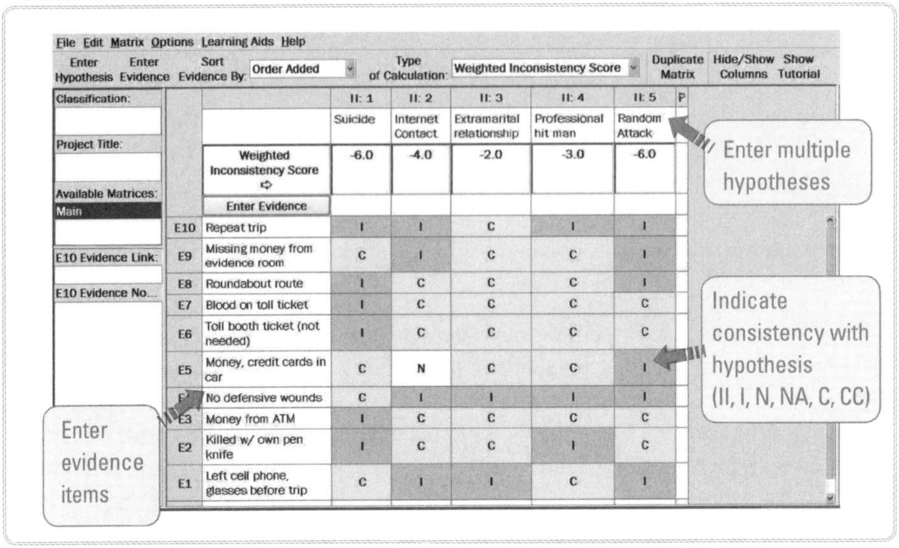

inconsistency score is tentatively the most likely hypothesis. The one with the most inconsistencies is the least likely.

＊ Analyze the sensitivity of your tentative conclusion to a change in the interpretation of a few critical items of evidence. Do this by using the ACH software to sort the evidence by diagnosticity. This identifies the most diagnostic evidence that is driving your conclusion. See Figure 7.3b. Consider the consequences for your analysis if one or more of these critical items of evidence were wrong or deceptive or subject to a different interpretation. If a different interpretation would be sufficient to change your conclusion, go back and do everything that is reasonably possible to double check the accuracy of your interpretation.

＊ Report the conclusions. Discuss the relative likelihood of all the hypotheses, not just the most likely one. State which items of evidence were the most diagnostic and how compelling a case they make in distinguishing the relative likelihood of the hypotheses.

＊ Identify indicators or milestones for future observation. Generate two lists: the first focusing on future events or what might be developed through additional research that would help prove the validity of your analytic judgment, and the

Figure 7.3b — ACH: Sorting Evidence for Diagnosticity

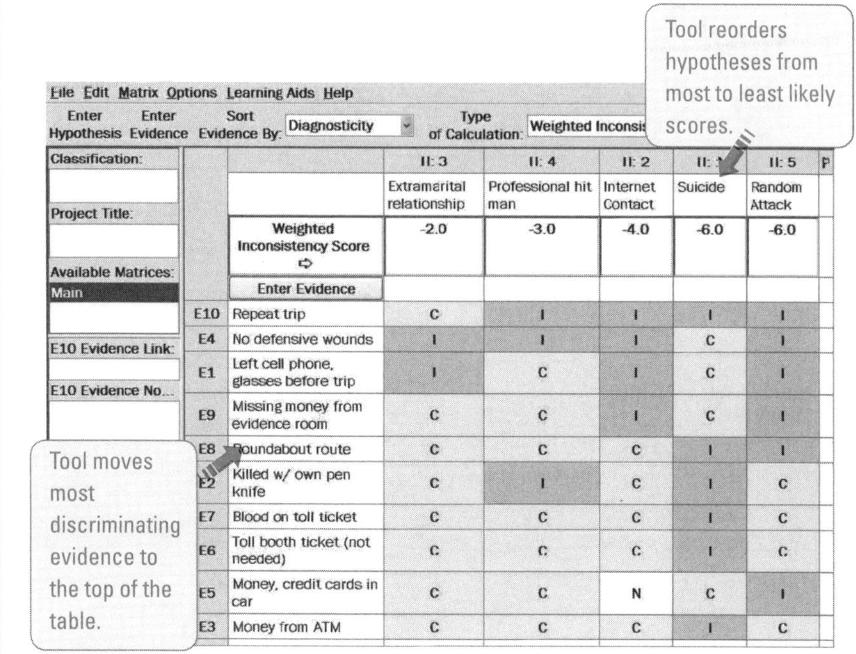

Tool reorders hypotheses from most to least likely scores.

File Edit Matrix Options Learning Aids Help

Enter Hypothesis | Enter Evidence | Sort Evidence By: Diagnosticity | Type of Calculation: Weighted Inconsi

Classification:				II: 3	II: 4	II: 2	II: 1	II: 5	P
				Extramarital relationship	Professional hit man	Internet Contact	Suicide	Random Attack	
Project Title:			Weighted Inconsistency Score ⇨	-2.0	-3.0	-4.0	-6.0	-6.0	
Available Matrices: Main			Enter Evidence						
	E10	Repeat trip		C	I	I	I	I	
E10 Evidence Link:	E4	No defensive wounds		I	I	I	C	I	
E10 Evidence No.	E1	Left cell phone, glasses before trip		I	C	I	C	I	
	E9	Missing money from evidence room		C	C	I	C	I	
	E8	Roundabout route		C	C	C	I	I	
	E2	Killed w/ own pen knife		C	I	C	I	C	
	E7	Blood on toll ticket		C	C	C	I	C	
	E6	Toll booth ticket (not needed)		C	C	C	I	C	
	E5	Money, credit cards in car		C	C	N	C	I	
	E3	Money from ATM		C	C	C	I	C	

Tool moves most discriminating evidence to the top of the table.

second, a list of indicators that would suggest that your judgment is less likely to be correct. Monitor both lists on a regular basis, remaining alert to whether new information strengthens or weakens your case.

Collaborative ACH

Web-based collaborative versions of ACH allow analysts to use the software tool in a Web-based environment working from multiple locations. Like ACH, the software analyzes the diagnosticity of the evidence (which includes arguments, assumptions, and the absence of evidence) to identify which items are most influential in judging the relative likelihood of each hypothesis. Analysts can propose hypotheses and enter data on the matrix from multiple locations, but they must agree to work from the same set of hypotheses and the same set of evidence. They can then disagree in their evaluation of the evidence and the conclusion they reach regarding the most likely hypothesis.

Figure 7.3c **Showing Levels of Disagreement with Collaborative ACH**

			Randy Pherson	Consistent
			Sarah Beebe	Neutral
			Kathy Hibbs	Inconsistent
			Dick Heuer	Neutral

	State-sponsored terrorism	Domestic extremists	Insider operational	Qa'eda terrorists
Note said Death to America	Strong	Moderate	Strong	Moderate
Suspect's résumé is misleading	Concensus **C**	Mild	Mild	Concensus **N**
Very high-grade Anthrax was used	Concensus **C**	Concensus **C**	Concensus **N**	Concensus **N**
Known terrorists rented from victim's wife	Mild	Mild	Concensus **N**	Mild

Extent of Disagreement

Concensus	Mild	Moderate	Strong

II Highly Inconsistent   I Inconsistent   N Neutral   NA Not Applicable   C Consistent   CC Highly Consistent

Source: 2009 Pherson Associates, LLC.

Collaborative ACH tools add a whole new functionality to ACH because they allow many analysts to work on the same project at the same time from different locations. With collaborative ACH tools, analysts working the same issue or case in different organizations or jurisdictions can conduct their analysis jointly, because each member can enter evidence as the story or the case progresses. Collaborative ACH also provides transparency in measuring the degree of agreement among analysts in their assessment of the evidence for each hypothesis. Analysts can keep track of how they personally evaluated the evidence, and compare it with how other team members evaluated the same evidence. They can also call up the Group Matrix which shows where there was group consensus, where differences of opinion exist, and how serious those differences are. This is shown in Figure 7.3c.

▶ **Potential Pitfalls**

The inconsistency or weighted inconsistency scores generated by the ACH software for each hypothesis are *not* the product of a magic formula that tells you which hypothesis to believe in! The ACH software takes you through a systematic analytic process, and the computer makes the calculation, but the judgment that emerges is only as accurate as your selection and evaluation of the evidence to be considered.

Because it is more difficult to refute hypotheses than to find information that confirms a favored hypothesis, the generation and testing of alternative hypotheses will often increase rather than reduce the analyst's level of uncertainty. Such uncertainty is frustrating, but it is usually an accurate reflection of the true situation. The ACH procedure has the offsetting advantage of focusing your attention on the few items of critical evidence that cause the uncertainty or which, if they were available, would alleviate it. ACH can guide future collection, research, and analysis to resolve the uncertainty and produce a more accurate judgment.

Analysts should be aware of five circumstances that can cause a divergence between an analyst's own beliefs and the inconsistency scores. In the first two circumstances described in the following list, the inconsistency scores seem to be wrong when they are actually correct. In the next three circumstances, the inconsistency scores may seem correct when they actually may be wrong. Analysts need to recognize these circumstances, understand the problem, and make adjustments accordingly.

∗ Assumptions or logical deductions omitted: If the scores in the matrix do not support what you believe is the most likely hypothesis, the matrix may be incomplete. Your thinking may be influenced by assumptions or logical deductions that have not been included in the list of evidence/arguments. If so, these should be included so that the matrix fully reflects everything that influences your judgment on this issue. It is important for all analysts to recognize the role that unstated or unquestioned (and sometimes unrecognized) assumptions play in their analysis. In political or military analysis, for example, conclusions may be driven by assumptions about another country's capabilities or intentions. A principal goal of the ACH process is to identify those factors that drive the analyst's thinking on an issue so that these factors can then be questioned and, if possible, validated.

∗ Insufficient attention to less likely hypotheses: If you think the scoring gives undue credibility to one or more of the less likely hypotheses, it may be because you have not assembled the evidence needed to refute them. You may have devoted insufficient attention to obtaining such evidence, or the evidence may simply not be there. If you cannot find evidence to refute a hypothesis, it may be necessary to adjust your thinking and recognize that the uncertainty is greater than you had originally thought.

∗ Definitive evidence: There are occasions when intelligence collectors obtain information from a trusted and well-placed inside source. The ACH analysis can assign a "High" weight for Credibility, but this is probably not enough to reflect the conclusiveness of such evidence and the impact it should have on an analyst's thinking about the hypotheses. In other words, in some circumstances one or two highly authoritative reports from a trusted source in a position to know may support one hypothesis so strongly that they refute all other hypotheses regardless of what other less reliable or less definitive evidence may show.

＊ Unbalanced set of evidence: Evidence and arguments must be representative of the problem as a whole. If there is considerable evidence on a related but peripheral issue and comparatively few items of evidence on the core issue, the inconsistency or weighted inconsistency scores may be misleading.

＊ Diminishing returns: As evidence accumulates, each new item of inconsistent evidence or argument has less impact on the inconsistency scores than does the earlier evidence. For example, the impact of any single item is less when there are fifty items than when there are only ten items. To understand this, consider what happens when you calculate the average of fifty numbers. Each number has equal weight, but adding a fifty-first number will have less impact on the average than if you start with only ten numbers and add one more. Stated differently, the accumulation of evidence over time slows down the rate at which the inconsistency score changes in response to new evidence. Therefore, these numbers may not reflect the actual amount of change in the situation you are analyzing. When you are evaluating change over time, it is desirable to delete the older evidence periodically or to partition the evidence and analyze the older and newer evidence separately.

▷ **Relationship to Other Techniques**

ACH is often used in conjunction with other techniques. For example, Structured Brainstorming, Nominal Group Technique, the Hypothesis Generator, or the Delphi Method may be used to identify hypotheses or evidence to be included in the ACH analysis or to evaluate the significance of evidence. Deception Detection may identify an opponent's motive, opportunity, or means to conduct deception, or past deception practices; information about these factors should be included in the list of ACH evidence. The Diagnostic Reasoning technique is incorporated within the ACH method. The final step in the ACH method identifies Indicators for monitoring future developments.

The ACH matrix is intended to reflect all evidence and arguments that affect one's thinking about a designated set of hypotheses. That means it should also include assumptions identified by a Key Assumptions Check (chapter 8). Conversely, rating the consistency of an item of evidence with a specific hypothesis is often based on an assumption. When rating the consistency of evidence in an ACH matrix, the analyst should ask, "If this hypothesis is true, would I see this item of evidence?" A common thought in response to this question is, "It all depends on. . . ." This means that however the consistency of that item of evidence is rated, that rating will be based on an assumption—whatever assumption the rating "depends on." These assumptions should be recorded and then considered in the context of a Key Assumptions Check.

The Delphi Method (chapter 9) can be used to double-check the conclusions of an ACH analysis. A number of outside experts are asked separately to assess the probability of the same set of hypotheses and to explain the rationale for their conclusions. If the two different groups of analysts using different methods arrive at the same conclusion, this is grounds for a significant increase in confidence in the conclusion. If they disagree, their lack of agreement would also be useful as one can then seek to understand the rationale for the different judgments.

ACH and Argument Mapping (described in the next section) are both used on the same types of complex analytic problems. They are both systematic methods for organizing evidence, but they work in fundamentally different ways and are best used at different stages in the analytic process. ACH is used during an early stage to analyze a range of hypotheses in order to determine which is most consistent with the broad body of evidence. At a later stage, when the focus is on developing, evaluating, or presenting the case for a specific conclusion, Argument Mapping is the appropriate method. Each method has strengths and weaknesses, and the optimal solution is to use both.

▷ **Origins of This Technique**

Richards Heuer originally developed the ACH technique as a method for dealing with a particularly difficult type of analytic problem at the CIA in the 1980s. It was first described publicly in his book *The Psychology of Intelligence Analysis* (Washington, D.C.: CIA Center for the Study of Intelligence, 1999); reprinted by Pherson Associates, LLC, 2007. Heuer and Randy Pherson helped the Palo Alto Research Center develop the ACH software. Pherson and Matthew Burton worked with Heuer in developing the Collaborative ACH software. Pherson Associates, together with Heuer, is currently engaged in activities for developing a collaborative version of ACH and for melding ACH software with other complementary analytic techniques.

7.4 ARGUMENT MAPPING

Argument Mapping is a technique that can be used to test a single hypothesis through logical reasoning. The process starts with a single hypothesis or tentative analytic judgment and then uses a box-and-arrow diagram to lay out visually the argumentation and evidence both for and against the hypothesis or analytic judgment.

▶ When to Use It

When making an intuitive judgment, use Argument Mapping to test your own reasoning. Creating a visual map of your reasoning and the evidence that supports this reasoning helps you better understand the strengths, weaknesses, and gaps in your argument.

Argument Mapping and Analysis of Competing Hypotheses (ACH) are complementary techniques that work well either separately or together. Argument Mapping is a detailed presentation of the argument for a single hypothesis, while ACH is a more general analysis of multiple hypotheses. The ideal is to use both.

＊ Before you generate an Argument Map, there is considerable benefit to be gained by using ACH to take a closer look at the viability of alternative hypotheses. After looking at alternative hypotheses, you can then select the best one to map.

＊ After you have identified a favored hypothesis through ACH analysis, there is much to be gained by using Argument Mapping to check and help present the rationale for this hypothesis.

▶ Value Added

An Argument Map makes it easier for both analysts and recipients of the analysis to evaluate the soundness of any conclusion. It helps clarify and organize one's thinking by showing the logical relationships between the various thoughts, both pro and con. An Argument Map also helps the analyst recognize assumptions and identify gaps in the available knowledge. The visualization of these relationships makes it easier to think about a complex issue and serves as a guide for clearly presenting to others the rationale for the conclusions. Having this rationale available in a visual form helps both the analyst and recipients of the report to focus on the key issues and arguments rather than meandering aimlessly or straying off to minor points.

The visual representation of an argument also makes it easier to recognize weaknesses in opposing arguments. It pinpoints the location of any disagreement, and it might also serve as an objective basis for mediating a disagreement.

▶ The Method

An Argument Map starts with a hypothesis—a single-sentence statement, judgment, or claim about which the analyst can, in subsequent statements, present general arguments and detailed evidence, both pro and con. Boxes with arguments are arrayed hierarchically below this statement, and these boxes are connected with arrows. The arrows signify that a statement in one box is a reason to believe, or not to believe, the statement in the box to which the arrow is pointing. Different types of boxes serve different functions in the reasoning process, and boxes use some combination of color-coding, icons, shapes, and labels so that one can quickly distinguish arguments supporting a hypothesis from arguments opposing it. Figure 7.4 is a very simple example of Argument Mapping, showing some of the arguments bearing on the assessment that North Korea has nuclear weapons.

Argument Mapping is a challenging skill. Training and practice are required to use the technique properly and so gain its benefits. Detailed instructions for effective use of this technique are available at the Web site listed under Sources. Assistance by someone experienced in using the technique is necessary for first-time users. Commercial software and freeware are available for various types of Argument Mapping. In the absence of software, a Post-it note for each box in the map can be very helpful, as it is easy to move the Post-its around as the map evolves and changes.

▶ Origins of This Technique

The history of Argument Mapping goes back to the early nineteenth century. In the early twentieth century John Henry Wigmore pioneered its use for legal argumentation. The availability of computers to create and modify the argument maps in the later twentieth century prompted broader interest in Argument Mapping for use in a variety of analytic domains. The short description here is based on the Austhink Web site, www.austhink.com/critical/pages/argument_mapping.html, and the CIA's Sherman Kent School for Intelligence Analysis training materials.

Figure 7.4

Argument Mapping: Does North Korea Have Nuclear Weapons?

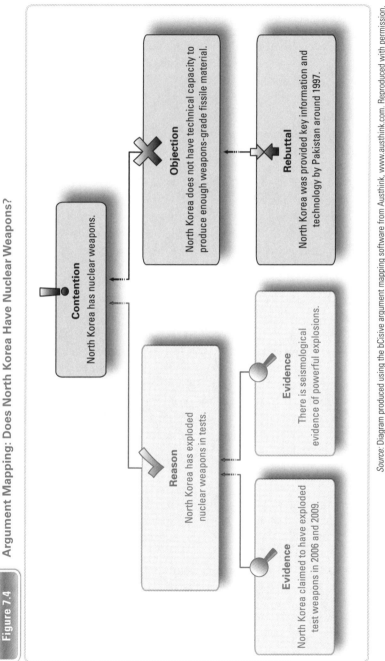

Source: Diagram produced using the bCisive argument mapping software from Austhink, www.austhink.com. Reproduced with permission.

DECEPTION DETECTION

Deception is an action intended by an adversary to influence the perceptions, decisions, or actions of another to the advantage of the deceiver. Deception Detection is a set of checklists that analysts can use to help them determine when to look for deception, discover whether deception actually is present, and figure out what to do to avoid being deceived. "The accurate perception of deception in counterintelligence analysis is extraordinarily difficult. If deception is done well, the analyst should not expect to see any evidence of it. If, on the other hand, it is expected, the analyst often will find evidence of deception even when it is not there."[4]

▶ **When to Use It**

Analysts should be concerned about the possibility of deception when:

* The potential deceiver has a history of conducting deception.

* Key information is received at a critical time, that is, when either the recipient or the potential deceiver has a great deal to gain or to lose.

* Information is received from a source whose bona fides are questionable.

* Analysis hinges on a single critical piece of information or reporting.

* Accepting new information would require the analyst to alter a key assumption or key judgment.

* Accepting the new information would cause the Intelligence Community, the U.S. government, or the client to expend or divert significant resources.

* The potential deceiver may have a feedback channel that illuminates whether and how the deception information is being processed and to what effect.

---

4. Richards J. Heuer Jr., "Cognitive Factors in Deception and Counterdeception," in *Strategic Military Deception*, ed. Donald C. Daniel & Katherine L. Herbig (New York: Pergamon Press, 1982).

▶ Value Added

Most analysts know they cannot assume that everything that arrives in their in-box is valid, but few know how to factor such concerns effectively into their daily work practices. If an analyst accepts the possibility that some of the information received may be deliberately deceptive, this puts a significant cognitive burden on the analyst. All the evidence is open then to some question, and it becomes difficult to draw any valid inferences from the reporting. This fundamental dilemma can paralyze analysis unless practical tools are available to guide the analyst in determining when it is appropriate to worry about deception, how best to detect deception in the reporting, and what to do in the future to guard against being deceived.

> *It is very hard to deal with deception when you are really just trying to get a sense of what is going on, and there is so much noise in the system, so much overload, and so much ambiguity. When you layer deception schemes on top of that, it erodes your ability to act.*
>
> —Robert Jervis, "Signaling and Perception in the Information Age," in *The Information Revolution and National Security*, ed. Thomas E. Copeland, U.S. Army War College Strategic Studies Institute, August 2000.

▶ The Method

Analysts should routinely consider the possibility that opponents are attempting to mislead them or to hide important information. The possibility of deception cannot be rejected simply because there is no evidence of it; if it is well done, one should not expect to see evidence of it. Some circumstances in which deception is most likely to occur are listed in the "When to Use It" section. When such circumstances occur, the analyst, or preferably a small group of analysts, should assess the situation using four checklists that are commonly referred to by their acronyms: MOM, POP, MOSES, and EVE. (See box.)

Analysts have also found the following "rules of the road" helpful in dealing with deception.[5]

* Avoid over-reliance on a single source of information.

* Seek and heed the opinions of those closest to the reporting.

* Be suspicious of human sources or sub-sources who have not been met with personally or for whom it is unclear how or from whom they obtained the information.

---

5. These rules are from Richards J. Heuer Jr., "Cognitive Factors in Deception and Counterdeception," in *Strategic Military Deception*, ed. Donald C. Daniel and Katherine L. Herbig (New York: Pergamon Press, 1982); and Michael I. Handel, "Strategic and Operational Deception in Historical Perspective, in *Strategic and Operational Deception in the Second World War*, ed. Michael I. Handel (London: Frank Cass, 1987).

DECEPTION DETECTION CHECKLISTS

Motion, Opportunity, and Means (MOM):

* *Motive:* What are the goals and motives of the potential deceiver?

* *Channels:* What means are available to the potential deceiver to feed information to us?

* *Risks:* What consequences would the adversary suffer if such a deception were revealed?

* *Costs:* Would the potential deceiver need to sacrifice sensitive information to establish the credibility of the deception channel?

* *Feedback:* Does the potential deceiver have a feedback mechanism to monitor the impact of the deception operation?

Past Opposition Practices (POP):

* Does the adversary have a history of engaging in deception?

* Does the current circumstance fit the pattern of past deceptions?

* If not, are there other historical precedents?

* If not, are there changed circumstances that would explain using this form of deception at this time?

Manipulability of Sources (MOSES):

* Is the source vulnerable to control or manipulation by the potential deceiver?

* What is the basis for judging the source to be reliable?

* Does the source have direct access or only indirect access to the information?

* How good is the source's track record of reporting?

Evaluation of Evidence (EVE):

* How accurate is the source's reporting? Has the whole chain of evidence including translations been checked?

* Does the critical evidence check out? Remember, the sub-source can be more critical than the source.

* Does evidence from one source of reporting (e.g., human intelligence) conflict with that coming from another source (e.g., signals intelligence or open source reporting)?

* Do other sources of information provide corroborating evidence?

* Is any evidence one would expect to see noteworthy by its absence?

* Do not rely exclusively on what someone says (verbal intelligence); always look for material evidence (documents, pictures, an address or phone number that can be confirmed, or some other form of concrete, verifiable information).

* Look for a pattern where on several occasions a source's reporting initially appears correct but later turns out to be wrong and the source can offer a seemingly plausible, albeit weak, explanation for the discrepancy.

* Generate and evaluate a full set of plausible hypothesis—including a deception hypothesis, if appropriate—at the outset of a project.

* Know the limitations as well as the capabilities of the potential deceiver.

▶ Relationship to Other Techniques

Analysts can combine Deception Detection with Analysis of Competing Hypotheses to assess the possibility of deception. The analyst explicitly includes deception as one of the hypotheses to be analyzed, and information identified through the MOM, POP, MOSES, and EVE checklists is then included as evidence in the ACH analysis.

▶ Origins of This Technique

Deception—and efforts to detect it—have always been an integral part of international relations. An excellent book on this subject is Michael Bennett and Edward Waltz, *Counterdeception Principles and Applications for National Security* (Boston: Artech House, 2007). The description of Deception Detection in this book was previously published in Randy Pherson, *Handbook of Analytic Tools and Techniques* (Reston, Va.: Pherson Associates, LLC, 2008).

8 Assessment of Cause and Effect

8

Assessment of Cause and Effect

8.1   Key Assumptions Check   [183]

8.2   Structured Analogies   [189]

8.3   Role Playing   [193]

8.4   Red Hat Analysis   [197]

8.5   Outside-In Thinking   [201]

8.6   Policy Outcomes Forecasting Model   [204]

8.7   Prediction Markets   [209]

CHAPTER 8

Assessment of Cause and Effect

Attempts to explain the past and forecast the future are based on an understanding of cause and effect. Such understanding is difficult, because the kinds of variables and relationships studied by the intelligence analyst are, in most cases, not amenable to the kinds of empirical analysis and theory development that are common in academic research. The best the analyst can do is to make an informed judgment, but such judgments depend upon the analyst's subject matter expertise and reasoning ability and are vulnerable to various cognitive pitfalls and fallacies of reasoning.

One of the most common causes of intelligence failures is mirror imaging, the unconscious assumption that other countries and their leaders will act as we would in similar circumstances. Another is the tendency to attribute the behavior of people, organizations, or governments to the nature of the actor and underestimate the influence of situational factors. Conversely, people tend to see their own behavior as conditioned almost entirely by the situation in which they find themselves. This is known as the "fundamental attribution error."

There is also a tendency to assume that the results of an opponent's actions are what the opponent intended, and we are slow to accept the reality of simple mistakes, accidents, unintended consequences, coincidences, or small causes leading to large effects. Analysts often assume that there is a single cause and stop their search for an explanation when the first seemingly sufficient cause is found. Perceptions of causality are partly determined by where one's attention is directed; as a result, information that is readily available, salient, or vivid is more likely to be perceived as causal than information that is not. Cognitive limitations and common errors in the perception of cause and effect are discussed in greater detail in Richards Heuer's *Psychology of Intelligence Analysis*.

People also make several common errors in logic. When two occurrences often happen at the same time, or when one follows the other, they are said to be correlated. A frequent assumption is that one occurrence causes the other, but correlation should not be confused with causation. It often happens that a third variable causes both. "A classic example of this is ice cream sales and the number of drownings in the summer. The fact that ice cream sales increase as drownings increase does not mean that either one caused the other. Rather, a third factor, such as hot weather, could have caused both."[1]

There is no single, easy technique for mitigating the pitfalls involved in making causal judgments, because analysts usually lack the information they need to be certain of a causal relationship. Moreover, the complex events that are the focus of intelligence analysis often have multiple causes that interact with each other. Appropriate use of the techniques in this chapter can, however, help mitigate a variety of common cognitive pitfalls and improve the analyst's odds of getting it right.

The Psychology of Intelligence Analysis describes three principal strategies that intelligence analysts use to make judgments to explain the cause of current events or forecast what might happen in the future:

＊ **Situational logic:** Making expert judgments based on the known facts and an understanding of the underlying forces at work at that particular time and place. When an analyst is working with incomplete, ambiguous, and possibly deceptive information, these expert judgments usually depend upon assumptions about capabilities, intent, or the normal workings of things in the country of concern. Key Assumptions Check, which is one of the most commonly used structured techniques, is described in this chapter.

＊ **Comparison with historical situations:** Combining an understanding of the facts of a specific situation with knowledge of what happened in similar situations in the past, either in one's personal experience or historical events. This strategy involves the use of analogies. The Structured Analogies technique described in this chapter adds rigor and increased accuracy to this process.

＊ **Applying theory:** Basing judgments on the systematic study of many examples of the same phenomenon. Theories or models often based on empirical academic research are used to explain how and when certain types of events normally happen. Many academic models are too generalized to be applicable to the unique characteristics of most intelligence problems. Many others involve quantitative analysis that is beyond the domain of structured analytic techniques as

---

1. David Roberts, "Reasoning: Errors in Causation," http://writing2.richmond.edu/WRITING/wweb/reason2b.html.

defined in this book. However, a conceptual model that simply identifies relevant variables and the diverse ways they might combine to cause specific outcomes can be a useful template for guiding collection and analysis of some common types of problems. The Policy Outcomes Forecasting Model is an example of this.

Overview of Techniques

Key Assumptions Check is one of the most important and frequently used techniques. Analytic judgment is always based on a combination of evidence and assumptions, or preconceptions, that influence how the evidence is interpreted. The Key Assumptions Check is a systematic effort to make explicit and question the assumptions (i.e., mental model) that guide an analyst's thinking.

Structured Analogies applies analytic rigor to reasoning by analogy. This technique requires that the analyst systematically compares the issue of concern with multiple potential analogies before selecting the one for which the circumstances are most similar to the issue of concern. It seems natural to use analogies when making decisions or forecasts as, by definition, they contain information about what has happened in similar situations in the past. People often recognize patterns and then consciously take actions that were successful in a previous experience or avoid actions that previously were unsuccessful. However, analysts need to avoid the strong tendency to fasten onto the first analogy that comes to mind and supports their prior view about an issue.

Role Playing, as described here, starts with the current situation, perhaps with a real or hypothetical new development that has just happened and to which the players must react. This type of Role Playing, unlike much military gaming, can often be completed in one or two days with little advance preparation. Even simple Role Playing like this will stimulate creative and systematic thinking about how a current complex situation might play out. A Role Playing game is also an effective mechanism for bringing together analysts who, although they work on a common problem, may have little opportunity to meet and discuss their perspectives on that problem.

Red Hat Analysis is a useful technique for trying to perceive threats and opportunities as others see them. Intelligence analysts frequently endeavor to forecast the behavior of a foreign leader, group, organization, or country. In doing so, they need to avoid the common error of mirror imaging, the natural tendency to assume that others think and perceive the world in the same way we do. Red Hat Analysis is of limited value without significant cultural understanding of the country and people involved. See chapter 9 for a discussion of how this technique differs from Red Team Analysis.

Outside-In Thinking broadens an analyst's thinking about the forces that can influence a particular issue of concern. This technique requires the analyst to reach beyond his or her specialty area to consider broader social, organizational, economic, environmental, technological, political, and global forces or trends that can affect the topic being analyzed.

Policy Outcomes Forecasting Model is a theory-based procedure for estimating the potential for political change. Formal models play a limited role in political/strategic analysis, since analysts generally are concerned with what they perceive to be unique events, rather than with any need to search for general patterns in events. Conceptual models that tell an analyst how to think about a problem and help the analyst through that thought process can be useful for frequently recurring issues, such as forecasting policy outcomes or analysis of political instability. Models or simulations that use a mathematical algorithm to calculate a conclusion are outside the domain of structured analytic techniques that are the topic of this book.

Prediction Markets are speculative markets created for the purpose of making predictions about future events. Just as betting on a horse race sets the odds on which horse will win, betting that some future occurrence will or will not happen sets the estimated probability of that future occurrence. Although the use of this technique has been successful in the private sector, it may not be a workable method for the Intelligence Community.

Analytic judgment is always based on a combination of evidence and assumptions, or preconceptions, which influence how the evidence is interpreted.[2] The Key Assumptions Check is a systematic effort to make explicit and question the assumptions (the mental model) that guide an analyst's interpretation of evidence and reasoning about any particular problem. Such assumptions are usually necessary and unavoidable as a means of filling gaps in the incomplete, ambiguous, and sometimes deceptive information with which the analyst must work. They are driven by the analyst's education, training, and experience, plus the organizational context in which the analyst works.

Key Assumptions Check is one of the most commonly used techniques, because intelligence analysts typically need to make assumptions to fill gaps. These are often assumptions about another country's intentions or capabilities, the way governmental processes usually work in that country, the relative strength of political forces, the trustworthiness or accuracy of key sources, the validity of previous analyses on the

> An organization really begins to learn when its most cherished assumptions are challenged by counterassumptions. Assumptions underpinning existing policies and procedures should therefore be unearthed, and alternative policies and procedures put forward based upon counterassumptions.
>
> —Ian I. Mitroff and Richard O. Mason, *Creating a Dialectical Social Science: Concepts, Methods, and Models* (1981).

same subject, or the presence or absence of relevant changes in the context in which the activity is occurring. It can be difficult to identify assumptions, because many are socio-cultural beliefs that are held unconsciously or so firmly that they are assumed to be truth and not subject to challenge.

▶ **When to Use It**

Any explanation of current events or estimate of future developments requires the interpretation of evidence. If the available evidence is incomplete or ambiguous, this interpretation is influenced by assumptions about how things normally work in the country of interest. These assumptions should be made explicit early in the analytic process.

---

2. Stuart K. Card, "The Science of Analytical Reasoning," in *Illuminating the Path: The Research and Development Agenda for Visual Analytics*, ed. James J. Thomas and Kristin A. Cook (National Visualization and Analytics Center, Pacific Northwest National Laboratory, 2005), http://nvac.pnl.gov/agenda.stm.

If a Key Assumptions Check is not done at the outset of a project, it can still prove extremely valuable if done during the coordination process or before conclusions are presented or delivered. If the Key Assumptions Check was done early in the process, it is often desirable to review the assumptions again later in the process, for example just before or just after drafting a report. Determine whether the assumptions still hold up or should be modified.

▷ **Value Added**

Preparing a written list of one's working assumptions at the beginning of any project helps the analyst:

* Identify the specific assumptions that underpin the basic analytic line.

* Achieve a better understanding of the fundamental dynamics at play.

* Gain a better perspective and stimulate new thinking about the issue.

* Discover hidden relationships and links between key factors.

* Identify any developments that would cause an assumption to be abandoned.

* Avoid surprise should new information render old assumptions invalid.

A sound understanding of the assumptions underlying an analytic judgment sets the limits for the confidence the analyst ought to have in making a judgment.

▷ **The Method**

The process of conducting a Key Assumptions Check is relatively straightforward in concept but often challenging to put into practice. One challenge is that participating analysts must be open to the possibility that they could be wrong. It helps to involve in this process several well-regarded analysts who are generally familiar with the topic but have no prior commitment to any set of assumptions about the issue at hand. Keep in mind that many "key assumptions" turn out to be "key uncertainties." Randy Pherson's extensive experience as a facilitator of analytic projects indicates that approximately one in every four key assumptions collapses on careful examination.

Here are the steps in conducting a Key Assumptions Check:

* Gather a small group of individuals who are working the issue along with a few "outsiders." The primary analytic unit already is working from an established mental model, so the "outsiders" are needed to bring other perspectives.

* Ideally, participants should be asked to bring their list of assumptions when they come to the meeting. If this was not done, start the meeting with a silent brainstorming session. Ask each participant to write down several assumptions on 3 × 5 cards.

* Collect the cards and list the assumptions on a whiteboard for all to see.

* Elicit additional assumptions. Work from the prevailing analytic line back to the key arguments that support it. Use various devices to help prod participants' thinking:
    - Ask the standard journalist questions. Who: Are we assuming that we know who all the key players are? What: Are we assuming that we know the goals of the key players? When: Are we assuming that conditions have not changed since our last report or that they will not change in the foreseeable future? Where: Are we assuming that we know where the real action is going to be? Why: Are we assuming that we understand the motives of the key players? How: Are we assuming that we know how they are going to do it?
    - Use of phrases such as "will always," "will never," or "would have to be" suggests that an idea is not being challenged. Perhaps it should be.
    - Use of phrases such as "based on" or "generally the case" suggests that a challengeable assumption is being made.
    - When the flow of assumptions starts to slow down, ask, "What else seems so obvious that one would not normally think about challenging it? If no one can identify more assumptions, then there is an assumption that they do not exist, which itself is an assumption subject to challenge.

* After identifying a full set of assumptions, go back and critically examine each assumption. Ask:
    - Why am I confident that this assumption is correct?
    - In what circumstances might this assumption be untrue?
    - Could it have been true in the past but no longer be true today?
    - How much confidence do I have that this assumption is valid?
    - If it turns out to be invalid, how much impact would this have on the analysis?

* Place each assumption in one of three categories:
    - Basically solid.
    - Correct with some caveats.
    - Unsupported or questionable—the "key uncertainties."

* Refine the list, deleting those that do not hold up to scrutiny and adding new assumptions that emerge from the discussion. Above all, emphasize those assumptions that would, if wrong, lead to changing the analytic conclusions.

* Consider whether key uncertainties should be converted into intelligence collection requirements or research topics.

When concluding the analysis, remember that the probability of your analytic conclusion being accurate cannot be greater than the weakest link in your chain of reasoning. Review your assumptions, review the quality of evidence and reliability of sources, and consider the overall difficulty and complexity of the issue. Then make a rough estimate of the probability that your analytic conclusion will turn out to be wrong. Use this number to calculate the rough probability of your conclusion turning out to be accurate. For example, a three in four chance (75 percent) of being right equates to one in four chance (25 percent) of being wrong. This focus on how and why we might be wrong is needed to offset the natural human tendency toward reluctance to admit we might be wrong.

Figure 8.1 on the next page shows apparently flawed assumptions made in the Wen Ho Lee espionage case during the 1990s and what further investigation showed about these assumptions. A Key Assumptions Check could have identified weaknesses in the case against Lee much earlier.

▶ Relationship to Other Techniques

The Key Assumptions Check is frequently paired with other techniques because assumptions play an important role in all structured analytic efforts, and it is important to get them right. For example, when an assumption is critical to an analysis, and questions remain about the validity of that assumption, it may be desirable to follow the Key Assumptions Check with a What If? Analysis. Imagine a future (or a present), in which the assumption is wrong. What could have happened to make it wrong, how could that have happened, and what are the consequences?

There is a particularly noteworthy interaction between Key Assumptions Check and Analysis of Competing Hypotheses (ACH). Key assumptions need to be included as "evidence" in an ACH matrix to ensure that the matrix is an accurate reflection of the analyst's thinking. And analysts frequently identify assumptions during the course of filling out an ACH matrix. This happens when an analyst assesses the consistency or inconsistency of an item of evidence with a hypothesis and concludes that this judgment is dependent upon something else—usually an assumption. Users of ACH should write down and keep track of the assumptions they make when evaluating evidence against the hypotheses.

Figure 8.1   Key Assumptions Check: The Case of Wen Ho Lee

U.S. scientists in the 1990s observed that China had made rapid advances in nuclear warhead miniaturization and that the new design closely resembled a U.S. design. The discovery occurred at a time when the United States sought to expand relations with China, and Chinese espionage against U.S. technology targets—especially nuclear weapons data at national laboratories—was receiving widespread publicity in the media. Department of Energy investigators opened an inquiry that focused on individuals who held special top secret clearances for work on nuclear data in the national labs, who dealt with visiting delegations from China, and who had traveled to China between 1984 and 1988. Investigators quickly narrowed their focus to Wen Ho Lee, a Taiwanese-American nuclear weapons specialist at Los Alamos National Laboratory in New Mexico. These and several other assumptions led investigators to seek Lee's indictment on fifty-nine counts of illegally removing highly classified information from Los Alamos. He ultimately pled guilty to only one count of mishandling a controlled document, was sentenced to time served, and released in September 2000.

Assumption	Assessment
China is developing good access to U.S. scientists.	**Solid.** In the post–Cold War environment, the United States was emphasizing the value of developing strategic partnerships with former adversaries.
China has an aggressive program to collect information and intelligence from U.S. scientists.	**Solid.** The Chinese have developed an extensive network of scientific colleagues and informants to gather data both openly and covertly.
A Taiwanese American would spy for China.	**Caveated.** Taiwan and China are rivals, and which country to spy for would be influenced by where one's close relatives resided and past loyalties.
Lee passed secret information	**Caveated.** The information was not classified information. It was protected as restricted data.
Wen Ho Lee is the spy.	**Unsupported.** Lee did not have access to the actual information allegedly passed. In fact, the information included revisions made to the design after he lost access to it.
China could have made rapid advances only with the help of stolen secrets; the Chinese could not have pieced together information from open sources or through sanctioned scientific contacts.	**Unsupported.** Almost all of the information was in the public domain.
The stolen data was unique to Los Alamos; individuals at other locations were unlikely to have provided the information.	**Unsupported.** The information could also have been obtained from other labs. It also could have come from 36 other Chinese employees working at the labs or from Russian scientists.

Source: 2009 Pherson Associates, LLC.

Quadrant Crunching (chapter 5) and Simple Scenarios (chapter 6) both use assumptions and their opposites to generate multiple explanations or outcomes.

▶ Origins of This Technique

Although assumptions have been a topic of analytic concern for a long time, the idea of a specific analytic technique to focus on assumptions originated in the CIA's Sherman Kent School for Intelligence Analysis. The discussion of Key Assumptions Check in this book is from Randy Pherson, *Handbook of Analytic Tools and Techniques* (Reston, Va.: Pherson Associates, LLC, 2008), and training materials from the Sherman Kent School.

8.2 STRUCTURED ANALOGIES

The Structured Analogies technique applies increased rigor to analogical reasoning by requiring that the issue of concern be compared systematically with multiple analogies rather than with a single analogy.

> One of the most widely used tools in intelligence analysis is the analogy. Analogies serve as the basis for constructing many predictive models, are the basis for most hypotheses, and rightly or wrongly, underlie many generalizations about what the other side will do and how they will go about doing it.
>
> —Jerome K. Clauser and Sandra M. Weir, *Intelligence Research Methodology*, Defense Intelligence School (1975).

▷ When to Use It

It seems natural to use analogies when making judgments or forecasts because, by definition, they contain information about what has happened in similar situations in the past. People do this in their daily lives, and analysts do it in their role as intelligence analysts. People recognize similar situations or patterns and then consciously take actions that were successful in a previous experience or avoid actions that previously were unsuccessful. People often turn to analogical reasoning in unfamiliar or uncertain situations where the available information is inadequate for any other approach.

An analogy involves a perception that two things are similar and a judgment that since they are similar in one way they are likely to be similar in other analytically relevant ways. Analysts may observe that a new military aircraft has several features that are similar to an existing aircraft and conclude that the new aircraft has been designed for similar missions. Examples of analogies on a larger scale and with a more tenuous basis include Vietnam as a reason for not undertaking military action in Iraq, and the successful occupation of Germany and Japan after World War II as a reason for believing that military occupation of Iraq will be successful. History records many analogies that have led to bad decisions as well as good decisions.

When one is making any analogy, it is important to think about more than just the similarities. It is also necessary to consider those conditions, qualities, or circumstances that are dissimilar between the two phenomena. This should be standard practice in all reasoning by analogy and especially in those cases when one cannot afford to be wrong.

Many analogies are used loosely and have a broad impact on the thinking of both decision makers and the public at large. One role for analysis is to take analogies that are already being used by others, and that are having an impact, and then subjecting these analogies to rigorous examination.

We recommend that analysts considering the use of this technique read Richard D. Neustadt and Ernest R. May, "Unreasoning from Analogies," chapter 4, in *Thinking in Time: The Uses of History for Decision Makers* (New York: Free Press, 1986). Also recommended is Giovanni Gavetti and Jan W. Rivkin, "How Strategists Really Think: Tapping the Power of Analogy," *Harvard Business Review* (April 2005).

▶ **Value Added**

Reasoning by analogy helps achieve understanding by reducing the unfamiliar to the familiar. In the absence of data required for a full understanding of the current situation, reasoning by analogy may be the only alternative. If this approach is taken, however, one should be aware of the significant potential for error, and the analyst should reduce the potential for error to the extent possible through the use of the Structured Analogies technique.

> *When resorting to an analogy, [people] tend to seize upon the first that comes to mind. They do not research more widely. Nor do they pause to analyze the case, test its fitness, or even ask in what ways it might be misleading.*
>
> —Ernest R. May, *Lessons of the Past: The Use and Misuse of History in American Foreign Policy* (1975).

The benefit of the Structured Analogies technique is that it avoids the tendency to fasten quickly on a single analogy and then focus only on evidence that supports the similarity of that analogy. Analysts should take into account the time required for this structured approach and may choose to use it only when the cost of being wrong is high.

Structured Analogies is one technique for which there has been an empirical study of its effectiveness. A series of experiments compared Structured Analogies with unaided judgments in predicting the decisions made in eight conflict situations. These were difficult forecasting problems, and the 32 percent accuracy of unaided experts was only slightly better than chance. In contrast, 46 percent of the forecasts made by using the Structured Analogies process described here were accurate. Among experts who were independently able to think of two or more analogies and who had direct experience with their closest analogy, 60 percent of the forecasts were accurate. (See "Origins of This Technique.")

▶ **Method**

Training in this technique is recommended prior to using it. A self-directed training module is available online at no cost at the International Institute of

Forecasters Web site (http://forecastingprinciples.com/practitioners.htm). The Structured Analogies course is listed under Courses for Forecasting.

The following is a step-by-step description of this technique.

* Describe the issue and the judgment or decision that needs to be made.

* Identify a group of experts who are familiar with the problem and who also have a broad background that enables them to identify analogous situations. The more varied the backgrounds the better. There should usually be at least five experts.

* Ask the group of experts to identify as many analogies as possible without focusing too strongly on how similar they are to the current situation. Various universities and international organizations maintain databases to facilitate this type of research. For example, the Massachusetts Institute of Technology (MIT) maintains its Cascon System for Analyzing International Conflict, a database of 85 post–World War II conflicts that are categorized and coded to facilitate their comparison with current conflicts of interest. The University of Maryland maintains the International Crisis Behavior Project database covering 452 international crises between 1918 and 2006. Each case is coded for eighty-one descriptive variables.

* Review the list of potential analogies and agree on which ones should be examined further.

* Develop a tentative list of categories for comparing the analogies to determine which analogy is closest to the issue in question. For example, the MIT conflict database codes each case according to the following broad categories as well as finer subcategories: previous or general relations between sides, great power and allied involvement, external relations generally, military-strategic, international organization (UN, legal, public opinion), ethnic (refugees, minorities), economic/resources, internal politics of the sides, communication and information, actions in disputed area.

* Write up an account of each selected analogy, with equal focus on those aspects of the analogy that are similar and those that are different. The task of writing accounts of all the analogies should be divided up among the experts. Each account can be posted on a wiki where each member of the group can read and comment on them.

* Review the tentative list of categories for comparing the analogous situations to make sure they are still appropriate. Then ask each expert to rate the similarity of each analogy to the issue of concern. The experts should do the rating

in private using a scale from 0 to 10, where 0 = not at all similar, 5 = somewhat similar, and 10 = very similar.

　✳　After combining the ratings to calculate an average rating for each analogy, discuss the results and make a forecast for the current issue of concern. This will usually be the same as the outcome of the most similar analogy. Alternatively, identify several possible outcomes, or scenarios, based on the diverse outcomes of analogous situations. Then use the analogous cases to identify drivers or policy actions that might influence the outcome of the current situation.

▶ **Origins of This Technique**
This technique is described in greater detail in Kesten C. Green and J. Scott Armstrong, "Structured Analogies for Forecasting," in *Principles of Forecasting: A Handbook for Researchers and Practitioners,* ed. J. Scott Armstrong (New York: Springer Science+Business Media, 2001), and www.forecastingprinciples.com/paperpdf/Structured_Analogies.pdf.

8.3 ROLE PLAYING

I n Role Playing, analysts assume the roles of the leaders who are the subject of their analysis and act out their responses to developments. This technique is also known as gaming, but we use the name Role Playing here to distinguish it from the more complex forms of military gaming. This technique is about simple Role Playing, when the starting scenario is the current existing situation, perhaps with a real or hypothetical new development that has just happened and to which the players must react.

▶ When to Use It

Role Playing is often used to improve understanding of what might happen when two or more people, organizations, or countries interact, especially in conflict situations or negotiations. It shows how each side might react to statements or actions from the other side. Many years ago Richards Heuer participated in several Role Playing exercises, including one with analysts of the Soviet Union from throughout the Intelligence Community playing the role of Politburo members deciding on the successor to Soviet leader Leonid Brezhnev. Randy Pherson has also organized several role playing games on Latin America involving intelligence analysts and senior policy officials. Role Playing has a desirable byproduct that might be part of the rationale for using this technique. It is a useful mechanism for bringing together people who, although they work on a common problem, may have little opportunity to meet and discuss their perspectives on this problem. A role-playing game may lead to the long-term benefits that come with mutual understanding and ongoing collaboration. To maximize this benefit, the organizer of the game should allow for participants to have informal time together.

▶ Value Added

Role Playing is a good way to see a problem from another person's perspective, to gain insight into how others think, or to gain insight into how other people might react to U.S. actions. Playing a role gives one license to think and act in a different manner. Simply trying to imagine how another leader or country will think and react, which analysts do frequently, is not Role Playing and is probably less effective than Role Playing. One must actually act out the role and become, in a sense, the person whose role is assumed. It is "living" the role that opens one's mental model and makes it possible to relate facts and ideas to each other in ways that differ from habitual patterns.

Role Playing is particularly useful for understanding the potential outcomes of a conflict situation. Parties to a conflict often act and react many times, and they can change as a result of their interactions. There is a body of research showing that experts using unaided judgment perform little better than chance in predicting the outcome of such conflict. Performance is improved significantly by the use of "simulated interaction" (Role Playing) to act out the conflicts.[3]

Role Playing does not necessarily give a "right" answer, but it typically enables the players to see some things in a new light. Players become more conscious that "where you stand depends on where you sit." By changing roles, the participants can see the problem in a different context. Most participants view their experiences as useful in providing new information and insights.[4] Bringing together analysts from various offices and agencies offers each participant a modest reality test of their views. Participants are forced to confront in a fairly direct fashion the fact that the assumptions they make about the problem are not inevitably shared by others.

▷ **Potential Pitfalls**

One limitation of Role Playing is the difficulty of generalizing from the game to the real world. Just because something happens in a role-playing game does not necessarily mean the future will turn out that way. This observation seems obvious, but it can actually be a problem. Because of the immediacy of the experience and the personal impression made by the simulation, the outcome may have a stronger impact on the participants' thinking than is warranted by the known facts of the case. As we shall discuss, this response needs to be addressed in the after-action review.

J. Scott Armstrong, a prominent specialist in forecasting methodologies, has researched the literature on the validity of Role Playing as a method for predicting decisions. He found that empirical evidence supports the hypothesis that Role Playing provides greater accuracy than individual expert opinion for predicting the outcome of conflicts. In five different studies, Role Playing predicted the correct outcome for 56 percent of 143 predictions, while unaided expert opinion was correct for 16 percent of 172 predictions. (See "Origins of This Technique.") Outcomes of conflict situations are difficult to predict because they involve a series of actions and reactions, with each action depending upon the other party's previous

---

3. Kesten C. Green, "Game Theory, Simulated Interaction, and Unaided Judgment for Forecasting Decisions in Conflicts," *International Journal of Forecasting* 21 (July–September 2005): 463–472; Kesten C. Green, "Forecasting Decisions in Conflict Situations: A Comparison of Game Theory, Role-Playing, and Unaided Judgment," *International Journal of Forecasting* 18 (July–September 2002): 321–344.

4. Ibid.

reaction to an earlier action, and so forth. People do not have the cognitive capacity to play out such a complex situation in their heads. Acting out situations and responses is helpful because it simulates this type of sequential interaction.

Armstrong's findings validate the use of Role Playing as a useful tool for intelligence analysis, but they do not validate treating the outcome as a valid prediction. Although Armstrong found Role Playing results to be more accurate than expert opinion, the error rate for Role Playing was still quite large. Moreover, the conditions in which Role Playing is used in intelligence analysis are quite different from the studies that Armstrong reviewed and conducted. When the technique is used for intelligence analysis, the goal is not an explicit prediction but better understanding of the situation and the possible outcomes. The method does not end with the conclusion of the Role Playing. There must be an after-action review of the key turning points and how the outcome might have been different if different choices had been made at key points in the game.

▶ **The Method**

Most of the gaming done in the Department of Defense and in the academic world is rather elaborate so it requires substantial preparatory work. It does not have to be that way. The preparatory work (such as writing scripts) can be avoided by starting the game with the current situation as already known to analysts, rather than with a notional scenario that participants have to learn. Just one notional news or intelligence report is sufficient to start the action in the game. In the authors' experience, it is possible to have a useful political game in just one day with only a modest investment in preparatory work.

Whenever possible, a Role Playing game should be conducted off site with cell phones turned off. Being away from the office precludes interruptions and makes it easier for participants to imagine themselves in a different environment with a different set of obligations, interests, ambitions, fears, and historical memories.

Each participant normally plays an individual foreign leader or stakeholder and, in some cases, may need to prepare by doing research on the role, interests, and personality of that individual prior to the game. The game may simulate decision making within the leadership of a single country or group, or the interaction between leaders in two or more countries or groups. To keep teams down to an easily manageable size and provide an active role for all participants, it may be appropriate for a single participant to play two or more of the less active roles.

The analyst who plans and organizes the game leads a control team. This team monitors time to keep the game on track, serves as the communication channel to pass messages between teams, leads the after-action review, and helps write the after-action report to summarize what happened and lessons learned. The control team also plays any role that becomes necessary but was not foreseen, for example, a United Nations mediator. If necessary to keep the game on track or lead it in a desired direction, the control team may introduce new events, such as a terrorist attack that inflames emotions or a new policy statement on the issue by the U.S. president.

After the game ends or on the following day, it is necessary to conduct an after-action review. If there is agreement that all participants played their roles well, there may be a natural tendency to assume that the outcome of the game is a reasonable forecast of what will eventually happen in real life. This natural bias in favor of the game outcome needs to be checked during the after-action review. The control team during the game should take notes on all statements or actions by any player that seem to have set the direction in which the game proceeded. The group should then discuss each of these turning points, including what other reasonable actions were available to that player and whether other actions would have caused the game to have a different outcome.

▶ Origins of This Technique

Role Playing is a basic technique in many different analytic domains. The description of it here is based on Richards Heuer's personal experience combined with information from the following sources: Robert Mandel, "Political Gaming and Foreign Policy Making During Crises," *World Politics* 29, no. 4 (July 1977); J. Scott Armstrong, "Role Playing: A Method to Forecast Decisions," in *Principles of Forecasting: A Handbook for Researchers and Practitioners,"* ed. J. Scott Armstrong (New York: Springer Science+Business Media, 2001).

Intelligence analysts frequently endeavor to forecast the actions of an adversary or a competitor. In doing so, they need to avoid the common error of mirror imaging, the natural tendency to assume that others think and perceive the world in the same way we do. Red Hat Analysis[5] is a useful technique for trying to perceive threats and opportunities as others see them, but this technique alone is of limited value without significant cultural understanding of the other country and people involved.

> To see the options faced by foreign leaders as these leaders see them, one must understand their values and assumptions and even their misperceptions and misunderstandings. Without such insight, interpreting foreign leaders' decisions or forecasting future decisions is often little more than partially informed speculation. Too frequently, behavior of foreign leaders appears 'irrational' or 'not in their own best interest.' Such conclusions often indicate analysts have projected American values and conceptual frameworks onto the foreign leaders and societies, rather than understanding the logic of the situation as it appears to them.
>
> —Richards J. Heuer Jr.,
> *Psychology of Intelligence Analysis* (1999).

▶ **When to Use It**

The chances of a Red Hat Analysis being accurate are better when one is trying to foresee the behavior of a specific person who has the authority to make decisions. Authoritarian leaders as well as small, cohesive groups, such as terrorist cells, are obvious candidates for this type of analysis. The chances of making an accurate forecast about an adversary's or a competitor's decision is significantly lower when the decision is constrained by a legislature or influenced by conflicting interest groups. In law enforcement, Red Hat Analysis can be used effectively to simulate the likely behavior of a criminal or a drug lord.

▶ **Value Added**

There is a great deal of truth to the maxim that "where you stand depends on where you sit." Red Hat Analysis is a reframing technique[6] that requires the analyst to adopt—and make decisions consonant with—the culture of a foreign leader, cohesive group, criminal, or competitor. This conscious effort to imagine the situation as the target perceives it helps the analyst gain a different and usually more accurate perspective on a problem or issue. Reframing the problem typically changes the

---

5. This technique should not be confused with Edward de Bono's Six Thinking Hats technique.
6. See the discussion of reframing in the introduction to chapter 9.

analyst's perspective from that of an analyst observing and forecasting an adversary's behavior to that of a leader who must make a difficult decision within that operational culture. This reframing process often introduces new and different stimuli that might not have been factored into a traditional analysis. For example, in a Red Hat exercise, participants might ask themselves these questions: "What are my supporters expecting from me?" "Do I really need to make this decision now?" What are the consequences of making a wrong decision?" "How will the United States respond?"

▶ **Potential Pitfalls**
Forecasting human decisions or the outcome of a complex organizational process is difficult in the best of circumstances. For example, how successful would you expect to be in forecasting the difficult decisions to be made by the U.S. president or even your local mayor? It is even more difficult when dealing with a foreign culture and significant gaps in the available information. Mirror imaging is hard to avoid because, in the absence of a thorough understanding of the foreign situation and culture, your own perceptions appear to be the only reasonable way to look at the problem.

A common error in our perceptions of the behavior of other people, organizations, or governments of all types is likely to be even more common when assessing the behavior of foreign leaders or groups. This is the tendency to attribute the behavior of people, organizations, or governments to the nature of the actor and to underestimate the influence of situational factors. This error is especially easy to make when one assumes that the actor has malevolent intentions but our understanding of the pressures on that actor is limited. Conversely, people tend to see their own behavior as conditioned almost entirely by the situation in which they find themselves. We seldom see ourselves as a bad person, but we often see malevolent intent in others. This is known to cognitive psychologists as the fundamental attribution error.[7]

Analysts should always *try* to see the situation from the other side's perspective, but if a sophisticated grounding in the culture and operating environment of their subject is lacking, they will often be wrong. Recognition of this uncertainty should prompt analysts to consider using wording such as "possibly" and "could happen" rather than "likely" or "probably" when reporting the results of Red Hat Analysis.

▶ **The Method**
    * Gather a group of experts with in-depth knowledge of the target, operating environment, and senior decision maker's personality, motives, and style

---

7. Richards J. Heuer Jr., *Psychology of Intelligence Analysis* (Washington, D.C.: CIA Center for the Study of Intelligence, 1999), reprinted by Pherson Associates, LLC, 2007, 134–138.

of thinking. If at all possible, try to include people who are well grounded in the adversary's culture, who speak the same language, share the same ethnic background, or have lived extensively in the region.

* Present the experts with a situation or a stimulus and ask the experts to put themselves in the adversary's or competitor's shoes and simulate how they would respond. For example, you might ask for a response to this situation: "The United States has just imposed sanctions on your country. Assume that you are the leader. What would you be thinking? What instructions would you issue?" Or this: "Your group wants to attack the U.S. Embassy to mark a special date. How would your group go about planning the attack? How would you go about simulating how the target would respond?" Or: "We are about to launch a new product. How will our key competitors respond?"

* Emphasize the need to avoid mirror imaging. The question is not "What would you do if you were in their shoes?" but "How would this person or group in that particular culture and circumstance most likely think, behave, and respond to the stimulus?"

* If trying to foresee the actions of a group or an organization, consider using the Role Playing technique. To gain cultural expertise that might otherwise be lacking, consider using the Delphi Method (chapter 9) to elicit the expertise of geographically distributed experts.

* In presenting the results, describe the alternatives that were considered and the rationale for selecting the path the person or group is most likely to take. Consider other less conventional means of presenting the results of your analysis, such as the following:
- Describing a hypothetical conversation in which the leader and other players discuss the issue in the first person.
- Drafting a document (set of instructions, military orders, policy paper, or directives) that the adversary or competitor would likely generate.

Figure 8.4 shows how one might use the Red Hat Technique to catch bank robbers.

▶ **Relationship to Other Techniques**

Red Hat Analysis differs from a Red Team Analysis in that it can be done or organized by any analyst who needs to understand or forecast foreign behavior and who has, or can gain access to, the required cultural expertise. A Red Team Analysis is a challenge analysis technique, described in chapter 9. It is usually conducted by a permanent organizational unit or a temporary group staffed by individuals

Most banking establishments utilize surveillance cameras to deter potential robberies, catch bank robbers, and avert internal loss. Multiple cameras usually are deployed near the ceiling to provide a broad panoramic view of all public spaces; some banks also put cameras behind the tellers to better acquire an image of the face of the bank robber. All of these camera locations are appropriate for various reasons. If Red Hat analytic techniques were employed during the development of surveillance strategies, however, many banks would discover that another, more optimal, camera placement for capturing the face of a bank robber merits serious consideration.

By putting themselves "in the shoes" of the robber, banks can gain a better understanding of what behaviors they are most likely to encounter. For instance, most bank robbers know that banks have surveillance cameras. For this reason they often wear baseball caps with visors, look down at their feet, and partially cover their faces when entering the bank to hide or obscure their image. Often when they confront the teller, they continue to look down to avoid showing their face. After they have collected their money, they turn around and look up to assess whether someone might impede their exit route.

By using Red Hat Analysis, security consultants would be more likely to conclude that the most effective location for a bank surveillance camera (for robbery suspect identification) is adjacent to the exit door at shoulder level. When the camera is placed at that location, it will catch the back of a robber entering the bank, but increase the chances of capturing an unobstructed image of the robber's face when the robber departs. Once bank robbers have their money, they only care about how quickly they can exit the bank, and they stop looking down.

Source: Eric Hess, Senior Biometric Product Manager, MorphoTrak, Inc. From an unpublished paper, "Facial Recognition for Criminal Investigations," delivered at the International Association of Law Enforcements Intelligence Analysts, Las Vegas, Nev., 2009. Reproduced with permission.

who are well qualified to think like or play the role of an adversary. The goal of Red Hat Analysis is to exploit the available resources to develop the best possible analysis of an adversary's or competitor's behavior. The goal of Red Team Analysis is usually to challenge the conventional wisdom or an opposing team.

▶ **Origins of This Technique**

Red Hat, Red Cell, and Red Team analysis became popular during the Cold War when "red" symbolized the Soviet Union, and it continues to have broad applicability. This description of Red Hat Analysis is a modified version of that in Randy Pherson, *Handbook of Analytic Tools and Techniques* (Reston, Va.: Pherson Associates, 2008).

8.5 OUTSIDE-IN THINKING

Outside-In Thinking identifies the broad range of global, political, environmental, technological, economic, or social forces and trends that are outside the analyst's area of expertise but that may profoundly affect the issue of concern. Many analysts tend to think from the inside out, focused on familiar factors in their specific area of responsibility with which they are most familiar.

▶ **When to Use It**

This technique is most useful in the early stages of an analytic process when analysts need to identify all the critical factors that might explain an event or could influence how a particular situation will develop. It should be part of the standard process for any project that analyzes potential future outcomes, for this approach covers the broader environmental context from which surprises and unintended consequences often come.

Outside-In Thinking also is useful if a large database is being assembled and needs to be checked to ensure that no important field in the database architecture has been overlooked. In most cases, important categories of information (or database fields) are easily identifiable early on in a research effort, but invariably one or two additional fields emerge after an analyst or group of analysts is well into a project, forcing them to go back and review all previous files, recoding for that new entry. Typically, the overlooked fields are in the broader environment over which the analysts have little control. By applying Outside-In Thinking, analysts can better visualize the entire set of data fields early on in the research effort.

▶ **Value Added**

Most analysts focus on familiar factors within their field of specialty, but we live in a complex, interrelated world where events in our little niche of that world are often affected by forces in the broader environment over which we have no control. The goal of Outside-In Thinking is to help analysts get an entire picture, not just the part of the picture with which they are already familiar.

Outside-In Thinking reduces the risk of missing important variables early in the analytic process. It encourages analysts to rethink a problem or an issue while employing a broader conceptual framework. This technique is illustrated in Figure 8.5. By casting their net broadly at the beginning, analysts are more likely to see an important dynamic or to include a relevant alternative hypothesis. The process

Figure 8.5   Inside-Out Analysis vs. Outside-In Approach

A key question in counterterrorism analysis is, "How are members of a terrorist group communicating with each other?" Analysts using the Inside-Out approach to answering the question constantly review incoming reporting to determine what techniques are being used and whether new methods have been adopted. One problem with this approach is that it might take months or even years before such tip-offs appear in official reporting. The use of Outside-In Thinking can help analysts overcome this obstacle. We recommend that analysts use both techniques.

Inside-Out Approach

- Monitor all-source reporting to detect any tip-offs, lead information, or evidence of new systems or techniques being used by the terrorist group under study.

- Review historical records for examples of techniques used by other terrorist groups.

Outside-In Approach

- Brainstorm what new technologies are emerging that could be used by terrorists (i.e., I-Pods, Voice over Internet Protocols, Second Life, social networking sites).

- Explore how each technology might be used, by whom, and in what circumstances.

- Once capabilities and vulnerabilities are determined, task intelligence collectors to check for evidence of any actual use of such techniques.

Source: 2009 Pherson Associates, LLC.

can provide new insights and uncover relationships that were not evident from the intelligence reporting. In doing so, the technique helps analysts think in terms that extend beyond day-to-day reporting and identify more fundamental forces and factors that should be considered.

▶ **The Method**

- ✳ Generate a generic description of the problem or phenomenon to be studied.

- ✳ Form a group to brainstorm the key forces and factors that could have an impact on the topic but over which the subject can exert little or no influence, such as globalization, the emergence of new technologies, historical precedent, and the growth of the Internet.

- ✳ Employ the mnemonic STEEP +2 to trigger new ideas (Social, Technical, Economic, Environmental, Political plus Military and Psychological).

* Move down a level of analysis and list the key factors about which some expertise is available.

* Assess specifically how each of these forces and factors could have an impact on the problem.

* Ascertain whether these forces and factors actually do have an impact on the issue at hand basing your conclusion on the available evidence.

* Generate new intelligence collection tasking to fill in information gaps.

▷ **Relationship to Other Techniques**
Outside-In Thinking is essentially the same as a business analysis technique that goes by different acronyms, such as STEEP, STEEPLED, PEST, or PESTLE. For example, PEST is an acronym for Political, Economic, Social, and Technological, while STEEPLED also includes Legal, Ethical, and Demographic. All require the analysis of external factors that may have either a favorable or unfavorable influence on an organization.

▷ **Origins of This Technique**
This technique has been used in a planning and management environment to ensure that outside factors that might affect an outcome have been identified. The Outside-In Thinking described here is from Randy Pherson, *Handbook of Analytic Tools and Techniques* (Reston, Va.: Pherson Associates, LLC, 2008); and training materials from the CIA's Sherman Kent School for Intelligence Analysis.

POLICY OUTCOMES FORECASTING MODEL

The Policy Outcomes Forecasting Model structures the analysis of competing political forces in order to forecast the most likely political outcome and the potential for significant political change. The model was originally designed as a quantitative method using expert-generated data, not as a structured analytic technique. However, like many quantitative models, it can also be used simply as a conceptual model to guide how an expert analyst thinks about a complex issue. That is what qualifies this technique for inclusion in this book about structured analytic techniques. Information about the software for quantitative analysis of the same problem is also included at the end of this discussion.

▶ When to Use It

The Policy Outcomes Forecasting Model has been used to analyze the following types of questions:

* What policy is Country W likely to adopt toward its neighbor?
* Is the U.S. military likely to lose its base in Country X?
* How willing is Country Y to compromise in its dispute with Country X?
* In what circumstances can the government of Country Z be brought down?

Use this model when you have substantial information available on the relevant actors (individual leaders or organizations), their positions on the issues, the importance of the issues to each actor, and the relative strength of each actor's ability to support or oppose any specific policy. Judgments about the positions and the strengths and weaknesses of the various political forces can then be used to forecast what policies might be adopted and to assess the potential for political change.

Use of this model is limited to situations when there is a single issue that will be decided by political bargaining and maneuvering, and when the potential outcomes can be visualized on a continuous line (see, for example, Figure 8.6). If the resolution of this issue depends upon the outcome of other issues, this model may not apply.

▶ Value Added

Like any model, Policy Outcomes Forecasting provides a systematic framework for generating and organizing information about an issue of concern. Once the basic analysis is done, it can be used to analyze the significance of changes in the position of any of the stakeholders. An analyst may also use the data to answer What If? questions such as the following:

* Would a leader strengthen her position if she modified her stand on a contentious issue?

* Would the military gain the upper hand if the current civilian leader were to die?

* What would be the political consequences if a traditionally apolitical institution—such as the church or the military—became politicized?

An analyst or group of analysts can make an informed judgment about an outcome by explicitly identifying all the stakeholders in the outcome of an issue and then determining how close or far apart they are on the issue, how influential each one is, and how strongly each one feels about it. Assembling all this data in a graphic such as Figure 8.6 helps the analyst manage the complexity, share and discuss the information with other analysts, and present conclusions in an efficient and effective manner.

▶ **Pitfalls**

Use of this technique requires an experienced facilitator. Analysts must also be very knowledgeable about the country or issue of concern, as results of the analysis are critically dependent upon the quality of information used. Methodological sophistication cannot compensate for a lack of expertise. Although this method provides insights into what will occur, it cannot forecast when or how fast events will unfold. It can, however, estimate the conditions in which changes might occur as a result of groups becoming stronger or weaker, altering their political agendas, modifying their positions on issues, or forming alliances with other stakeholders.

▶ **The Method**

Define the problem in terms of a policy or leadership choice issue. The issue must vary along a single dimension so that options can be arrayed from one extreme to another in a way that makes sense within the country in which the decision will be made. These alternative policies are rated on a scale from 0 to 100, with the position on the scale reflecting the distance or difference between the policies. Figure 8.6 illustrates this by showing seven policies the fictional country of Zambria might pursue for investment in energy resources. These options range between the two extremes—full nationalization of energy investment at the left end of the

Figure 8.6

Zambia Energy Investment Diagram

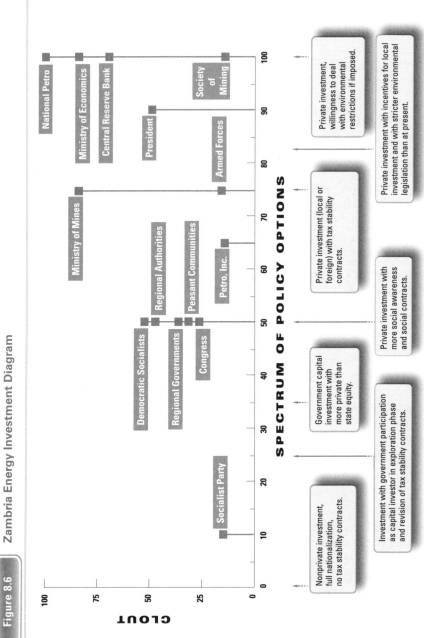

Source: 2009 Pherson Associates, LLC.

scale and private investment only at the right end. Note that the position of these policies on the horizontal scale captures the full range of the policy debate and reflects the estimated political distance or difference between each of the policies.

The next step is to identify all the actors, no matter how strong or weak, that will try to influence the policy outcome. As in the Zambria model, these actors are then positioned above the scale in a manner that shows two things. First, their position on the horizontal scale shows where the actor stands on the issue, and, second, their height above the scale is a measure of the relative amount of clout each actor has and is prepared to use to influence the outcome of the policy decision. To judge the relative height of each actor, identify the strongest actor and arbitrarily assign that actor a strength of 100. Assign proportionately lower values to other actors based on your judgment or gut feeling about how their strength and political clout compare with those of the actor assigned a strength of 100.

This graphic representation of the relevant variables is used as an aid in assessing and communicating to others the current status of the most influential forces on this issue and the potential impact of various changes in this status.

▶ Origins of This Technique

The Policy Outcomes Forecasting Model described here is a simplified, nonquantitative version of a policy forecasting model developed by Bruce Bueno de Mesquita and described in his book *The War Trap* (New Haven: Yale University Press, 1981). It was further refined by Bueno de Mesquita et al., in *Forecasting Political Events: The Future of Hong Kong* (New Haven: Yale University Press, 1988).

Software to implement this model for intelligence analysis was originally developed in the 1980s by Policon Corporation (now Decision Insights, Inc.) for use at the CIA and, subsequently, in the private sector. Stanley A. Feder and programmers in the CIA's Office of Research and Development developed software, called Factions, to run the original version.

In the 1980s, CIA analysts used this method with the implementing software to analyze scores of policy and political instability issues in more than thirty countries. Analysts used their subject expertise to assign numeric values to the variables. The simplest version of this methodology uses the positions of each actor, the relative strength of each actor, and the relative importance of the issue to each actor to calculate which actor's or group's position would get the most support if each policy position had to compete with every other policy position in a series of "pairwise "contests. In other words, the model finds the policy option around which a coalition will form that can defeat every other possible coalition in every possible contest between any two policy options (the "median voter" model). The model can also test how sensitive the policy forecast is to various changes in the relative strength of the actors or in their positions or in the importance each attaches to the issue.

A testing program at that time found that traditional analysis and analyses using the policy forces analysis software were both accurate in hitting the target about 90 percent of the time, but the software hit the bull's-eye twice as often. Also, reports based on the policy forces software gave greater detail on the political dynamics leading to the policy outcome and were less vague in their forecasts than were traditional analyses. See Stanley A. Feder, "Factions and Policon: New Ways to Analyze Politics," in *Inside CIA's Private World: Declassified Articles from the Agency's Internal Journal, 1955–1992*, ed. H. Bradford Westerfield (New Haven: Yale University Press, 1995), 274–292.

Later, another version of the methodology, now known as Policy Forces Analysis, became available to the government and private sector from PolicyFutures, LLC. Decision Insights has continued to develop the methodology and its own implementing software for the Department of Defense and the commercial sector. The Intelligence Community has also developed a software tool based on the model, and other implementations are found in the private sector.

Our description of the Policy Outcomes Forecasting Model draws heavily from communications with Stanley Feder and his previously cited book chapter "Factions and Policon: New Ways to Analyze Politics." We are also grateful for contributions received from Alan Schwartz and Grace Scarborough on this topic.

8.7   PREDICTION MARKETS

Prediction Markets are speculative markets created solely for the purpose of allowing participants to make predictions in a particular area. Just as betting on a horse race sets the odds on which horse will win, supply and demand in the prediction market sets the estimated probability of some future occurrence. Two books, *The Wisdom of Crowds* by James Surowiecki and *Infotopia* by Cass Sunstein, have popularized the concept of Prediction Markets.[8]

We do not support the use of Prediction Markets for intelligence analysis for reasons that are discussed below. We have included Prediction Markets in this book because it is an established analytic technique and it has been suggested for use in the Intelligence Community.[9]

▶ When to Use It

Large corporations such as Google, Microsoft, Motorola, Intel, and General Electric use Prediction Markets to forecast developments and to make decisions within their own corporations. Such markets might predict next year's revenue, gauge consumer demand for a new product, identify future trends, or determine whether a project will finish on time. Employees, partners, and customers of the corporation who believe they have some insight into the issue in question buy and sell prediction contracts. The predictions have often proved to be more correct than the corporations' own internal forecasts. Their success rate lends support to the wisdom of crowds theory that "the many are smarter than the few," that is, that the collective wisdom is often smarter than the average expert. A number of Prediction Markets that cover a wide range of fields are available to the public on the Internet. A Prediction Market Industry Association was recently formed to promote the field, and there is now an academic *Journal of Prediction Markets*.

The following arguments have been made against the use of Prediction Markets for intelligence analysis:[10]

---

8. James Surowiecki, *The Wisdom of Crowds* (New York: Doubleday, 2004); and Cass R. Sunstein, *Infotopia, How Many Minds Produce Knowledge* (New York: Oxford University Press, 2006). See also Sunstein, "Deliberating Groups Versus Prediction Markets," The Law School, University of Chicago, Working Paper No. 321 (January 2007).

9. Cass R. Sunstein, "Improving Intelligence Analysis: What Works? How Can We Tell? Lessons from Outside the Intelligence Community," presentation and subsequent discussion at the Director of National Intelligence Conference, Chantilly, Va., January 9–10, 2007.

10. Kesten C. Green, J. Scott Armstrong, and Andreas Graefe, "Methods to Elicit Forecasts from Groups: Delphi and Prediction Markets Compared," *Foresight: The International Journal of Applied Forecasting* (Fall 2007), www.forecastingprinciples.com/paperpdf/Delphi-WPlatestV.pdf.

* Prediction Markets can be used only in situations that will have an unambiguous outcome, usually within a predictable time period. Such situations are commonplace in business and industry, though much less so in intelligence analysis.

* Prediction Markets do have a strong record of near-term forecasts, but intelligence analysts and their customers are likely to be uncomfortable with their predictions. No matter what the statistical record of accuracy with this technique might be, consumers of intelligence are unlikely to accept any forecast without understanding the rationale for the forecast and the qualifications of those who voted on it.

* If people in the crowd are offering their unsupported opinions, and not informed judgments, the utility of the prediction is questionable. Prediction Markets are more likely to be useful in dealing with commercial preferences or voting behavior and less accurate, for example, in predicting the next terrorist attack in the United States, a forecast that would require special expertise and knowledge.

* Like other financial markets, such as commodities futures markets, Prediction Markets are subject to liquidity problems and speculative attacks mounted in order to manipulate the results. Financially and politically interested parties may seek to manipulate the vote. The fewer the participants, the more vulnerable a market is.

* Ethical objections have been raised to the use of a Prediction Market for national security issues. The Defense Advanced Research Projects Agency (DARPA) proposed a Policy Analysis Market in 2003. It would have worked in a manner similar to the commodities market, and it would have allowed investors to earn profits by betting on the likelihood of such events as regime changes in the Middle East and the likelihood of terrorist attacks. The DARPA plan was attacked on grounds that "it was unethical and in bad taste to accept wagers on the fate of foreign leaders and a terrorist attack. The project was canceled a day after it was announced."[11] Although attacks on the DARPA plan in the media may have been overdone, there is a legitimate concern about government-sponsored betting on international events.

▶ **The Method**
A number of Prediction Markets are open to the public. For example, Intrade manages public markets for trading contracts in the categories of politics,

---

11. Robert Looney, "DARPA's Policy Analysis Market for Intelligence: Outside the Box or Off the Wall?" *Strategic Insight* (September 2003).

entertainment, financial indicators, weather, current events, and legal affairs. Each contract is for a specific event that will have an unambiguous result. The value of the contract ranges from 0 to 100 points. The contract's value at any given point in time is set by market supply and demand and is therefore the market prediction of the probability that an event will occur.

▶ Relationship to Other Techniques

The Delphi Method (chapter 9) is a more appropriate method for intelligence agencies to use to aggregate outside expert opinion; Delphi also has a broader applicability for other types of intelligence analysis.

▶ Origins of This Technique

The modern version of Prediction Markets started in about 1990. It was popularized by works of James Surowiecki and Cass Sunstein. The sources used for this discussion of Prediction Markets are cited in the text.

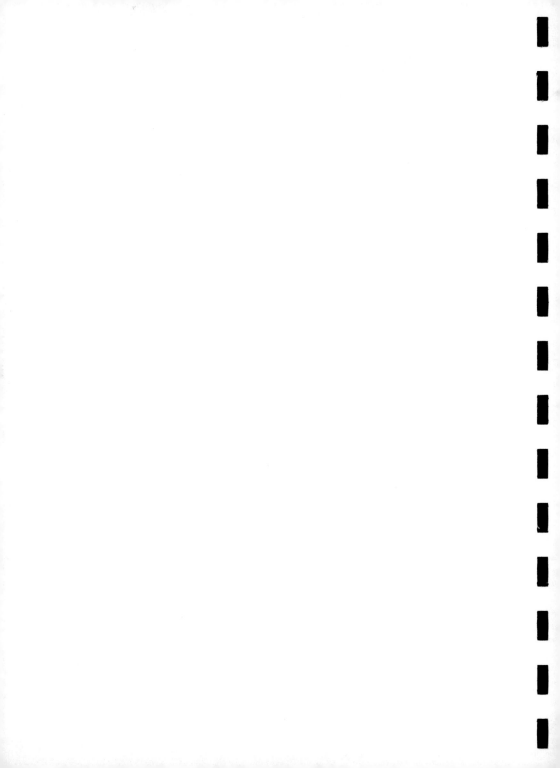

9 Challenge
Analysis

9

Challenge Analysis

9.1   Premortem Analysis   [221]

9.2   Structured Self-Critique   [226]

9.3   What If? Analysis   [231]

9.4   High Impact/Low Probability Analysis   [235]

9.5   Devil's Advocacy   [240]

9.6   Red Team Analysis   [242]

9.7   Delphi Method   [245]

CHAPTER 9

Challenge Analysis

C hallenge analysis encompasses a set of analytic techniques that have also been called contrarian analysis, alternative analysis, competitive analysis, red team analysis, and devil's advocacy. What all of these have in common is the goal of challenging an established mental model or analytic consensus in order to broaden the range of possible explanations or estimates that are seriously considered. The fact that this same activity has been called by so many different names suggests there has been some conceptual diversity about how and why these techniques are being used and what might be accomplished by their use.

There is a broad recognition in the Intelligence Community that failure to question a consensus judgment, or a long-established mental model, has been a consistent feature of most significant intelligence failures. The postmortem analysis of virtually every major U.S. intelligence failure since Pearl Harbor has identified an analytic mental model (mindset) as a key factor contributing to the failure. The situation changed, but the analyst's mental model did not keep pace with that change or did not recognize all the ramifications of the change.

This record of analytic failures has generated discussion about the "paradox of expertise."[1] The experts can be the last to recognize the reality and significance of change. For example, few experts on the Soviet Union foresaw its collapse, and the experts on Germany were the last to accept that Germany was going to be reunified. Going all the way back to the Korean War, experts on China were saying that China would not enter the war—until it did.

As we noted in chapter 1, an analyst's mental model can be regarded as a distillation of everything the analyst knows about how things normally work in a certain country or a specific scientific field. It tells the analyst, sometimes

---

1. Rob Johnston, *Analytic Culture in the U.S. Intelligence Community* (Washington, D.C.: CIA Center for the Study of Intelligence, 2005), 64.

subconsciously, what to look for, what's important, and how to interpret what he or she sees. A mental model formed through education and experience serves an essential function; it is what enables the analyst to provide on a daily basis reasonably good intuitive assessments or estimates about what is happening or likely to happen.

> What gets us into trouble is not what we don't know, it's what we know for sure that just ain't so.
>
> —Mark Twain, American author and humorist

The problem is that a mental model that has previously provided accurate assessments and estimates for many years can be slow to change. New information received incrementally over time is easily assimilated into one's existing mental model, so the significance of gradual change over time is easily missed. It is human nature to see the future as a continuation of the past. As a general rule, major trends and events evolve slowly, and the future is often foreseeable to skilled intelligence analysts. However, life does not always work this way. The most significant intelligence failures have been failures to foresee historical discontinuities, when history pivots and changes direction. Such surprising events are not foreseeable unless they are first imagined so that one can start examining the world from a different perspective. That is what this chapter is about—techniques that enable the analyst, and eventually the intelligence consumer, to evaluate events from a different perspective—in other words, with a different mental model.

There is also another logical rationale for consistently challenging conventional wisdom. Former CIA Director Michael Hayden has stated that "our profession deals with subjects that are inherently ambiguous, and often deliberately hidden. Even when we're at the top of our game, we can offer policymakers insight, we can provide context, and we can give them a clearer picture of the issue at hand, but we cannot claim certainty for our judgments." The director went on to suggest that getting it right seven times out of ten might be a realistic expectation.[2]

Director Hayden's estimate of seven times out of ten is supported by a quick look at verbal expressions of probability used in intelligence reports. "Probable" seems to be the most common verbal expression of the likelihood of an assessment or estimate. Unfortunately, there is no consensus within the Intelligence Community on what "probable" and other verbal expressions of likelihood mean when they are converted to numerical percentages. For discussion here, we

---

2. Paul Bedard, "CIA Chief Claims Progress with Intelligence Reforms," *U.S. News and World Report,* May 16, 2008, www.usnews.com/articles/news/2008/05/16/cia-chief-claims-with-intelligence-reforms.html.

accept Sherman Kent's definition of "probable" as meaning "75% plus or minus 12%."[3] This means that analytic judgments described as "probable" are expected to be correct roughly 75 percent of the time—and, therefore, incorrect or off target about 25 percent of the time.

Logically, therefore, one might expect that one of every four judgments that intelligence analysts describe as "probable" will turn out to be wrong. This perspective broadens the scope of what challenge analysis might accomplish. It should not be limited to questioning the dominant view to be sure it's right. Even if the challenge analysis confirms the initial probability judgment, it should go further to seek a better understanding of the other 25 percent. In what circumstances might there be a different assessment or outcome, what would that be, what would constitute evidence of events moving in that alternative direction, how likely is it, and what would be the consequences? As we will discuss in the next chapter, on conflict management, an understanding of these probabilities should reduce the frequency of unproductive conflict between opposing views. Analysts who recognize a one in four chance of being wrong should at least be open to consideration of alternative assessments or estimates to account for the other 25 percent.

This chapter describes three types of challenge analysis techniques: self-critique, critique *of* others, and solicitation of critique *by* others.

＊ Self-critique: Two techniques that help analysts challenge their own thinking are Premortem Analysis and Structured Self-Critique. These techniques can counteract the pressures for conformity or consensus that often suppress the expression of dissenting opinions in an analytic team or group. We adapted Premortem Analysis from business and applied it to intelligence analysis.

＊ Critique of others: Analysts can use What If? Analysis or High Impact/Low Probability Analysis to tactfully question the conventional wisdom by making the best case for an alternative explanation or outcome.

＊ Critique by others: Several techniques are available for seeking out critique by others. Devil's Advocacy is a well-known example of that. The term "Red Team" is used to describe a group that is assigned to take an adversarial perspective. The Delphi Method is a structured process for eliciting opinions from a panel of outside experts.

---

3. Donald P. Steury, ed., *Sherman Kent and the Board of National Estimates: Collected Essays* (Washington, D.C.: CIA Center for the Study of Intelligence, 1994), 133.

Reframing Techniques

Three of the techniques in this chapter work by a process called reframing. A frame is any cognitive structure that guides the perception and interpretation of what one sees. A mental model of how things normally work can be thought of as a frame through which an analyst sees and interprets evidence. An individual or a group of people can change their frame of reference, and thus challenge their own thinking about a problem, simply by changing the questions they ask or changing the perspective from which they ask the questions. Analysts can use this reframing technique when they need to generate new ideas, when they want to see old ideas from a new perspective, or any other time when they sense a need for fresh thinking.[4]

Reframing helps analysts break out of a mental rut by activating a different set of synapses in their brain. To understand the power of reframing and why it works, it is necessary to know a little about how the human brain works. The brain is now believed to have roughly 100 billion neurons, each analogous to a computer chip capable of storing information. Each neuron has octopus-like arms called axons and dendrites. Electrical impulses flow through these arms and are ferried by neurotransmitting chemicals across the synaptic gap between neurons. Whenever two neurons are activated, the connections, or synapses, between them are strengthened. The more frequently those same neurons are activated, the stronger the path between them.

Once a person has started thinking about a problem one way, the same mental circuits or pathways are activated and strengthened each time the person thinks about it. The benefit of this is that it facilitates the retrieval of information one wants to remember. The downside is that these pathways become mental ruts that make it difficult to see the information from a different perspective. When an analyst reaches a judgment or decision, this thought process is embedded in the brain. Each time the analyst thinks about it, the same synapses are triggered, and the analyst's thoughts tend to take the same well-worn pathway through the brain. Getting the same answer each time one thinks about it builds confidence, and often overconfidence, in that answer.

Fortunately, it is fairly easy to open the mind to think in different ways. The trick is to restate the question, task, or problem from a different perspective that activates a different set of synapses in the brain. Each of the three applications of reframing described in this chapter does this in a different way. Premortem

---

4. Reframing is similar to the Problem Restatement technique Morgan Jones described in his book, *The Thinker's Toolkit* (New York: Three Rivers Press, 1995). Jones observed that "the moment we define a problem our thinking about it quickly narrows considerably." We create a frame through which we view the problem and which tends to obscure other interpretations of the problem. A group can change that frame of reference, and challenge its own thinking, simply by redefining the problem.

Analysis asks analysts to imagine themselves at some future point in time, after having just learned that a previous analysis turned out to be completely wrong. The task then is to figure out how and why it might have gone wrong. What If? Analysis asks the analyst to imagine that some unlikely event has occurred, and then to explain how it could happen and the implications of the event. Structured Self-Critique asks a team of analysts to reverse its role from advocate to critic in order to explore potential weaknesses in the previous analysis. This change in role can empower analysts to express concerns about the consensus view that might previously have been suppressed. These techniques are generally more effective in a small group than with a single analyst. Their effectiveness depends in large measure on how fully and enthusiastically participants in the group embrace the imaginative or alternative role they are playing. Just going through the motions is of limited value.

Overview of Techniques

Premortem Analysis reduces the risk of analytic failure by identifying and analyzing a potential failure *before* it occurs. Imagine yourself several years in the future. You suddenly learn from an unimpeachable source that your estimate was wrong. Then imagine what could have happened to cause the estimate to be wrong. Looking back from the future to explain something that has happened is much easier than looking into the future to forecast what will happen, and this exercise helps identify problems one has not foreseen.

Structured Self-Critique is a procedure that a small team or group uses to identify weaknesses in its own analysis. All team or group members don a hypothetical black hat and become critics rather than supporters of their own analysis. From this opposite perspective, they respond to a list of questions about sources of uncertainty, the analytic processes that were used, critical assumptions, diagnosticity of evidence, anomalous evidence, information gaps, changes in the broad environment in which events are happening, alternative decision models, availability of cultural expertise, and indicators of possible deception. Looking at the responses to these questions, the team reassesses its overall confidence in its own judgment.

What If? Analysis is an important technique for alerting decision makers to an event that could happen, or is already happening, even if it may seem unlikely at the time. It is a tactful way of suggesting to decision makers the possibility that they may be wrong. What If? Analysis serves a function similar to that of Scenario Analysis—it creates an awareness that prepares the mind to recognize early signs of a significant change, and it may enable a decision maker to plan ahead for that contingency. The analyst imagines that an event has occurred and then considers how the event could have unfolded.

High Impact/Low Probability Analysis is used to sensitize analysts and decision makers to the possibility that a low-probability event might actually happen and stimulate them to think about measures that could be taken to deal with the danger or to exploit the opportunity if it does occur. The analyst assumes the event has occurred, and then figures out how it could have happened and what the consequences might be.

Devil's Advocacy is a technique in which a person who has been designated the Devil's Advocate, usually by a responsible authority, makes the best possible case against a proposed analytic judgment, plan, or decision.

Red Team Analysis as described here is any project initiated by management to marshal the specialized substantive, cultural, or analytic skills required to challenge conventional wisdom about how an adversary or competitor thinks about an issue. See also Red Hat Analysis in chapter 8.

Delphi Method is a procedure for obtaining ideas, judgments, or forecasts electronically from a geographically dispersed panel of experts. It is a time-tested, extremely flexible procedure that can be used on any topic or issue for which expert judgment can contribute. It is included in this chapter because it can be used to identify divergent opinions that challenge conventional wisdom. It can also be used as a double check on any research finding. If two analyses from different analysts who are using different techniques arrive at the same conclusion, this is grounds for a significant increase in confidence in that conclusion. If the two conclusions disagree, this is also valuable information that may open a new avenue of research.

PREMORTEM ANALYSIS

The goal of a Premortem Analysis is to reduce the risk of surprise and the subsequent need for a postmortem investigation of what went wrong. It is an easy-to-use technique that enables a group of analysts who have been working together on any type of future-oriented analysis to challenge effectively the accuracy of their own conclusions. It is a specific application of the reframing method, in which restating the question, task, or problem from a different perspective enables one to see the situation differently and come up with different ideas.

▶ **When to Use It**

Premortem Analysis should be used by analysts who can devote a few hours to challenging their own analytic conclusions about the future to see where they might be wrong. It may be used by a single analyst but, like all structured analytic techniques, it is most effective when used in a small group.

A Premortem as an analytic aid was first used in the context of decision analysis by Gary Klein in his 1998 book, *Sources of Power: How People Make Decisions.* He reported using it in training programs to show decision makers that they typically are overconfident that their decisions and plans will work. After the trainees formulated a plan of action, they were asked to imagine that it is several months or years into the future, and their plan has been implemented but has failed. They were then asked to describe how it might have failed, and, despite their original confidence in the plan, they could easily come up with multiple explanations for failure—reasons that were not identified when the plan was first proposed and developed. This assignment provided the trainees with evidence of their overconfidence, and it also demonstrated that the premortem strategy can be used to expand the number of interpretations and explanations that decision makers consider. Klein explains, "We devised an exercise to take them out of the perspective of defending their plan and shielding themselves from flaws. We tried to give them a perspective where they would be actively searching for flaws in their own plan." [5] Klein reported his trainees showed a "much higher level of candor" when evaluating their own plans after being exposed to the premortem exercise, as compared with other more passive attempts at getting them to self-critique their own plans. [6]

---

5. Gary Klein, *Sources of Power: How People Make Decisions* (Cambridge, Mass.: MIT Press, 1998), 71.

6. Gary Klein, *Intuition at Work: Why Developing Your Gut Instinct Will Make You Better at What You Do* (New York, Doubleday, 2002), 91.

▶ **Value Added**

It is important to understand what it is about the Premortem Analysis approach that helps analysts identify potential causes of error that previously had been overlooked. Briefly, there are two creative processes at work here. First, the questions are reframed, an exercise that typically elicits responses that are different from the original ones. Asking questions about the same topic, but from a different perspective, opens new pathways in the brain, as we noted in the introduction to this chapter. Second, the Premortem approach legitimizes dissent. For various reasons, many members of small groups suppress dissenting opinions, leading to premature consensus. In a Premortem Analysis, all analysts are asked to make a positive contribution to group goals by identifying *weaknesses* in the previous analysis.

Research has documented that an important cause of poor group decisions is the desire for consensus. This desire can lead to premature closure and agreement with majority views regardless of whether they are perceived as right or wrong. Attempts to improve group creativity and decision making often focus on ensuring that a wider range of information and opinions are presented to the group and given consideration.[7]

There are many reasons why group members tend to go along with the group leader, with the first group member to stake out a position, or with an emerging majority viewpoint. Most benign is the common rule of thumb that when we have no firm opinion, we take our cues from the opinions of others. We follow others because we believe (often rightly) they know what they are doing. There may also be a concern that one's own views will be critically evaluated by others, or that dissent will be perceived as disloyalty or as an obstacle to progress that will just make the meeting last longer.

In a candid newspaper column written long before he became CIA Director, Leon Panetta wrote that "an unofficial rule in the bureaucracy says that to 'get along, go along.' In other words, even when it is obvious that mistakes are being made, there is a hesitancy to report the failings for fear of retribution or embarrassment. That is true at every level, including advisers to the president. The result is a 'don't make waves' mentality . . . that is just another fact of life you tolerate in a big bureaucracy."[8] We can hope that, as CIA Director, Panetta may be able to

> *It is not bigotry to be certain we are right; but it is bigotry to be unable to imagine how we might possibly have gone wrong.*
>
> —G. K. Chesterton, English writer

---

7. Charlan J. Nemeth and Brendan Nemeth-Brown, "Better than Individuals? The Potential Benefits of Dissent and Diversity for Group Creativity," in *Group Creativity*, ed. Paul B. Paulus and Bernard A Nijstad (New York: Oxford University Press, 2003), 63.

8. Leon Panetta, "Government: A Plague of Incompetence," *Monterey County Herald*, March 11, 2007, F1.

change this "unofficial rule." A significant value of Premortem Analysis is that it legitimizes dissent.

▶ The Method

The best time to conduct a Premortem Analysis is shortly after a group has reached a conclusion on an action plan, but before any serious drafting of the report has been done. If the group members are not already familiar with the Premortem technique, the group leader, another group member, or a facilitator steps up and makes a statement along the lines of the following. "Okay, we now think we know the right answer, but we need to double-check this. To free up our minds to consider other possibilities, let's imagine that we have made this judgment, our report has gone forward and been accepted, and now, x months or years later, we gain access to a crystal ball. Peering into this ball, we learn that our analysis was wrong, and things turned out very differently from the way we had expected. Now, working from that perspective in the future, let's put our imaginations to work and brainstorm what could have possibly happened to cause our analysis to be so wrong."

Ideally, a separate meeting should be held for the Premortem discussion so that participants have time prior to the meeting to think about what might have happened to cause the analytic judgment to be wrong. They might be asked to bring to the meeting a list of things that might have gone differently than expected. To set the tone for the Premortem meeting, analysts should be advised not to focus only on the hypotheses, assumptions, and key evidence already discussed during their group meetings. Rather, they should also look at the situation from the perspective of their own life experiences. They should think about how fast the world is changing, how many government programs are unsuccessful or have unintended consequences, or how difficult it is to see things from the perspective of a foreign culture. This type of thinking may bring a different part of analysts' brains into play as they are mulling over what could have gone wrong with their analysis. Outside-In Thinking (chapter 8) can also be helpful for this purpose.

At the Premortem meeting, the group leader or a facilitator writes the ideas on a whiteboard or flip chart. To ensure that no single person dominates the presentation of ideas, the Nominal Group version of brainstorming might be used. With that technique, the facilitator goes around the room in round-robin fashion taking one idea from each participant until all have presented every idea on their lists. (See Nominal Group Technique in chapter 5.) After all ideas are posted on the board and visible to all, the group discusses what it has learned by this exercise, and what action, if any, the group should take. This generation and initial discussion of ideas can often be accomplished in a single two-hour meeting, which is a small investment of time to undertake a systematic challenge to the group's thinking.

One expected result is an increased appreciation of the uncertainties inherent in any assessment of the future. Another outcome might be identification of indicators which, if observed, would provide early warning that events are not proceeding as expected. Such findings may lead to modification of the existing analytic framework.

On the other hand, the Premortem Analysis may identify problems, conditions, or alternatives that require rethinking the group's original position. In such a case, the Premortem has done its job by alerting the group to the fact that it has a problem, but it does not necessarily tell the group exactly what the problem is or how to fix it. That is beyond the scope of the Premortem. The Premortem makes a start by alerting the group to the fact that it has a problem, but it has not systematically assessed the likelihood of these things happening, nor has it evaluated other possible sources of analytic error or made a comprehensive assessment of alternative courses of action.

If the Premortem Analysis leads the group to reconsider and revise its analytic judgment, the questions shown in Figure 9.1 are a good starting point. For a more thorough set of self-critique questions, see the discussion of Structured Self-Critique, which involves changing one's role from advocate to critic of one's previous analysis.

▶ **Relationship to Other Techniques**

If the Premortem Analysis identifies significant problems, a good follow-up technique to address these problems may be the Structured Self-Critique, described in the next section.

▶ **Origins of This Technique**

Richards Heuer adapted Premortem Analysis as an intelligence analysis technique. As noted, it was originally developed by Gary Klein to train managers to recognize their habitual overconfidence that their plans and decisions will lead to success. For original references on this subject, see Klein, *Sources of Power: How People Make Decisions* (Cambridge, Mass.: MIT Press, 1998); Klein, *Intuition at Work: Why Developing Your Gut Instinct Will Make You Better at What You Do* (New York, Doubleday, 2002); and Klein, "Performing a Project *Pre*Mortem," *Harvard Business Review* (September 2007).

Figure 9.1   Structured Self-Critique: Key Questions

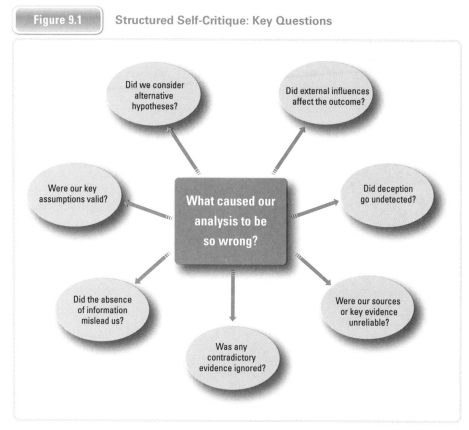

Source: 2009 Pherson Associates, LLC.

9.2 STRUCTURED SELF-CRITIQUE

Structured Self-Critique is a systematic procedure that a small team or group can use to identify weaknesses in its own analysis. All team or group members don a hypothetical black hat and become critics rather than supporters of their own analysis. From this opposite perspective, they respond to a list of questions about sources of uncertainty, the analytic processes that were used, critical assumptions, diagnosticity of evidence, anomalous evidence, information gaps, changes in the broad environment in which events are happening, alternative decision models, availability of cultural expertise, and indicators of possible deception.

> *Begin challenging your own assumptions. Your assumptions are your windows on the world. Scrub them off every once in a while, or the light won't come in.*
>
> —Alan Alda, American actor

As it reviews responses to these questions, the team reassesses its overall confidence in its own judgment.

▶ **When to Use It**

You can use Structured Self-Critique productively to look for weaknesses in any analytic explanation of events or estimate of the future. It is specifically recommended for use in the following ways:

* As the next step after a Premortem Analysis raises unresolved questions about any estimated future outcome or event.

* As a double check prior to the publication of any major product such as a National Intelligence Estimate.

* As one approach to resolving conflicting opinions (as discussed in chapter 10 under Adversarial Collaboration).

The amount of time required to work through the Structured Self-Critique will vary greatly depending upon how carefully the previous analysis was done. The questions listed in the method as described later in this section are actually just a prescription for very careful analysis. To the extent that these same questions have been explored during the initial analysis, the time required for the Structured Self-Critique is reduced. If these questions are being asked for the first time, the process will take longer. As analysts gain experience with the self-critique, they may have less need for certain parts of it, as those parts will have been internalized and will have been done during the initial analysis (as they should have been).

▶ Value Added

When people are asked questions about the same topic but from a different perspective, they often give different answers than the ones they gave before. For example, if a team member is asked if he or she supports the team's conclusions, the answer will usually be "yes." However, if all team members are asked to look for weaknesses in the team's argument, that member may give a quite different response.

This change in the frame of reference is intended to change the group dynamics. The critical perspective should always generate more critical ideas. Team members who previously may have suppressed questions or doubts because they lacked confidence or wanted to be good team players are now empowered to express those divergent thoughts. If the change in perspective is handled well, all team members will know that they win points with their colleagues for being critical of the previous judgment, not for supporting it.

▶ Potential Pitfalls

The success of this technique depends in large measure on the team members' willingness and ability to make the transition from supporters to critics of their own ideas. Some individuals lack the intellectual flexibility to do this well. It must be very clear to all members that they are no longer performing the same function as before. Their new task is to critique an analytic position taken by some other group (actually themselves but with a different hat on).

To emphasize the different role analysts are playing, Structured Self-Critique meetings should be scheduled exclusively for this purpose. The meetings should be led by a different person from the usual leader, and, preferably, held at a different location. It will be helpful if an experienced facilitator is available to lead the meeting(s). This formal reframing of the analysts' role from advocate to critic is an important part of helping analysts see an issue from a different perspective.

▶ The Method

Start by re-emphasizing that all analysts in the group are now wearing a black hat. They are now critics, not advocates, and they will now be judged by their ability to find weaknesses in the previous analysis, not on the basis of their support for the previous analysis. Then work through the following topics or questions:

  * Sources of uncertainty: Identify the sources and types of uncertainty in order to set reasonable expectations for what the team might expect to achieve. Should one expect to find: (a) a single correct or most likely

answer, (b) a most likely answer together with one or more alternatives that must also be considered, or (c) a number of possible explanations or scenarios for future development? To judge the uncertainty, answer these questions:

- Is the question being analyzed a puzzle or a mystery? Puzzles have answers, and correct answers can be identified if enough pieces of the puzzle are found. A mystery has no single definitive answer; it depends upon the future interaction of many factors, some known and others unknown. Analysts can frame the boundaries of a mystery only "by identifying the critical factors and making an intuitive judgment about how they have interacted in the past and might interact in the future."[9]
- How does the team rate the quality and timeliness of its evidence?
- Are there a greater than usual number of assumptions because of insufficient evidence or the complexity of the situation?
- Is the team dealing with a relatively stable situation or with a situation that is undergoing, or potentially about to undergo, significant change?

＊ Analytic process: In the initial analysis, did the team do the following. Did it identify alternative hypotheses and seek out information on these hypotheses? Did it identify key assumptions? Did it seek a broad range of diverse opinions by including analysts from other offices, agencies, academia, or the private sector in the deliberations? If these steps were not taken, the odds of the team having a faulty or incomplete analysis are increased. Either consider doing some of these things now or lower the team's level of confidence in its judgment.

＊ Critical assumptions: Assuming that the team has already identified key assumptions, the next step is to identify the one or two assumptions that would have the greatest impact on the analytic judgment if they turned out to be wrong. In other words, if the assumption is wrong, the judgment will be wrong. How recent and well-documented is the evidence that supports each such assumption? Brainstorm circumstances that could cause each of these assumptions to be wrong, and assess the impact on the team's analytic judgment if the assumption is wrong. Would the reversal of any of these assumptions support any alternative hypothesis? If the team has not previously identified key assumptions, it should do a Key Assumptions Check now.

---

9. Gregory F. Treverton, "Risks and Riddles," *Smithsonian Magazine*, June 1, 2007.

* Diagnostic evidence: Identify alternative hypotheses and the several most diagnostic items of evidence that enable the team to reject alternative hypotheses. For each item, brainstorm for any reasonable alternative interpretation of this evidence that could make it consistent with an alternative hypothesis. See Diagnostic Reasoning in chapter 7.

* Information gaps: Are there gaps in the available information, or is some of the information so dated that it may no longer be valid? Is the absence of information readily explainable? How should absence of information affect the team's confidence in its conclusions?

* Missing evidence: Is there any evidence that one would expect to see in the regular flow of intelligence or open source reporting if the analytic judgment is correct, but that turns out not to be there?

* Anomalous evidence: Is there any anomalous item of evidence that would have been important if it had been believed or if it could have been related to the issue of concern, but that was rejected as unimportant because it was not believed or its significance was not known? If so, try to imagine how this item might be a key clue to an emerging alternative hypothesis.

* Changes in the broad environment: Driven by technology and globalization, the world as a whole seems to be experiencing social, technical, economic, environmental, and political changes at a faster rate than ever before in history. Might any of these changes play a role in what is happening or will happen? More broadly, what key forces, factors, or events could occur independently of the issue that is the subject of analysis that could have a significant impact on whether the analysis proves to be right or wrong?

* Alternative decision models: If the analysis deals with decision making by a foreign government or nongovernmental organization (NGO), was the group's judgment about foreign behavior based on a rational actor assumption? If so, consider the potential applicability of other decision models, specifically that the action was or will be the result of bargaining between political or bureaucratic forces, the result of standard organizational processes, or the whim of an authoritarian leader.[10] If information for a more thorough analysis is lacking, consider the implications of that for confidence in the team's judgment.

---

10. For information about these three decision-making models, see Graham T. Allison and Philip Zelikov, *Essence of Decision,* 2nd ed. (New York: Longman, 1999).

* Cultural expertise: If the topic being analyzed involves a foreign or otherwise unfamiliar culture or subculture, does the team have or has it obtained cultural expertise on thought processes in that culture?[11]

* Deception: Does another country, NGO, or commercial competitor about which the team is making judgments have a motive, opportunity, or means for engaging in deception to influence U.S. policy or to change your behavior? Does this country, NGO, or competitor have a past history of engaging in denial, deception, or influence operations?

After responding to these questions, the analysts take off the black hats and reconsider the appropriate level of confidence in the team's previous judgment. Should the initial judgment be reaffirmed or modified?

▷ **Relationship to Other Techniques**
One version of what has been called Devil's Advocacy is similar to Structured Self-Critique in that one member of the team is designated to play the role of Devil's Advocate. That member takes one of the team's critical assumptions, reverses it, and then argues from that perspective against the team's conclusions. We believe it is more effective for the entire team to don the hypothetical black hat and play the role of critic. It should not be one team member trying to persuade the rest of the team that they are wrong while acting out a role that he or she may actually disagree with. See information on Devil's Advocacy later in this chapter.

▷ **Origins of This Technique**
Richards Heuer and Randy Pherson developed Structured Self-Critique. A simpler version of this technique appears in Randy Pherson, "The Pre-Mortem Assessment," in *Handbook of Analytic Tools and Techniques* (Reston, Va.: Pherson Associates, LLC, 2008).

---

11. For information on fundamental differences in how people think in different cultures, see Richard Nisbett, *The Geography of Thought: How Asians and Westerners Think Differently and Why* (New York: Free Press, 2003).

W hat If? Analysis imagines that an unexpected event has occurred with potential major impact. Then, with the benefit of "hindsight," the analyst figures out how this event could have come about and what the consequences might be.

▷ **When to Use It**

This technique should be in every analyst's toolkit. It is an important technique for alerting decision makers to an event that could happen, even if it may seem unlikely at the present time. What If? Analysis serves a function similar to Scenario Analysis—it creates an awareness that prepares the mind to recognize early signs of a significant change, and it may enable the decision maker to plan ahead for that contingency. It is most appropriate when two conditions are present:

* A mental model is well ingrained within the analytic or the customer community that a certain event will not happen.

* There is a perceived need for others to focus on the possibility that this event could actually happen and to consider the consequences if it does occur.

What If? Analysis is also a logical follow-up after any Key Assumptions Check that identifies an assumption that is critical to an important estimate but about which there is some doubt. In that case, the What If? Analysis would imagine that the opposite of this assumption is true. Analysis would then focus on how this outcome could possibly occur and what the consequences would be.

> *When analysts are too cautious in estimative judgments on threats, they brook blame for failure to warn. When too aggressive in issuing warnings, they brook criticism for 'crying wolf.'*
>
> —Jack Davis, "Improving CIA Analytic Performance: Strategic Warning," Sherman Kent School for Intelligence Analysis, September 2002.

▷ **Value Added**

Shifting the focus from asking whether an event will occur to imagining that it has occurred and then explaining how it might have happened opens the mind to think in different ways. What If? Analysis shifts the discussion from, "How likely is it?" to these questions:

* How could it possibly come about?
* What would be the impact?
* Has the possibility of the event happening increased?

The technique also gives decision makers the following additional benefits:

* A better sense of what they might be able to do today to prevent an untoward development from occurring, or what they might do today to leverage an opportunity for advancing their interests.
* A list of specific indicators to monitor to help determine if the chances of a development actually occurring are increasing.

The What If? technique is a useful tool for exploring unanticipated or unlikely scenarios that are within the realm of possibility and that would have significant consequences should they come to pass. Figure 9.3 is an example of this. It posits a dramatic development—the emergence of India as a new international hub for finance—and then explores how this scenario could come about. In this example, the technique spurs the analyst to challenge traditional analysis and rethink the underlying dynamics of the situation.

▷ **The Method**

* A What If? Analysis can be done by an individual or as a team project. The time required is about the same as that for drafting a short paper. It usually helps to initiate the process with a brainstorming session and/or to interpose brainstorming sessions at various stages of the process.

* Begin by assuming that what could happen has actually occurred. Often it is best to pose the issue in the following way: "The *New York Times* reported yesterday that. . . ." Be precise in defining both the event and its impact. Sometimes it is useful to posit the new contingency as the outcome of a specific triggering event, such as a natural disaster, an economic crisis, a major political miscalculation, or an unexpected new opportunity that vividly reveals that a key analytic assumption is no longer valid.

* Develop a chain of argumentation—based on both evidence and logic—to explain how this outcome could have come about. In developing the scenarios, focus on what must actually occur at each stage of the process. Work backwards from the event to the present day. This is called "backwards thinking."

* Often more than one scenario or chain of argument can be envisioned.

India's Success Story

In sharp contrast to the rest of the world, India remained relatively insulated from the global economic downturn that began in late 2008. By 2012, and much to everyone's surprise, India is now regarded as one of the world's strongest economies and is known for its continued growth and stability. Although India does not yet dominate global trade and continues to exhibit fairly conservative economic policies, its careful stewardship of its own financial markets has made it a new international hub for finance.

How Did This Happen?

Indian economic policies have always been conservative and strongly controlled by New Delhi. As a result, India's industries have not participated fully in global trade, focusing more on the internal market. Throughout the 1990s and early 2000s, India's economy grew largely because the government eased restrictions on internal competition. When the global economy began to sag in 2008, India used its large foreign exchange reserves to prop up the rupee and institute import controls. The immediate impact was on China and South Korea, both of which had exported consumer goods—cell phones, refrigerators, fans, air conditioners, and televisions—to India. By cutting off imports, Indian producers of these same commodities reaped the benefits of the cessation of competition. Demand for quality consumer goods in India grew quickly, forcing Indian manufacturers to improve their production levels and their quality standards.

The Indian financial sector began to allow foreign banks to operate in India only in 2004 and even then only under strict guidelines. A small number of Indians were only gradually beginning to use banks for savings. Mortgages were uncommon. The majority of Indians continued to use informal financial mechanisms. By 2009, India was largely left out of the global bank crisis.

Meanwhile, the financial crisis in Europe and North America continued unabated throughout 2009–2010. Bailouts and stimulus packages, while showing initial promise, failed to prompt a sustained economic recovery. With high unemployment, no purchasing power, and eroding confidence in the markets, businesses closed, bankruptcies soared, and the service sector declined. Chinese manufacturing for export markets, a critical part of China's economic growth in the 1990s and early 2000s, evaporated in 2010, leaving China's boom cities struggling as workers flocked back to rural areas to eke out their living from the land.

Although these developments undercut India's role as an outsource center for Western companies, the resultant stable of unemployed Western-trained talent enabled Indian entrepreneurs to augment their ranks at a fraction of the previous cost. With a huge internal demand for goods and services, Indian entrepreneurs had room to grow and did.

Source: This example was developed by Ray Converse and Elizbeth Manak, Pherson Associates, LLC.

* Generate a list of indicators or "observables" for each scenario that would help to detect whether events are starting to play out in a way envisioned by that scenario.

* Assess the level of damage or disruption that would result from a negative scenario and estimate how difficult it would be to overcome or mitigate the damage incurred. For new opportunities, assess how well developments could turn out and what can be done to ensure that such a positive scenario might actually come about.

* Rank order the scenarios according to how much attention they merit, taking into consideration both difficulty of implementation and the potential significance of the impact.

* Monitor the indicators or observables on a regular or periodic basis.

▶ **Relationship to Other Techniques**

What If? Analysis is sometimes confused with the High Impact/Low Probability technique, as each deal with low-probability events. However, only What If? Analysis uses the reframing technique of assuming that a future event has happened and then thinking backwards in time to imagine how it could have happened. High Impact/Low Probability requires new or anomalous information as a trigger and then projects forward to what might occur and the consequences if it does occur.

▶ **Origins of This Technique**

The term What If? Analysis has been applied to a variety of different techniques for a long time. The version described here is based on Randy Pherson, "What If? Analysis," in *Handbook of Analytic Tools and Techniques* (Reston, Va.: Pherson Associates, LLC, 2008); and training materials from the Sherman Kent School for Intelligence Analysis.

HIGH IMPACT/LOW PROBABILITY ANALYSIS

High Impact/Low Probability Analysis provides decision makers with early warning that a seemingly unlikely event with major policy and resource repercussions might actually occur.

▶ When to Use It

High Impact/Low Probability Analysis should be used when one wants to alert decision makers to the possibility that a seemingly long-shot development that would have a major policy or resource impact may be more likely than previously anticipated. Events that would have merited such treatment before they occurred include the reunification of Germany in 1989 and the collapse of the Soviet Union in 1991. This technique might now be used in discussing the potential impact of an outbreak of H5N1 (avian influenza) or applied to a terrorist attack when intent is well-established but there are multiple variations on how and when an attack might be carried out. With regard to the risk of an avian influenza attack, some in the Homeland Security community maintain that this technique is better described as High Impact/Uncertain Probability Analysis.

A High Impact/Low Probability study usually is initiated when some new and often fragmentary information is received suggesting that a previously unanticipated event might actually occur. For example, it is conceivable that such a tip-off could be received suggesting the need to alert decision makers to the susceptibility of the United States to a major information warfare attack or a dramatic terrorist attack on a national holiday.

> A thoughtful senior policy official has opined that most potentially devastating threats to U.S. interests start out being evaluated as unlikely. The key to effective intelligence-policy relations in strategic warning is for analysts to help policy officials in determining which seemingly unlikely threats are worthy of serious consideration.
>
> —Jack Davis, "Improving CIA Analytic Performance: Strategic Warning," Sherman Kent School for Intelligence Analysis, September 2002.

The technique can also be used to sensitize analysts and decision makers to the possible effects of low-probability events and stimulate them to think early on about measures that could be taken to deal with the danger or to exploit the opportunity.

▶ Value Added

The High Impact/Low Probability Analysis format allows analysts to explore the consequences of an event—particularly one not deemed likely by conventional wisdom—without having to challenge the mainline judgment or to argue with others about how likely an event is to happen. In other words, this technique provides a tactful way of communicating a viewpoint that some recipients might prefer not to hear.

The analytic focus is not on whether something *will* happen but to take it as a given that an event *could* happen that would have a major and unanticipated impact. The objective is to explore whether an increasingly credible case can be made for an unlikely event occurring that could pose a major danger—or offer great opportunities. The more nuanced and concrete the analyst's depiction of the plausible paths to danger, the easier it is for a decision maker to develop a package of policies to protect or advance vital U.S. interests.

▷ **Potential Pitfalls**
Analysts need to be careful when communicating the likelihood of unlikely events. The meaning of the word "unlikely" can be interpreted as meaning anywhere from 1 percent to 25 percent probability, while "highly unlikely" may mean from 1 percent to 10 percent.[12] Customers receiving an intelligence report that uses words of estimative probability such as "very unlikely" will typically interpret the report as consistent with their own prior thinking, if at all possible. If the report says a terrorist attack against a specific U.S. embassy abroad within the next year is very unlikely, it is quite possible, for example, that the analyst may be thinking of about a 10 percent possibility, while a decision maker sees that as consistent with his or her own thinking that the likelihood is less than 1 percent. Such a difference in likelihood can make the difference between a decision to pay or not to pay for expensive contingency planning or a proactive preventive countermeasure. When an analyst is describing the likelihood of an unlikely event, it is desirable to express the likelihood in numeric terms, either as a range (such as less than 5 percent or 10 to 20 percent) or as bettor's odds (such as 1 chance in 10).

Figure 9.4 shows an example of an unlikely event—the outbreak of conflict in the Arctic Ocean—that could have major geopolitical consequences for the United States and other neighboring countries. Analysts can employ the technique to sensitize decision makers to the possible effects of the melting of Arctic ice and stimulate them to think about measures that could be taken to deal with the danger.

---

12. Richards J. Heuer Jr., *Psychology of Intelligence Analysis* (Washington, D.C.: CIA Center for the Study of Intelligence, 1999), reprinted by Pherson Associates, LLC, 2007), 155.

An effective High Impact/Low Probability Analysis involves these steps:

* Clearly describe the unlikely event.

* Define the high-impact consequences if this event occurs. Consider both the actual event and the secondary impacts of the event.

* Identify any recent information or reporting suggesting that the likelihood of the unlikely event occurring may be increasing.

* Postulate additional triggers that would propel events in this unlikely direction or factors that would greatly accelerate timetables, such as a botched government response, the rise of an energetic challenger, a major terrorist attack, or a surprise electoral outcome that benefits U.S. interests.

* Develop one or more plausible pathways that would explain how this seemingly unlikely event could unfold. Focus on the specifics of what must happen at each stage of the process for the train of events to play out.

* Generate a list of indicators that would help analysts and decision makers recognize that events were beginning to unfold in this way.

* Identify factors that would deflect a bad outcome or encourage a positive outcome.

Once the list of indicators has been developed, the analyst must periodically review the list. Such periodic reviews help analysts overcome prevailing mental models that the events being considered are too unlikely to merit serious attention.

▷ **Relationship to Other Techniques**
High Impact/Low Probability Analysis is sometimes confused with What If? Analysis. Both deal with low-probability or unlikely events. High Impact/Low Probability Analysis is primarily a vehicle for warning decision makers that recent, unanticipated developments suggest that an event previously deemed highly unlikely might actually occur. Based on recent evidence or information, it projects forward to discuss what could occur and the consequences if

Figure 9.4 High Impact/Low Probability Scenario: Conflict in the Arctic

Unlikely Event

Recent trends in the Arctic spur a military conflict among regional players over conflicting claims to Arctic resources within the next five years.

Background

The United Nations Law of the Sea prohibits any country from owning the North Pole or the Arctic Ocean surrounding it. The treaty permits each bordering country (Canada, Denmark, Norway, Russia, and the United States) to expand its claim beyond its permitted 200-mile economic zone if its continental shelf is geographically linked to the Arctic seabed. The United States has not ratified the treaty, however, and does not recognize any rights beyond the 200-mile economic zone or Canada's claim that the Northwest Passage represents internal Canadian waters to which it may limit access.

Events and Triggers

In 2001, Russia made an unsuccessful bid for more of the Arctic, and Canada and Denmark subsequently submitted claims on the region. Since 2006, NATO forces, including Norwegian and Dutch troops, have conducted annual training exercises in the Arctic. Russia planted its flag on the seabed below the North Pole in 2007, raising concerns by other states that Russia was trying to claim more territory.

Polar melting is expanding access to untapped energy and mineral reserves that are increasingly attractive to both polar and nonpolar states in a resource-scarce world with escalating energy prices. Long-term overfishing could spur nations dependent on this source of protein to begin fishing in the Arctic Ocean as it becomes more accessible. The melting of Arctic ice is likely to open the Northwest Passage to year-round shipping in the coming years, undercutting the commercial utility of the Panama Canal.

the event does occur. It challenges the conventional wisdom. What If? Analysis does not require new or anomalous information to serve as a trigger. It reframes the question by assuming that a surprise event has happened. It then looks backwards from that surprise event to map several ways it could have come about. It also tries to identify actions which, if taken in a timely manner, might have prevented it.

Pathways to Unlikely Outcome

An almost certain race to tap the Arctic's newly available resources will increase the chances of a violent incident leading to conflict. For example, nonpolar states starved for resources could claim underwater energy reserves. Canada could require ships using the Northwest Passage to pay high licensing fees. Fishing vessels of some polar states might harass those of other states, such as Japan.

Armed conflict could take many forms including the following: Russia versus NATO, the United States versus Canada, and polar states versus nonpolar states. A possible armed grab for resources and control of shipping lanes could undermine existing alliances and open the door to resource grabs by other states. If the "Battle over the Arctic" becomes a clarion call in various national media, pressure will grow on all the players to assert their "sovereign rights," possibly ushering in a new era of interstate tension and conflict.

Indicators to Watch For

- Russian calls to renegotiate the treaty limiting land claims in the Arctic.
- Canada increases patrols in Arctic waters and starts searching ships to demonstrate that these are internal waterways.
- Border states send "scientific teams" year round to key Arctic locations.
- More nations plant their flags in Arctic waters.
- Special oil carriers and drilling platforms are built for the Arctic.

Factors to Encourage Positive Outcome

- International bodies or regional states propose new legal principles to reflect changed circumstances caused by sea ice melting.
- Support grows for the creation of an international ecological zone that sets parameters for resource sharing.

Source: This example was developed by Michael Bannister and Ray Converse, Pherson Associates, LLC.

▷ **Origins of This Technique**
The description here is based on Randy Pherson, "High Impact/Low Probability Analysis," in *Handbook of Analytic Tools and Techniques* (Reston, Va.: Pherson Associates, LLC, 2008); and Sherman Kent School for Intelligence Analysis training materials.

9.5   DEVIL'S ADVOCACY

Devil's Advocacy is a process for critiquing a proposed analytic judgment, plan, or decision, usually by a single analyst not previously involved in the deliberations that led to the proposed judgment, plan, or decision. The origins of devil's advocacy "lie in a practice of the Roman Catholic Church in the early 16th century. When a person was proposed for beatification or canonization to sainthood, someone was assigned the role of critically examining the life and miracles attributed to that individual; his duty was to especially bring forward facts that were unfavorable to the candidate."[13]

▶ **When to Use It**

Devil's Advocacy is most effective when initiated by a manager as part of a strategy to ensure that alternative solutions are thoroughly considered. The following are examples of well-established uses of Devil's Advocacy that are widely regarded as good management practices:

   ✳ Before making a decision, a policymaker or military commander asks for a Devil's Advocate analysis of what could go wrong.

   ✳ An intelligence organization designates a senior manager as a Devil's Advocate to oversee the process of reviewing and challenging selected assessments.

   ✳ A manager commissions a Devil's Advocacy analysis when he or she is concerned about seemingly widespread unanimity on a critical issue throughout the Intelligence Community, or when the manager suspects that the mental model of analysts working an issue for a long time has become so deeply ingrained that they are unable to see the significance of recent changes.

Within the Intelligence Community, Devil's Advocacy is sometimes defined as a form of self-critique. Rather than being done by an outsider, a member of the analytic team volunteers or is asked to play the Devil's Advocate role. A common approach is to consider the key assumptions, select one or more assumptions that seem most vulnerable to challenge, and then have the designated Devil's

---

13. Charlan J. Nemeth and Brendan Nemeth-Brown. "Better than Individuals? The Potential Benefits of Dissent and Diversity for Group Creativity," in *Group Creativity: Innovation Through Collaboration*, ed. Paul B. Paulus and Bernard A. Nijstad (New York: Oxford University Press, 2003), 75–76.

Advocate develop the arguments for and the logical implications of that different assumption. This single team member then tries to persuade the rest of the team that this assumption is valid or at least a serious possibility.[14] This approach is critiqued in the "Value Added" discussion.

▶ **Value Added**

The unique attribute and value of Devil's Advocacy as described here is that the critique is initiated at the discretion of management to test the strength of the argument for a proposed analytic judgment, plan, or decision. It looks for what could go wrong and often focuses attention on questionable assumptions, evidence, or lines of argument that undercut the generally accepted conclusion, or on the insufficiency of current evidence on which to base such a conclusion.

As we noted earlier, a current practice in the Intelligence Community is to use Devil's Advocacy as a form of self-critique. One team member plays the role of Devil's Advocate and presents arguments to the team against its own conclusion. We do not support this approach for the following reasons:

* Calling such a technique Devil's Advocacy is inconsistent with the historic concept of Devil's Advocacy that calls for investigation by an independent outsider.

* Research shows that a person playing the role of a Devil's Advocate, without actually believing it, is significantly less effective than a true believer and may even be counterproductive. Apparently, more attention and respect is accorded to someone with the courage to advance their own minority view than to someone who is known to be only playing a role. If group members see the Devil's Advocacy as an analytic exercise they have to put up with, rather than the true belief of one of their members who is courageous enough to speak out, this exercise may actually enhance the majority's original belief—"a smugness that may occur because one assumes one has considered alternatives though, in fact, there has been little serious reflection on other possibilities."[15] What the team learns from the Devil's Advocate presentation may be only how to better defend the team's own entrenched position.

* There are other forms of self-critique, especially Premortem Analysis and Structured Self-Critique as described in this chapter, which may be more effective in prompting even a cohesive, heterogeneous team to question their mental model and to analyze alternative perspectives.

---

14. Sherman Kent School for Intelligence Analysis training materials.
15. Nemeth and Brown, "Better than Individuals," 77–78.

▷ The Method

The Devil's Advocate is charged with challenging the proposed judgment by building the strongest possible case against it. There is no prescribed procedure. Devil's Advocates may be selected because of their expertise with a specific technique. Or they may decide to use a different technique from that used in the original analysis or to use a different set of assumptions. They may also simply review the evidence and the analytic procedures looking for weaknesses in the argument. In the latter case, an ideal approach would be asking the questions about how the analysis was conducted that are listed in this chapter under Structured Self-Critique. These questions cover sources of uncertainty, the analytic processes that were used, critical assumptions, diagnosticity of evidence, anomalous evidence, information gaps, changes in the broad environment in which events are happening, alternative decision models, availability of cultural expertise, and indicators of possible deception.

▷ Relationship to Other Techniques

Proponents of the current practice of having a team designate a single Devil's Advocate should see the discussion of Structured Self-Critique.

▷ Origins of This Technique

As noted, this technique dates back to sixteenth-century practices of the Roman Catholic Church. Since then, it has been used in different ways and for different purposes. The discussion of Devil's Advocacy here is based on the authors' analysis of current practices and on Sherman Kent School for Intelligence Analysis training materials; Charlan Jeanne Nemeth and Brendan Nemeth-Brown, "Better than Individuals? The Potential Benefits of Dissent and Diversity for Group Creativity," in *Group Creativity: Innovation Through Collaboration,* ed. Paul B. Paulus and Bernard A. Nijstad (New York: Oxford University Press, 2003); Alexander L. George and Eric K. Stern, "Harnessing Conflict in Foreign Policy Making: From Devil's to Multiple Advocacy," *Presidential Studies Quarterly* 32 (September 2002).

9.6 RED TEAM ANALYSIS

The term "red team" or "red teaming" has several meanings. One definition is that red teaming is "the practice of viewing a problem from an adversary or competitor's perspective."[16] This is how red teaming is commonly viewed by intelligence analysts.

A broader definition, described by the Defense Science Board's task force on red teaming activities in the Department of Defense, is that red teaming is a strategy for challenging an organization's plans, programs, and assumptions at all levels—strategic, operational, and tactical. This "includes not only 'playing' adversaries or competitors, but also serving as devil's advocates, offering alternative interpretations (team B) and otherwise challenging established thinking within an enterprise."[17] This is red teaming as a management strategy rather than as a specific analytic technique. It is in this context that red teaming is sometimes used as a synonym for *any form* of challenge analysis or alternative analysis.

To accommodate these two different ways that red teaming is used, in this book we identify two separate techniques called Red Team Analysis and Red Hat Analysis.

✳ Red Team Analysis, as described in this section, is a challenge analysis technique. It is usually initiated by a leadership decision to create a special project or cell or office with analysts whose cultural and analytical skills qualify them for dealing with this special type of analysis. A Red Team Analysis is often initiated to challenge the conventional wisdom as a matter of principle to ensure that other reasonable alternatives have been carefully considered. It is, in effect, a modern version of Devil's Advocacy.

✳ Red Hat Analysis, described in chapter 8, is a culturally sensitive analysis of an adversary's or competitor's behavior and decision making initiated by a regular line analyst or analytic team. It can and should be done, to the maximum extent possible, as part of standard analytic practice.

▷ When to Use It

Management should initiate a Red Team Analysis whenever there is a perceived need to challenge the conventional wisdom on an important issue or whenever

---

16. This definition is from the *Red Team Journal,* http://redteamjournal.com.

17. Defense Science Board Task Force, *The Role and Status of DoD Red Teaming Activities* (Washington, D.C.: Office of the Under Secretary of Defense for Acquisition, Technology, and Logistics, September 2003).

the responsible line office is perceived as lacking the level of cultural expertise required to fully understand an adversary's or competitor's point of view.

▶ Value Added

Red Team Analysis can help free analysts from their own well-developed mental model—their own sense of rationality, cultural norms, and personal values. When analyzing an adversary, the Red Team approach requires that an analyst change his or her frame of reference from that of an "observer" of the adversary or competitor, to that of an "actor" operating within the adversary's cultural and political milieu. This reframing or role playing is particularly helpful when an analyst is trying to replicate the mental model of authoritarian leaders, terrorist cells, or non-Western groups that operate under very different codes of behavior or motivations than those to which most Americans are accustomed.

▶ The Method

The function of Red Team Analysis is to challenge a proposed or existing judgment by building the strongest possible case against it. If the goal is to understand the thinking of an adversary or a competitor, the method is similar to that described in chapter 8 under Red Hat Analysis. The difference is that additional resources for cultural, substantive expertise and analytic skills may be available to implement the Red Team Analysis. The use of Role Playing or the Delphi Method to cross-check or supplement the Red Team approach is encouraged.

▶ Relationship to Other Techniques

The Red Team technique is closely related to Red Hat Analysis, described in chapter 8.

▶ Origins of This Technique

The term "Red Team" evolved during the Cold War, with the word "red" symbolizing any Communist adversary. The following materials were used in preparing this discussion of Red Team Analysis. *Red Team Journal,* http://redteamjournal.com; Defense Science Board Task Force, *The Role and Status of DoD Red Teaming Activities* (Washington, D.C.: Office of the Under Secretary of Defense for Acquisition, Technology, and Logistics, September 2003); Michael K. Keehan, "Red Teaming for Law Enforcement," *Police Chief* 74, no. 2 (February 2007); Sherman Kent School for Intelligence Analysis training materials.

DELPHI METHOD

Delphi is a method for eliciting ideas, judgments, or forecasts from a group of experts who may be geographically dispersed. It is different from a survey in that there are two or more rounds of questioning. After the first round of questions, a moderator distributes all the answers and explanations of the answers to all participants, often anonymously. The expert participants are then given an opportunity to modify or clarify their previous responses, if so desired, on the basis of what they have seen in the responses of the other participants. A second round of questions builds on the results of the first round, drills down into greater detail, or moves to a related topic. There is great flexibility in the nature and number of rounds of questions that might be asked.

▷ **When to Use It**

The Delphi Method was developed by the RAND Corporation at the beginning of the Cold War in the 1950s to forecast the impact of new technology on warfare. It was also used to assess the probability, intensity, or frequency of future enemy attacks. In the 1960s and 1970s, Delphi became widely known and used as a method for futures research, especially forecasting long-range trends in science and technology. Futures research is similar to intelligence analysis in that the uncertainties and complexities one must deal with often preclude the use of traditional statistical methods, so explanations and forecasts must be based on the experience and informed judgments of experts.

Over the years, Delphi has been used in a wide variety of ways, and for an equally wide variety of purposes. Although many Delphi projects have focused on developing a consensus of expert judgment, a variant called Policy Delphi is based on the premise that the decision maker is *not* interested in having a group make a consensus decision, but rather in having the experts identify alternative policy options and present all the supporting evidence for and against each option. That is the rationale for including Delphi in this chapter on challenge analysis. It can be used to identify divergent opinions that may be worth exploring.

One group of Delphi scholars advises that the Delphi technique "can be used for nearly any problem involving forecasting, estimation, or decision making"—as long as the problem is not so complex or so new as to preclude the use of expert judgment. These Delphi advocates report using it for diverse purposes that range from "choosing between options for regional development, to predicting election outcomes, to deciding which applicants should be hired for academic positions, to predicting how many meals to order for a conference luncheon."[18]

▶ Value Added

One of Sherman Kent's "Principles of Intelligence Analysis," which are taught at the CIA's Sherman Kent School for Intelligence Analysis, is "Systematic Use of Outside Experts as a Check on In-House Blinders." Consultation with relevant experts in academia, business, and nongovernmental organizations is also encouraged by Intelligence Community Directive No. 205, on Analytic Outreach, dated July 2008. As an effective process for eliciting information from outside experts, Delphi has several advantages:

∗ Outside experts can participate from their home locations, thus reducing the costs in time and travel commonly associated with the use of outside consultants.

∗ Delphi can provide analytic judgments on any topic for which outside experts are available. That means it can be used as an independent cross-check of conclusions reached in house. If the same conclusion is reached in two analyses using different analysts and different methods, this is grounds for a significant increase in confidence in that conclusion. If the conclusions disagree, this is also valuable information that may open a new avenue of research.

∗ Delphi identifies any outliers who hold an unusual position. Recognizing that the majority is not always correct, researchers can then focus on gaining a better understanding of the grounds for any views that diverge significantly from the consensus. In fact, identification of experts who have an alternative perspective and are qualified to defend it might be the objective of a Delphi project.

∗ The process by which the expert panel members are provided feedback from other experts and are given an opportunity to modify their responses makes it easy for experts to adjust their previous judgments in response to new evidence.

∗ In many Delphi projects, the experts remain anonymous to other panel members so that no one can use his or her position of authority, reputation,

---

18. Kesten C. Green, J. Scott Armstrong, and Andreas Graefe, "Methods to Elicit Forecasts from Groups: Delphi and Prediction Markets Compared," *Foresight: The International Journal of Applied Forecasting* (Fall 2007), www.forecastingprinciples.com/paperpdf/Delphi-WPlatestV.pdf.

or personality to influence others. Anonymity also facilitates the expression of opinions that go against the conventional wisdom and may not otherwise be expressed.

On the down side, a Delphi project involves administrative work to identify the experts, communicate with panel members, and collate and tabulate their responses through several rounds of questioning. Several software programs have been developed to handle these tasks, and one of these is hosted for public use (http://armstrong.wharton.upenn.edu/delphi2). The distributed decision support systems now publicly available to support virtual teams include some or all of the functions necessary for Delphi as part of a larger package of analytic tools.

We believe the development of Delphi panels of experts on areas of critical concern should be standard procedure for outreach to experts outside the Intelligence Community.

▶ **The Method**

In a Delphi project, a moderator (analyst) sends a questionnaire to a panel of experts who may be in different locations. The experts respond to these questions and usually are asked to provide short explanations for their responses. The moderator collates the results from this first questionnaire and sends the collated responses back to all panel members, requesting them to reconsider their responses based on what they see and learn from the other experts' responses and explanations. Panel members may also be asked to answer another set of questions. This cycle of question, response, and feedback continues through several rounds using the same or a related set of questions. It is often desirable for panel members to remain anonymous so that they are not unduly influenced by the responses of senior members. This method is illustrated in Figure 9.7.

▶ **Examples**

To show how Delphi can be used for intelligence analysis, we have developed three illustrative applications:

∗ Evaluation of another country's policy options: The Delphi project manager or moderator identifies several policy options that a foreign country might choose. The moderator then asks a panel of experts on the country to rate the desirability and feasibility of each option, from the other country's point of view, on a five-point scale ranging from "Very Desirable" or "Feasible" to "Very Undesirable" or "Definitely Infeasible." Panel members are also asked to identify and assess any other policy options that ought to be considered and to identify the top two

Figure 9.7

The Delphi Technique

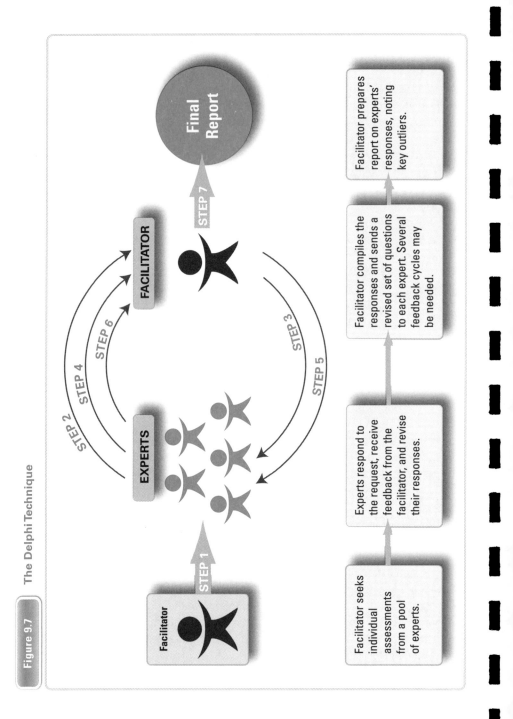

or three arguments or items of evidence that guided their judgments. A collation of all responses is sent back to the panel with a request for members to do one of the following: reconsider their position in view of others' responses, provide further explanation of their judgments, or reaffirm their previous response. In a second round of questioning, it may be desirable to list key arguments and items of evidence and ask the panel to rate them on their validity and their importance, again from the other country's perspective.

* Analysis of Alternative Hypotheses: A panel of outside experts is asked to estimate the probability of each hypothesis in a set of mutually exclusive hypotheses where the probabilities must add up to 100 percent. This could be done as a stand-alone project or to double-check an already completed Analysis of Competing Hypotheses (ACH) analysis (chapter 7). If two analyses using different analysts and different methods arrive at the same conclusion, this is grounds for a significant increase in confidence in the conclusion. If the analyses disagree, that may also be useful to know as one can then seek to understand the rationale for the different judgments.

* Warning analysis or monitoring a situation over time: An analyst asks a panel of experts to estimate the probability of a future event. This might be either a single event for which the analyst is monitoring early warning indicators or a set of scenarios for which the analyst is monitoring milestones to determine the direction in which events seem to be moving. There are two ways to manage a Delphi project that monitors change over time. One is to have a new round of questions and responses at specific intervals to assess the extent of any change. The other is what is called either Dynamic Delphi or Real Time Delphi where participants can modify their responses at any time as new events occur or as new information is submitted by one of the participants.[19] The probability estimates provided by the Delphi panel can be aggregated to provide a measure of the significance of change over time. They can also be used to identify differences of opinion between the experts that warrant further examination.

▶ **Relationship to Other Techniques**
Delphi is easily combined with other techniques, such as Virtual Brainstorming, and techniques for prioritizing, ranking, or scaling lists of information.

---

19. See Real Time Delphi, www.realtimedelphi.org.

▶ Origins of This Technique

The origin of Delphi as an analytic method was described under "When to Use It." The following references were useful in researching this topic: Murray Turoff and Starr Roxanne Hiltz, "Computer Based Delphi Processes," 1996, http://web.njit.edu/~turoff/Papers/delphi3.html; and Harold A. Linstone and Murray Turoff, *The Delphi Method: Techniques and Applications* (Reading, Mass.: Addison-Wesley, 1975). A 2002 digital version of Linstone and Turoff's book is available online at http://is.njit.edu/pubs/delphibook; see in particular the chapter by Turoff on "The Policy Delphi" (http://is.njit.edu/pubs/delphibook/ch3b1.pdf). For more current information on validity and optimal techniques for implementing a Delphi project, see Gene Rowe and George Wright, "Expert Opinions in Forecasting: The Role of the Delphi Technique," in *Principles of Forecasting*, ed. J. Scott Armstrong (New York: Springer Science+Business Media, 2001).

10 Conflict Management

10

Conflict Management

10.1   Adversarial Collaboration   [256]

10.2   Structured Debate   [262]

CHAPTER 10

Conflict Management

As we discussed in the previous chapter, challenge analysis frequently leads to the identification and confrontation of opposing views. That is, after all, the purpose of challenge analysis, but two important questions are raised. First, how can confrontation be managed so that it becomes a learning experience rather than a battle between determined adversaries? Second, in an analysis of any topic with a high degree of uncertainty, how can one decide if one view is wrong or if both views have merit and need to be discussed in an analytic report? This chapter offers a conceptual framework and two new techniques for dealing with analytic conflicts.

A widely distributed article in the *Harvard Business Review* stresses that improved collaboration among organizations or organizational units that have different interests can be achieved only by accepting and actively managing the inevitable—and desirable—conflicts between these units:

> The disagreements sparked by differences in perspective, competencies, access to information, and strategic focus . . . actually generate much of the value that can come from collaboration across organizational boundaries. Clashes between parties are the crucibles in which creative solutions are developed. . . . So instead of trying simply to reduce disagreements, senior executives need to embrace conflict and, just as important, institutionalize mechanisms for managing it.[1]

The Intelligence Community's procedure for dealing with differences of opinion has often been to force a consensus, water down the differences, or add a dissenting footnote to an estimate. Efforts are under way to move away from this practice, and we share the hopes of many in the community that this approach will become increasingly rare as members of the Intelligence Community embrace greater

---

1. Jeff Weiss and Jonathan Hughes, "Want Collaboration? Accept—and Actively Manage—Conflict," *Harvard Business Review*, March 2005.

interagency collaboration early in the analytic process, rather than mandated coordination at the *end* of the process after all parties are locked into their positions. One of the principal benefits of using structured analytic techniques for interoffice and interagency collaboration is that these techniques identify differences of opinion early in the analytic process. This gives time for the differences to be at least understood, if not resolved, at the working level before management becomes involved.

How one deals with conflicting analytic assessments or estimates depends, in part, upon one's expectations about what intelligence can achieve. Mark Lowenthal has written persuasively of the need to recalibrate expectations of what intelligence analysis can accomplish.[2] More than in any other discipline, intelligence analysts typically work with incomplete, ambiguous, and potentially deceptive evidence. Combine this with the fact that intelligence analysts are seeking to understand human behavior, which is often difficult to predict even in our own culture, and it should not be surprising that intelligence analysis sometimes turns out to be "wrong." Acceptance of the basic principle that it's okay for intelligence analysts to be uncertain, because they are dealing with uncertain matters, helps to set the stage for appropriate management of conflicting views. In some cases, one position will be refuted and rejected. In other cases, however, two or more positions may be reasonable assessments or estimates, usually one more likely than the others. In such cases, conflict is mitigated when it is recognized that each position has some value in covering the full range of options.

In the previous chapter we noted that an assessment or estimate that is properly described as "probable" has about a one-in-four chance of being wrong. This has clear implications for appropriate action when analysts hold conflicting views. If an analysis meets rigorous standards and conflicting views still remain, decision makers are best served by an analytic product that deals directly with the uncertainty rather than minimizing it or suppressing it. The greater the uncertainty, the more appropriate it is to go forward with a product that discusses the most likely assessment or estimate and gives one or more alternative possibilities. Factors to be considered when assessing the amount of uncertainty include the following:

* An estimate of the future generally has more uncertainty than an assessment of a past or current event.

* Mysteries, for which there are no knowable answers, are far more uncertain than puzzles, for which an answer does exist if one could only find it.[3]

---

2. Mark M. Lowenthal, "Towards a Reasonable Standard for Analysis: How Right, How Often on Which Issues?" *Intelligence and National Security* 23 (June 2008).

3. Gregory F. Treverton, "Risks and Riddles," *Smithsonian,* June 2007.

* The more assumptions that are made, the greater the uncertainty. Assumptions about intent or capability, and whether or not they have changed, are especially critical.

* Analysis of human behavior or decision making is far more uncertain than analysis of technical data.

* The behavior of a complex dynamic system is more uncertain than that of a simple system. The more variables and stakeholders involved in a system, the more difficult it is to foresee what might happen.

If the decision is to go forward with a discussion of alternative assessments or estimates, the next step might be to produce any of the following:

* A comparative analysis of opposing views in a single report. This calls for analysts to identify the sources and reasons for the uncertainty (e.g., assumptions, ambiguities, knowledge gaps), consider the implications of alternative assessments or estimates, determine what it would take to resolve the uncertainty, and suggest indicators for future monitoring that might provide early warning of which alternative is correct.

* An analysis of alternative scenarios as described in chapter 6.

* A What If? Analysis or High Impact/Low Probability Analysis as described in chapter 9.

* A report that is clearly identified as a "second opinion."

Overview of Techniques

Adversarial Collaboration in essence is an agreement between opposing parties on how they will work together in an effort to resolve their differences, to gain a better understanding of how and why they differ, or as often happens to collaborate on a joint paper explaining the differences. Six approaches to implementing adversarial collaboration are described.

Structured Debate is a planned debate of opposing points of view on a specific issue in front of a "jury of peers," senior analysts, or managers. As a first step, each side writes up its best possible argument for its position and passes this summation to the opposing side. The next step is an oral debate that focuses on refuting the other side's arguments rather than further supporting one's own arguments. The goal is to elucidate and compare the arguments *against* each side's argument. If neither argument can be refuted, perhaps both merit some consideration in the analytic report.

10.1 ADVERSARIAL COLLABORATION

Adversarial Collaboration is an agreement between opposing parties about how they will work together to resolve or at least gain a better understanding of their differences. Adversarial Collaboration is a relatively new concept championed by Daniel Kahneman, the psychologist who along with Amos Tversky initiated much of the research on cognitive biases described in Richards Heuer's *Psychology of Intelligence Analysis.* Kahneman received a Nobel Prize in 2002 for his research on behavioral economics, and he wrote an intellectual autobiography in connection with this in which he commented as follows on Adversarial Collaboration:

> One line of work that I hope may become influential is the development of a procedure of *adversarial collaboration* which I have championed as a substitute for the format of critique-reply-rejoinder in which debates are currently conducted in the social sciences. Both as a participant and as a reader I have been appalled by the absurdly adversarial nature of these exchanges, in which hardly anyone ever admits an error or acknowledges learning anything from the other. Adversarial collaboration involves a good-faith effort to conduct debates by carrying out joint research—in some cases there may be a need for an agreed arbiter to lead the project and collect the data. Because there is no expectation of the contestants reaching complete agreement at the end of the exercise, adversarial collaboration will usually lead to an unusual type of joint publication, in which disagreements are laid out as part of a jointly authored paper.[4]

Kahneman's approach to Adversarial Collaboration involves agreement on empirical tests for resolving a dispute and conducting those tests with the help of an impartial arbiter. A joint report describes the tests, states what has been learned that both sides agree on, and provides interpretations of the test results on which they disagree.[5]

---

4. Daniel Kahneman, *Autobiography*, 2002, available on the Nobel Prize Web site, http://nobelprize.org/nobel_prizes/economics/laureates/2002/kahneman-autobio.html. For a pioneering example of a report on an adversarial collaboration, see Barbara Mellers, Ralph Hertwig, and Daniel Kahneman, "Do Frequency Representations Eliminate Conjunction Effects? An Exercise in Adversarial Collaboration," *Psychological Science* 12 (July 2001).

5. Richards Heuer is grateful to Steven Rieber of the Office of the Director of National Intelligence, Analytic Integrity and Standards office, for referring him to Kahneman's work on Adversarial Collaboration.

Although differences of opinion on intelligence judgments can seldom be resolved through empirical research, the Adversarial Collaboration concept

> *Truth springs from argument amongst friends.*
> —David Hume, Scottish philosopher

can, nevertheless, be adapted to apply to intelligence analysis. There are a number of approaches that analysts might agree to use to reduce, resolve, or more clearly define or explain their differences. These are grouped together here under the overall heading of Adversarial Collaboration.

▷ When to Use It

Adversarial Collaboration should be used only if both sides are open to discussion of an issue. If one side is fully locked into its position and has repeatedly rejected the other side's arguments, this technique is unlikely to be successful. It is then more appropriate to use Structured Debate in which a decision is made by an independent arbiter after listening to both sides.

▷ Value Added

Adversarial Collaboration can help opposing analysts see the merit of another group's perspective. If successful, it will help both parties gain a better understanding of what assumptions or evidence is behind their opposing opinions on an issue and to explore the best way of dealing with these differences. Can one side be shown to be wrong, or should both positions be reflected in any report on the subject? Can there be agreement on indicators to show the direction in which events seem to be moving?

▷ The Method

Six approaches to Adversarial Collaboration are described here. What they all have in common is the forced requirement to understand and address the other side's position rather than simply dismiss it. Mutual understanding of the other side's position is the bridge to productive collaboration. These six techniques are not mutually exclusive; in other words, one might use several of them for any specific project.

Key Assumptions Check: The first step in understanding what underlies conflicting judgments is a Key Assumptions Check, as described in chapter 8. Evidence is always interpreted in the context of a mental model about how events normally transpire in a given country or situation, and a Key Assumptions Check is one way to make a mental model explicit. If a Key Assumptions Check has not already been done, each side can apply this technique and then share the results with the other side.

Discussion should then focus on the rationale for each assumption and suggestions for how the assumption might be either confirmed or refuted. If the discussion focuses on the probability of Assumption A versus Assumption B, it is often helpful to express probability as a numerical range, for example, 65 percent to 85 percent for probable. When analysts go through these steps, they sometimes discover they are not as far apart as they thought. The discussion should focus on refuting the other side's assumptions rather than supporting one's own.

Analysis of Competing Hypotheses: When opposing sides are dealing with a collegial difference of opinion, with neither side firmly locked into its position, Analysis of Competing Hypotheses (ACH), described in chapter 7, may be a good structured format for helping to identify and discuss their differences. One important benefit of ACH is that it pinpoints the exact sources of disagreement. Both parties agree on a set of hypotheses and then rate each item of evidence as consistent or inconsistent with each hypothesis. When analysts disagree on these consistency ratings, the differences are often quickly resolved. When not resolved, the differences often point to previously unrecognized assumptions or to some interesting rationale for a different interpretation of the evidence. Using ACH one can also trace the significance of each item of evidence in making the overall conclusion.

The use of ACH may not result in the elimination of all the differences of opinion, but it can be a big step toward understanding these differences and determining which might be reconcilable through further intelligence collection or research. The analysts can then make a judgment about the potential productivity of further efforts to resolve the differences. ACH may not be helpful, however, if two sides are already locked into their positions. It is all too easy in ACH for one side to interpret the evidence and enter assumptions in a way that deliberately supports its preconceived position. To challenge a well-established mental model, it may be necessary to use other challenge or conflict management techniques.

Argument Mapping: Argument Mapping, which was described in chapter 7, maps the logical relationship between each element of an argument. Two sides might agree to work together to create a single argument map with the rationale both for and against a given conclusion. Such an argument map will show where the two sides agree, and where they diverge, and why. The visual representation of the argument makes it easier to recognize weaknesses in opposing arguments. This technique pinpoints the location of any disagreement, and it could serve as an objective basis for mediating a disagreement.

An alternative approach might be to focus the discussion on alternative contrasting Argument Maps.

Mutual Understanding: When analysts in different offices or agencies disagree, the disagreement is often exacerbated by the fact that they have a limited understanding of the other side's position and logical reasoning. The Mutual Understanding approach addresses this problem directly.

After an exchange of information on their positions, the two sides meet together with a facilitator, moderator, or decision maker. Side 1 is required to explain to Side 2 its understanding of Side 2's position. Side 1 must do this in a manner that satisfies Side 2 that its position is appropriately represented. Then the roles are reversed, and Side 2 explains its understanding of Side 1's position. This mutual exchange is often difficult to do without really listening to and understanding the opposing view and what it is based upon. Once all the analysts accurately understand each side's position, they can discuss their differences more rationally and with less emotion. Experience shows that this technique normally prompts some movement of the opposing parties toward a common ground.[6]

> There are two ways to measure the health of a debate: the kinds of questions being asked and the level of listening.
>
> —David A. Garvin and Michael A. Roberto, "What You Don't Know About Making Decisions," Harvard Business Review, September 2001.

Joint Escalation: When disagreement occurs within an analytic team, the disagreement is often referred to a higher authority. This escalation often makes matters worse. What typically happens is that a frustrated analyst takes the problem up to his or her boss, briefly explaining the conflict in a manner that is clearly supportive of the analyst's own position. The analyst then returns to the group armed with the boss's support. However, the opposing analyst(s) have also gone to their boss and come back with support for their solution. Each analyst is then locked into what has become "my manager's view" of the issue. An already thorny problem has become even more intractable.

This situation can be avoided by an agreement between team members, or preferably an established organization policy, that requires joint escalation.[7] The analysts should be required to prepare a joint statement describing the disagreement and to present it jointly to their superiors. This requires each analyst to understand and address, rather than simply dismiss, the other side's position. It also ensures that managers have access to multiple perspectives on the conflict, its causes, and the various ways it might be resolved.

---

6. Richards Heuer is grateful to Jay Hillmer of the Defense Intelligence Agency for sharing his experience in using this technique to resolve coordination disputes.

7. Jeff Weiss and Jonathan Hughes, "Want Collaboration? Accept—and Actively Manage—Conflict," Harvard Business Review, March 2005.

Just the need to prepare such a joint statement discourages escalation and often leads to an agreement. The proponents of this approach report their experience that "companies that require people to share responsibility for the escalation of a conflict often see a decrease in the number of problems that are pushed up the management chain. Joint escalation helps create the kind of accountability that is lacking when people know they can provide their side of an issue to their own manager and blame others when things don't work out."[8]

The Nosenko Approach: Yuriy Nosenko was a Soviet intelligence officer who defected to the United States in 1964. Whether he was a true defector or a Soviet plant was a subject of intense and emotional controversy within the CIA for more than a decade. In the minds of some, this historic case is still controversial.

At a critical decision point in 1968, the leadership of the CIA's Soviet Bloc Division set up a three-man team to review all the evidence and make a recommendation for the division's action in this case. The amount of evidence is illustrated by the fact that just one single report arguing that Nosenko was still under Soviet control was 1,000 pages long. The team consisted of one leader who was of the view that Nosenko was a Soviet plant, one leader who believed that he was a bona fide defector, and an experienced officer who had not previously been involved but was inclined to think Nosenko might be a plant.

The interesting point here is the ground rule that the team was instructed to follow. After reviewing the evidence, each officer identified those items of evidence thought to be of critical importance in making a judgment on Nosenko's bona fides. Any item that one officer stipulated as critically important had to be addressed by the other two members.

It turned out that fourteen items were stipulated by at least one of the team members and had to be addressed by both of the others. Each officer prepared his own analysis, but they all had to address the same fourteen issues. Their report became known as the "Wise Men" report.

The team did not come to a unanimous conclusion. However, it was significant that the thinking of all three moved in the same direction. When the important evidence was viewed from the perspective of searching for the truth, rather than proving Nosenko's guilt, the case that Nosenko was a plant began to unravel. The officer who had always believed that Nosenko was bona fide felt he could now prove the case. The officer who was relatively new to the case changed his mind in favor of Nosenko's bona fides. The officer who had been one of the principal analysts and advocates for the position that Nosenko was a plant became

8. Ibid.

substantially less confident in that conclusion. There were now sufficient grounds for management to make the decision.

The ground rules used in the Nosenko case can be applied in any effort to abate a long-standing analytic controversy. The key point that makes these rules work is the requirement that each side must directly address the issues that are important to the other side and thereby come to understand the other's perspective. This process guards against the common propensity of analysts to make their own arguments and then simply dismiss the other side's arguments as unworthy of consideration.[9]

---

9. This discussion is based on Richards J. Heuer Jr., "Nosenko: Five Paths to Judgment," in *Inside CIA's Private World: Declassified Articles from the Agency's Internal Journal, 1955–1992,* ed. H. Bradford Westerbrook (New Haven: Yale University Press, 1995).

10.2 STRUCTURED DEBATE

AStructured Debate is a planned debate between analysts or analytic teams holding opposing points of view on a specific issue. It is conducted according to a set of rules before an audience, which may be a "jury of peers" or one or more senior analysts or managers.

▶ **When to Use It**

Structured Debate is called for when there is a significant difference of opinion within or between analytic units or within the policymaking community, or when Adversarial Collaboration has been unsuccessful or is impractical, and it is necessary to make a choice between two opposing opinions or to go forward with a comparative analysis of both. A Structured Debate requires a significant commitment of analytic time and resources. A long-standing policy issue, a critical decision that has far-reaching implications, or a dispute within the analytic community that is obstructing effective interagency collaboration would be grounds for making this type of investment in time and resources.

▶ **Value Added**

In the method proposed here, each side presents its case in writing, and the written report is read by the other side and the audience prior to the debate. The oral debate then focuses on *refuting* the other side's position. Glib and personable speakers can always make their arguments for a position sound persuasive. Effectively refuting the other side's position is a very different ball game, however. The requirement to refute the other side's position brings to the debate an important feature of the scientific method, that the most likely hypothesis is actually the one with the least evidence against it as well as good evidence for it. (The concept of refuting hypotheses is discussed in chapter 7.)

> *He who knows only his own side of the case, knows little of that. His reasons may be good, and no one may have been able to refute them. But if he is equally unable to refute the reasons on the opposite side, if he does not so much as know what they are, he has no ground for preferring either opinion.*
>
> —John Stuart Mill, *On Liberty* (1859).

The goal of the debate is to decide what to tell the customer. If neither side can effectively refute the other, then arguments for and against both sides should be recognized in any report. Customers of intelligence analysis gain more benefit by weighing well-argued conflicting views than from reading an assessment that masks substantive differences among analysts or drives the analysis toward the lowest common denominator.

If participants routinely interrupt one another or pile on rebuttals before digesting the preceding comment, the teams are engaged in emotional conflict rather than constructive debate.

▶ The Method

Start by defining the conflict to be debated. If possible, frame the conflict in terms of competing and mutually exclusive hypotheses. Ensure that all sides agree with the definition. Then follow these steps:

* Identify individuals or teams to develop the best case that can be made for each hypothesis.

* Each side writes up the best case for its point of view. This written argument must be structured with an explicit presentation of key assumptions, key pieces of evidence, and careful articulation of the logic behind the argument.

* The written arguments are exchanged with the opposing side, and the two sides are given time to develop counterarguments to refute the opposing side's position.

The debate phase is conducted in the presence of a jury of peers, senior analysts, or managers who will provide guidance after listening to the debate. If desired, there might also be an audience of interested observers.

* The debate starts with each side presenting a brief (maximum five minutes) summary of its argument for its position. The jury and the audience are expected to have read each side's full argument.

* Each side then presents to the audience its *rebuttal* of the other side's written position. The purpose here is to proceed in the oral arguments by systematically *refuting* alternative hypotheses rather than by presenting more evidence to support one's own argument. This is the best way to evaluate the strengths of the opposing arguments.

* After each side has presented its rebuttal argument, the other side is given an opportunity to refute the rebuttal.

* The jury asks questions to clarify the debaters' positions or gain additional insight needed to pass judgment on the debaters' positions.

* The jury discusses the issue and passes judgment. The winner is the side that makes the best argument refuting the other side's position, not the side that

makes the best argument supporting its own position. The jury may also recommend possible next steps for further research or intelligence collection efforts. If neither side can refute the other's arguments, it may be that both sides have a valid argument that should be represented in any subsequent analytic report.

▷ Relationship to Other Techniques

Structured Debate is similar to the Team A/Team B technique which has been taught and practiced in parts of the Intelligence Community. Structured Debate differs from Team A/Team B in its focus on refuting the other side's argument. And it avoids the historical association with the infamous 1976 Team A/Team B exercise, which is not an appropriate role model for how analysis should be done today.[10]

▷ Origins of This Technique

The history of debate goes back to the Socratic dialogues in ancient Greece and even before, and many different forms of debate have evolved since then. Richards Heuer formulated the idea of focusing the debate between intelligence analysts on refuting the other side's argument rather than supporting one's own argument.

---

10. The term Team A/Team B is taken from a historic analytic experiment conducted in 1976. A team of CIA Soviet analysts (Team A) and a team of outside critics (Team B) prepared competing assessments of the Soviet Union's strategic military objectives. This exercise was characterized by entrenched and public warfare between long-term adversaries. In other words, the historic legacy of Team A/Team B is exactly the type of trench warfare between opposing sides that we need to avoid. The 1976 experiment did not achieve its goals, and it is not a model that most analysts who are familiar with it would want to follow. We recognize that some recent Team A/Team B exercises have been quite fruitful, but we believe other conflict management techniques described in this chapter are a better way to proceed.

11 Decision Support

11 Decision Support

11.1   Complexity Manager   [271]

11.2   Decision Matrix   [278]

11.3   Force Field Analysis   [281]

11.4   Pros-Cons-Faults-and-Fixes   [284]

11.5   SWOT Analysis   [288]

CHAPTER 11

Decision Support

Managers, commanders, planners, and other decision makers all make choices or tradeoffs among competing goals, values, or preferences. Because of limitations in human short-term memory, we usually cannot keep all the pros and cons of multiple options in mind at the same time. That causes us to focus first on one set of problems or opportunities and then another, a situation that often leads to vacillation or procrastination in making a firm decision. Some decision-support techniques help overcome this cognitive limitation by laying out all the options and interrelationships in graphic form so that analysts can test the results of alternative options while still keeping the problem as a whole in view. Other techniques help decision makers untangle the complexity of a situation or define the opportunities and constraints in the environment in which the choice needs to be made.

It is not the analyst's job to make the choices or decide on the tradeoffs, but intelligence analysts can and should use decision-support techniques to provide timely support to managers, commanders, planners, and decision makers who do make these choices. The Director of National Intelligence's *Vision 2015* foresees intelligence driven by customer needs and a "shifting focus from today's product-centric model toward a more interactive model that blurs the distinction between producer and consumer."[1] When analysis is done collaboratively on the Intelligence

> *The role of the analyst in the policymaking process is similar to that of the scout in relation to the football coach. The job of the scout is not to predict in advance the final score of the game, but to assess the strengths and weaknesses of the opponent so that the coach can devise a winning game plan. Then the scout sits in a booth with powerful binoculars, to report on specific vulnerabilities the coach can exploit.*
>
> —Douglas MacEachin, CIA Deputy Director for Intelligence, 1993–1995

---

1. *Vision 2015: A Globally Networked and Integrated Intelligence Enterprise* (Washington, D.C.: Director of National Intelligence, 2008), 9–10.

Community's secure Web-based network, A-Space, a decision maker may even participate in the analysis or have an aide monitor the work as it is being done.

To engage in this type of customer support analysis, analysts must understand the operating environment of the decision maker and anticipate how the decision maker is likely to approach an issue. They must understand the dynamics of the decision-making process in order to recognize when and how they can be most useful. Most of the decision-support techniques described here are used in both government and industry. By using such techniques, analysts can see a problem from the decision maker's perspective. They can use these techniques without overstepping the limits of their role as intelligence analysts because the technique doesn't make the decision; it just structures all the relevant information in a format that makes it easier for the manager, commander, planner, or other decision maker to make a choice.

The decision aids described in this chapter also provide a framework for analyzing why or how an individual leader, group, organization, or country has made or is likely to make a decision. If an analyst can describe an adversary's or a competitor's goals and preferences, it may be easier to foresee their decision. Similarly, when the decisions are known, the technique makes it easier to infer the competitor's or adversary's goals and preferences.

Caution is in order, however, whenever one thinks of predicting or even explaining another person's decision, regardless of whether the person is of similar background or not. People do not always act rationally in their own best interests. Their decisions are influenced by emotions and habits, as well as by what others might think or values of which others may not be aware.

The same is true of organizations and governments. One of the most common analytic errors is the assumption that an organization or a government will act rationally, that is, in its own best interests. There are three major problems with this assumption:

* Even if the assumption is correct, the analysis may be wrong, because foreign organizations and governments typically see their own best interests quite differently from the way Americans see them.

* Organizations and governments do not always have a clear understanding of their own best interests. Governments in particular typically have a variety of conflicting interests.

* The assumption that organizations and governments commonly act rationally in their own best interests is not always true. All intelligence analysts seeking to understand the behavior of another country should be familiar with Graham

Allison's analysis of U.S. and Soviet decision making during the Cuban missile crisis.[2] It describes three different models for how governments make decisions—bureaucratic bargaining processes and standard organizational procedures as well as the rational actor model.

Instead of trying to predict a foreign organization or government's decision, an analyst will often find that the best course is to use one or more of these decision-support techniques to describe the forces that are expected to shape the decision, identify several potential outcomes, and then select indicators or signs to look for that would provide early warning of the direction in which events are headed. (See chapter 6 for a discussion of Scenarios and Indicators.)

Decision making and decision analysis are large and diverse fields of study and research. The decision-support techniques described in this chapter are only a small sample of what is available, but they do meet many of the basic requirements for intelligence analysis.

Overview of Techniques

Complexity Manager is a simplified approach to understanding complex systems—the kind of systems in which many variables are related to each other and may be changing over time. Government policy decisions are often aimed at changing a dynamically complex system. It is because of this dynamic complexity that many policies fail to meet their goals or have unforeseen and unintended consequences. Use Complexity Manager to assess the chances for success or failure of a new or proposed policy, identify opportunities for influencing the outcome of any situation, determine what would need to change in order to achieve a specified goal, or identify potential unintended consequences from the pursuit of a policy goal.

Decision Matrix is a simple but powerful device for making tradeoffs between conflicting goals or preferences. An analyst lists the decision options or possible choices, the criteria for judging the options, the weights assigned to each of these criteria, and an evaluation of the extent to which each option satisfies each of the criteria. This process will show the best choice—based on the values the analyst or a decision maker puts into the matrix. By studying the matrix, one can also analyze how the best choice would change if the values assigned to the selection criteria were changed or if the ability of an option to satisfy a specific criterion were changed. It is almost impossible for an analyst to keep track of these factors

---

2. See Graham T. Allison and Philip Zelikow, *Essence of Decision: Explaining the Cuban Missile Crisis,* 2nd ed. (New York: Addison-Wesley, 1999).

effectively without such a matrix, as one cannot keep all the pros and cons in working memory at the same time. A Decision Matrix helps the analyst see the whole picture.

Force Field Analysis is a technique that analysts can use to help a decision maker decide how to solve a problem or achieve a goal, or to determine whether it is possible to do so. The analyst identifies and assigns weights to the relative importance of all the factors or forces that are either a help or a hindrance in solving the problem or achieving the goal. After organizing all these factors in two lists, pro and con, with a weighted value for each factor, the analyst or decision maker is in a better position to recommend strategies that would be most effective in either strengthening the impact of the driving forces or reducing the impact of the restraining forces.

Pros-Cons-Faults-and-Fixes is a strategy for critiquing new policy ideas. It is intended to offset the human tendency of analysts and decision makers to jump to conclusions before conducting a full analysis of a problem, as often happens in group meetings. The first step is for the analyst or the project team to make lists of Pros and Cons. If the analyst or team is concerned that people are being unduly negative about an idea, he or she looks for ways to "Fix" the Cons, that is, to explain why the Cons are unimportant or even to transform them into Pros. If concerned that people are jumping on the bandwagon too quickly, the analyst tries to "Fault" the Pros by exploring how they could go wrong. The analyst can also do both Pros and Cons. Of the various techniques described in this chapter, this one is probably the easiest and quickest to use.

SWOT Analysis is used to develop a plan or strategy for achieving a specified goal. (SWOT is an acronym for Strengths, Weaknesses, Opportunities, and Threats.) In using this technique, the analyst first lists the strengths and weaknesses in the organization's ability to achieve a goal, and then lists opportunities and threats in the external environment that would either help or hinder the organization from reaching the goal.

COMPLEXITY MANAGER

Complexity Manager helps analysts and decision makers understand and anticipate changes in complex systems. As used here, the word *complexity* encompasses any distinctive set of interactions that are more complicated than even experienced intelligence analysts can think through solely in their head.[3]

▶ **When to Use It**

As a policy support tool, Complexity Manager can be used to assess the chances for success or failure of a new or proposed program or policy, and opportunities for influencing the outcome of any situation. It also can be used to identify what would have to change in order to achieve a specified goal, as well as unintended consequences from the pursuit of a policy goal. In chapter 14, the final chapter of this book, we use Complexity Manager to make a forecast of how the Intelligence Community might be using structured analytic techniques in the year 2015.

When trying to foresee future events, the Intelligence Community has typically dealt with complexity by:

* Assuming that the future is unpredictable and generating alternative future scenarios and indicators that can be tracked to obtain early warning of which future is emerging.

* Developing or contracting for complex computer models and simulations of how the future might play out. This practice is costly in time and money and often of limited practical value to the working intelligence analyst.

* Making a number of assumptions and relying on the analyst's unaided expert judgment to generate a best guess of how things will work out.

The use of Complexity Manager is a fourth approach that may be preferable in some circumstances, especially in cases of what one might call "manageable complexity." It can help decision makers ask better questions and anticipate problems.

Complexity Manager is different from other methods for dealing with complexity, because it can be used by the average analyst who does not have

---

3. Seth Lloyd, a specialist in complex systems, has listed thirty-two definitions of complexity. See Seth Lloyd, *Programming the Universe* (New York: Knopf, 2006).

advanced quantitative skills. It can be used by analysts who do not have access to software for programs such as Causal Loop Diagramming or Block-Flow Diagramming commonly used in System Dynamics analysis.

▶ **Value Added**

We all know that we live in a complex world of interdependent political, economic, social, and technological systems in which each event or change has multiple impacts. These impacts then have additional impacts on other elements of the system. Although we understand this, we usually do not analyze the world in this way, because the multitude of potential interactions is too difficult for the human brain to track simultaneously. As a result, analysts often fail to foresee future problems or opportunities that may be generated by current trends and developments. Or they fail to foresee the undesirable side effects of well-intentioned policies.[4]

Complexity Manager can often improve an analyst's understanding of a complex situation without the time delay and cost required to build a computer model and simulation. The steps in the Complexity Manager technique are the same as the initial steps required to build a computer model and simulation. These are identification of the relevant variables or actors, analysis of all the interactions between them, and assignment of rough weights or other values to each variable or interaction.

Scientists who specialize in the modeling and simulation of complex social systems report that "the earliest—and sometimes most significant—insights occur while reducing a problem to its most fundamental players, interactions, and basic rules of behavior," and that "the frequency and importance of additional insights diminishes exponentially as a model is made increasingly complex."[5] Thus there is reason to expect that in many cases the Complexity Manager technique will provide much, although not all, of the benefit one could gain from computer modeling and simulation but without the time lag and contract costs. However, if key variables are quantifiable with changes that are trackable over time, it would be more appropriate to use a quantitative modeling technique such as System Dynamics.

Complexity Manager does not itself provide analysts with answers. It enables analysts to find a best possible answer by organizing in a systematic manner the

---

4. Dietrich Dorner, *The Logic of Failure* (New York: Basic Books, 1996).

5. David S. Dixon and William N. Reynolds, "The BASP Agent-Based Modeling Framework: Applications, Scenarios, and Lessons Learned," Hawaii International Conference on System Sciences, 2003, www2.computer.org/portal/web/csdl/doi/10.1109/HICSS.2003.1174225. Also see Donnella H. Meadows and J. M. Robinson, *The Electronic Oracle: Computer Models and Social Decisions* (New York: Wiley, 1985).

jumble of information about many relevant variables. It enables analysts to get a grip on the whole problem, not just one part of the problem at a time. Analysts can then apply their expertise in making an informed judgment about the problem. This structuring of the analyst's thought process also provides the foundation for a well-organized report that clearly presents the rationale for each conclusion. This may also lead to some form of visual presentation, such as a Concept Map or Mind Map, or a causal or influence diagram.

It takes time to work through the Complexity Manager process, but it may save time in the long run. This structured approach helps analysts work efficiently without getting mired down in the complexity of the problem. Because it produces a better and more carefully reasoned product, it also saves time during the editing and coordination processes.

▷ **The Method**
Complexity Manager requires the analyst to proceed through eight specific steps:

1. *Define the problem:* State the problem (plan, goal, outcome) to be analyzed, including the time period to be covered by the analysis.

2. *Identify and list relevant variables:* Use one of the brainstorming techniques described in chapter 4 to identify the significant variables (factors, conditions, people, etc.) that may affect the situation of interest during the designated time period. Think broadly to include organizational or environmental constraints that are beyond anyone's ability to control. If the goal is to estimate the status of one or more variables several years in the future, those variables should be at the top of the list. Group the other variables in some logical manner with the most important variables at the top of the list.

3. *Create a Cross-Impact Matrix:* Create a matrix in which the number of rows and columns are each equal to the number of variables plus one. Leaving the cell at the top left corner of the matrix blank, enter all the variables in the cells in the row across the top of the matrix and the same variables in the column down the left side. The matrix then has a cell for recording the nature of the relationship between all pairs of variables. This is called a Cross-Impact Matrix—a tool for assessing the two-way interaction between each pair of variables. Depending on the number of variables and the length of their names, it may be convenient to use the variables' letter designations across the top of the matrix rather than the full names.

When deciding whether or not to include a variable, or to combine two variables into one, keep in mind that the number of variables has a significant impact on the complexity and the time required for an analysis. If an analytic problem has 5 variables, there are 20 possible two-way interactions between those variables. That number increases rapidly as the number of variables increases. With 10 variables, as in Figure 11.1, there are 90 possible interactions. With 15 variables, there are 210. Complexity Manager may be impractical with more than 15 variables.

4. *Assess the interaction between each pair of variables:* Use a diverse team of experts on the relevant topic to analyze the strength and direction of the interaction between each pair of variables, and enter the results in the relevant cells of the matrix. For each pair of variables, ask the question: Does this variable impact the paired variable in a manner that will increase or decrease the impact or influence of that variable?

When entering ratings in the matrix, it is best to take one variable at a time, first going down the column and then working across the row. Note that the matrix requires each pair of variables to be evaluated twice—for example, the impact of variable A on variable B and the impact of variable B on variable A. To record what variables impact variable A, work down *column* A and ask yourself whether each variable listed on the left side of the matrix has a positive or negative influence, or no influence at all, on variable A. To record the reverse impact of variable A on the other variables, work across *row* A to analyze how variable A impacts the variables listed across the top of the matrix.

There are two different ways one can record the nature and strength of impact that one variable has on another. Figure 11.1 uses plus and minus signs to show whether the variable being analyzed has a positive or negative impact on the paired variable. The size of the plus or minus sign signifies the strength of the impact on a three-point scale. The small plus or minus shows a weak impact, the medium size a medium impact, and the large size a strong impact. If the variable being analyzed has no impact on the paired variable, the cell is left empty. If a variable might change in a way that could reverse the direction of its impact, from positive to negative or vice versa, this is shown by using both a plus and a minus sign.

The completed matrix shown in Figure 11.1 is the same matrix you will see in chapter 14, when the Complexity Manager technique is used to forecast the future of structured analytic techniques in the Intelligence Community. The plus and minus signs work well for the finished matrix. When first populating the matrix, however, it may be easier to use letters (*P* and *M* for plus and minus) to show whether each variable has a positive or negative impact on the other variable with which it is paired, Each *P* or *M* is then followed by a number to show the strength of that impact. A three-point scale is used, with 3 indicating a strong impact, 2 medium, and 1 weak.

Figure 11.1

Variables Affecting the Future Use of Structured Analysis

	A	B	C	D	E	F	G	H	I	J
A Increased use of Structured Analytic Techniques		+	+	+	+	–	+	+	+	–
B DNI promotes sharing, collaboration	+		+	+	+	–	+	+	+	–
C Availability of technical infrastructure	+	+		+	+		+	+	+	+
D Generational change of analysts	+	+	+		+	–		+	–	–
E Availability/depth of analytic support	+/–	+/–				–	+	+	–	–
F Reduced budget for analysis	–	–	–	–	–			–	–	–
G Change in customer needs/preferences	+/–	+			+			+	–	–
H Research on effectiveness of Structured Analytic Techniques	+/–	+/–	+		+				+/–	+/–
I Analyst perception of time pressure	–	–								+
J Lack of openness to change among senior analysts and managers	–	–							+	

Reading the Matrix: The cells in each *row* show the impact of the variable represented by that row on each of the variables listed across the top of the matrix. The cells in each *column* show the impact of each variable listed down the left side of the matrix on the variable represented by the column.

Direction and magnitude of the impact:

+	strong positive impact
+	medium positive impact
+	weak positive impact
–	strong negative impact
–	medium negative impact
–	weak negative impact

Combination of + and – means impact could go either direction.
Empty cell = no impact.

After rating each pair of variables, and before doing further analysis, consider pruning the matrix to eliminate variables that are unlikely to have a significant effect on the outcome. It is possible to measure the relative significance of each variable by adding up the weighted values in each row and column. The sum of the weights in each row is a measure of each variable's impact on the system as a whole. The sum of the weights in each column is a measure of how much each variable is affected by all the other variables. Those variables most impacted by the other variables should be monitored as potential indicators of the direction in which events are moving or as potential sources of unintended consequences.

5. *Analyze direct impacts:* Write several paragraphs about the impact of each variable, starting with variable A. For each variable, describe the variable for further clarification if necessary. Identify all the variables that impact on that variable with a rating of 2 or 3, and briefly explain the nature, direction, and, if appropriate, the timing of this impact. How strong is it and how certain is it? When might these impacts be observed? Will the impacts be felt only in certain conditions? Next, identify and discuss all variables on which this variable has an impact with a rating of 2 or 3 (strong or medium effect), including the strength of the impact and how certain it is to occur. Identify and discuss the potentially good or bad side effects of these impacts.

6. *Analyze loops and indirect impacts:* The matrix shows only the direct impact of one variable on another. When you are analyzing the direct impacts variable by variable, there are several things to look for and make note of. One is feedback loops. For example, if variable A has a positive impact on variable B, and variable B also has a positive impact on variable A, this is a positive feedback loop. Or there may be a three-variable loop, from A to B to C and back to A. The variables in a loop gain strength from each other, and this boost may enhance their ability to influence other variables. Another thing to look for is circumstances where the causal relationship between variables A and B is necessary but not sufficient for something to happen. For example, variable A has the potential to influence variable B, and may even be trying to influence variable B, but it can do so effectively only if variable C is also present. In that case, variable C is an enabling variable and takes on greater significance than it ordinarily would have.

All variables are either static or dynamic. Static variables are expected to remain more or less unchanged during the period covered by the analysis. Dynamic variables are changing or have the potential to change. The analysis should focus on the dynamic variables as these are the sources of surprise in any complex system. Determining how these dynamic variables interact with other variables and with each other is critical to any forecast of future developments. Dynamic variables can be either predictable or unpredictable. Predictable change includes established trends or established policies that are in the process of being implemented. Unpredictable change may be a change in leadership or an unexpected change in policy or available resources.

7. *Draw conclusions:* Using data about the individual variables assembled in Steps 5 and 6, draw conclusions about the system as a whole. What is the most likely outcome or what changes might be anticipated during the specified time period? What are the driving forces behind that outcome? What things could happen to cause a different outcome? What desirable or undesirable side effects should be anticipated? If you need help to sort out all the relationships, it may be useful to sketch out by hand a diagram showing all the causal relationships. A Concept Map (chapter 4) may be useful for this purpose. If a diagram is helpful during the analysis, it may also be helpful to the reader or customer to include such a diagram in the report.

8. *Conduct an opportunity analysis:* When appropriate, analyze what actions could be taken to influence this system in a manner favorable to the primary customer of the analysis.

▶ **Relationship to Other Techniques**
The same procedures for creating a matrix and coding data can be applied in using a Cross-Impact Matrix (chapter 5). The difference is that the Cross-Impact Matrix technique is used only to identify and share information about the cross-impacts in a group or team exercise. The goal of Complexity Manager is to build on the Cross-Impact Matrix to analyze the working of a complex system.

Use a form of Scenario Analysis rather than Complexity Manager when the future is highly uncertain and the goal is to identify alternative futures and indicators that will provide early warning of the direction in which future events are headed. Use a computerized modeling system such as System Dynamics rather than Complexity Manager when changes over time in key variables can be quantified or when there are more than fifteen variables to be considered.[6]

▶ **Origins of This Technique**
Complexity Manager was developed by Richards Heuer to fill an important gap in structured techniques that are available to the average analyst. It is a very simplified version of older quantitative modeling techniques, such as system dynamics.

---

6. John Sterman, *Business Dynamics: Systems Thinking and Modeling for a Complex World* (McGraw Hill, 2000).

A Decision Matrix helps analysts identify the course of action that best achieves specified goals or preferences.

▶ When to Use It

The Decision Matrix technique should be used when a decision maker has multiple options to choose from, multiple criteria for judging the desirability of each option, and/or needs to find the decision that maximizes a specific set of goals or preferences. For example, it can be used to help choose among various plans or strategies for improving intelligence analysis, to select one of several IT systems one is considering buying, to determine which of several job applicants is the right choice, or to consider any personal decision, such as what to do after retiring.

A Decision Matrix is not applicable to most intelligence analysis, which typically deals with evidence and judgments rather than goals and preferences. It can be used, however, for supporting a decision maker's consideration of alternative courses of action. It might also be used to support a Red Hat Analysis that examines decision options from an adversary's or competitor's perspective.

▶ Value Added

This technique deconstructs a decision problem into its component parts, listing all the options or possible choices, the criteria for judging the options, the weights assigned to each of these criteria, and an evaluation of the extent to which each option satisfies each of these criteria. All these judgments are apparent to anyone looking at the matrix. Because it is so explicit, the matrix can play an important role in facilitating communication between those who are involved in or affected by the decision process. It can be easy to identify areas of disagreement and to determine whether such disagreements have any material impact on the decision. One can also see how sensitive the decision is to changes that might be made in the values assigned to the selection criteria or to the ability of an option to satisfy the criteria. If circumstances or preferences change, it is easy to go back to the matrix, make changes, and calculate the impact of the changes on the proposed decision.

▶ The Method

Create a Decision Matrix table. To do this, break the decision problem down into two main components by making two lists—a list of options or alternatives for making a choice and a list of criteria to be used when judging the desirability of the options. Then follow these steps:

* Create a matrix with one column for each option. Write the name of each option at the head of one of the columns. Add two more blank columns on the left side of the table.

* Count the number of selection criteria, and then adjust the table so that it has that many rows plus two more, one at the top to list the options and one at the bottom to show the scores for each option. In the first column on the left side, starting with the second row, write in all the selection criteria down the left side of the table. There is some value in listing them roughly in order of importance, but doing so is not critical. Leave the bottom row blank. (Note: Whether you enter the options across the top row and the criteria down the far left column, or vice versa, depends on what fits best on the page. If one of the lists is significantly longer than the other, it usually works best to put the longer list in the left-hand column.)

* Assign weights based on the importance of each of the selection criteria. There are easier ways to do this, but the preferred way is to take 100 percent and divide these percentage points among the selection criteria. Be sure that the weights for all the selection criteria combined add to 100 percent. Also be sure that all the criteria are phrased in such a way that a higher weight is more

| Figure 11.2 | **Example of a Decision Matrix** |

	% Weight	Option 1	Option 2	Option 3
Criterion 1	30%	3.5 x 30 = 105	3 x 30 = 90	3.5 x 30 = 105
Criterion 2	10%	3.5 x 10 = 35	2 x 10 = 20	4.5 x 10 = 45
Criterion 3	20%	2.5 x 20 = 50	4.5 x 20 = 90	3 x 20 = 60
Criterion 4	20%	4 x 20 = 80	2.5 x 20 = 50	3.5 x 20 = 70
Criterion 5	15%	3 x 15 = 45	4 x 15 = 60	3 x 15 = 45
Criterion 6	5%	3.5 x 5 = 17.5	2.5 x 5 = 12.5	4 x 5 = 20
Totals	100%	**332.5**	**322.5**	**345**

desirable. (Note: If this technique is being used by an intelligence analyst to support decision making, this step should not be done by the analyst. The assignment of relative weights is up to the decision maker.)

＊ Work across the matrix one row at a time to evaluate the relative ability of each of the options to satisfy each of the selection criteria. For example, assign ten points to each row and divide these points according to an assessment of the degree to which each of the options satisfies each of the selection criteria. Then multiply this number by the weight for that criterion. Figure 11.2 is an example of a Decision Matrix with three options and six criteria.

＊ Add the columns for each of the options. If you accept the judgments and preferences expressed in the matrix, the option with the highest number will be the best choice.

When using this technique, many analysts will discover relationships or opportunities not previously recognized. A sensitivity analysis may find that plausible changes in some values would lead to a different choice. For example, the analyst might think of a way to modify an option in a way that makes it more desirable or might rethink the selection criteria in a way that changes the preferred outcome. The numbers calculated in the matrix do not make the decision. The matrix is just an aid to help the analyst and the decision maker understand the tradeoffs between multiple competing preferences.

▷ **Origins of This Technique**

This may be the most commonly used decision analysis technique. Many variations of this basic technique have been called by many different names, including Multiple Criteria Decision Analysis (MCDA), Multiple Criteria Decision Making (MCDM), Multiple Attribute Utility Analysis (MAU), Utility Matrix, Pugh Matrix, and decision grid. For a comparison of various approaches to this type of analysis, see Panos M. Parlos and Evangelos Triantaphyllou, eds., *Multi-Criteria Decision Making Methods: A Comparative Study* (Dordrecht, The Netherlands: Kluwer Academic Publishers, 2000).

FORCE FIELD ANALYSIS

Force Field Analysis is a simple technique for listing and assessing all the forces for and against a change, problem, or goal. Kurt Lewin, one of the fathers of modern social psychology, believed that all organizations are systems in which the present situation is a dynamic balance between forces driving for change and restraining forces. In order for any change to occur, the driving forces must exceed the restraining forces, and the relative strength of these forces is what this technique measures. This technique is based on Lewin's theory.[7]

▷ When to Use It

Force Field Analysis is useful in the early stages of a project or research effort, when the analyst is defining the issue, gathering data, or developing recommendations for action. It requires that the analyst clearly define the problem in all its aspects. It can aid an analyst in structuring the data and assessing the relative importance of each of the forces affecting the issue. The technique can also help the analyst overcome the natural human tendency to dwell on the aspects of the data that are most comfortable. The technique can be used by an individual analyst or by a small team.

▷ Value Added

The primary benefit of Force Field Analysis is that it requires an analyst to consider the forces and factors that influence a situation. It helps the analyst think through the ways various forces affect the issue and fosters the recognition that forces can be divided into two categories: the driving forces and the restraining forces. By sorting the evidence into driving and restraining forces, the analyst must delve deeply into the issue and consider the less obvious factors and issues. By weighing all the forces for and against an issue, the analyst can better recommend strategies that would be most effective in reducing the impact of the restraining forces and strengthening the effect of the driving forces. Force Field Analysis also offers a

> *An issue is held in balance by the interaction of two opposing sets of forces—those seeking to promote change (driving forces) and those attempting to maintain the status quo (restraining forces).*
>
> —Kurt Lewin, *Resolving Social Conflicts* (1948).

---

7. Kurt Lewin, *Resolving Social Conflicts: Selected Papers on Group Dynamics* (New York: Harper and Row, 1948).

Figure 11.3

Force Field Analysis: Removing Abandoned Cars from City Streets

Arguments For		Arguments Against	
5	The public service director supports the plan.	A location is needed to put the abandoned cars once identified.	4
5	Local auto salvage yards will remove cars for free.	Locating and disposing of cars will be expensive.	3
4	The City Council supports the plan.	The owners of old cars feel threatened.	3
3	Advocacy groups have expressed interest.	A procedure is needed to verify a car's status and notify owners.	3
2	Health Department has cited old and abandoned vehicles as potential health hazards.	It is difficult to locate abandoned cars.	2
2	The public climate favors cleaning up the city.	The definition of "abandoned cars" is unclear to the public.	1

Note: The number value and size of the type indicate the significance of each argument.

Source: 2007 Pherson Associates, LLC.

powerful way to visualize the key elements of the problem by providing a simple tally sheet for displaying the different levels of intensity of the forces individually and as a whole. With the data sorted into two lists, decision makers can more easily identify which forces deserve the most attention and develop strategies to overcome the negative elements while promoting the positive elements. Figure 11.3 is an example of a Force Field diagram.

▶ **The Method**

* Define the problem, goal, or change clearly and concisely.

* Brainstorm to identify the main forces that will influence the issue. Consider such topics as needs, resources, costs, benefits, organizations, relationships, attitudes, traditions, interests, social and cultural trends, rules and regulations,

policies, values, popular desires, and leadership to develop the full range of forces promoting and restraining the factors involved.

* Make one list showing the forces or people "driving" the change and a second list showing the forces or people "restraining" the change.

* Assign a value (the intensity score) to each driving or restraining force to indicate its strength. Assign the weakest intensity scores a value of 1 and the strongest a value of 5. The same intensity score can be assigned to more than one force if you consider the factors equal in strength. List the intensity scores in parentheses beside each item.

* Calculate a total score for each list to determine whether the driving or the restraining forces are dominant.

* Examine the two lists to determine if any of the driving forces balance out the restraining forces.

* Devise a manageable course of action to strengthen those forces that lead to the preferred outcome and weaken the forces that would hinder the desired outcome.

You should keep in mind that the preferred outcome may be either promoting a change or restraining a change. For example, if the problem is increased drug use or criminal activity, you would focus the analysis on the factors that would have the most impact on restraining criminal activity or drug use. On the other hand, if the preferred outcome is improved border security, you would highlight the drivers that, if strengthened, would be most likely to promote border security.

▶ **Origins of This Technique**
Force Field Analysis is widely used in social science and business research. (A Google search on the term brings up more than 80,000 hits.) This version of the technique is largely from Randy Pherson, *Handbook of Analytic Tools and Techniques* (Reston, Va.: Pherson Associates, LLC, 2008); and Pherson Associates teaching materials.

PROS-CONS-FAULTS-AND-FIXES

Pros-Cons-Faults-and-Fixes is a strategy for critiquing new policy ideas. It is intended to offset the human tendency of a group of analysts and decision makers to jump to a conclusion before full analysis of the problem has been completed.

▶ **When to Use It**

Making lists of pros and cons for any action is a very common approach to decision making. The "Faults" and "Fixes" are what is new in this strategy. Use this technique to make a quick appraisal of a new idea or a more systematic analysis of a choice between two options.

One advantage of Pros-Cons-Faults-and-Fixes is its applicability to virtually all types of decisions. Of the various structured techniques for decision making, it is probably the easiest and quickest to use. It requires only a certain procedure for making the lists and discussing them with others to solicit divergent input.

▶ **Value Added**

It is unusual for a new idea to meet instant approval. What often happens in meetings is that a new idea is brought up, one or two people immediately explain why they don't like it or believe it won't work, and the idea is then dropped. On the other hand, there are occasions when just the opposite happens. A new idea is immediately welcomed, and a commitment to support it is made before the idea is critically evaluated. The Pros-Cons-Faults-and-Fixes technique helps to offset this human tendency toward jumping to conclusions.

The technique first requires a list of Pros and Cons about the new idea or the choice between two alternatives. If there seems to be excessive enthusiasm for an idea and a risk of acceptance without critical evaluation, the next step is to look for "Faults." A Fault is any argument that a Pro is unrealistic, won't work, or will have unacceptable side effects. On the other hand, if there seems to be a bias toward negativity or a risk of the idea being dropped too quickly without careful consideration, the next step is to look for "Fixes." A Fix is any argument or plan that would neutralize or minimize a Con, or even change it into a Pro. In some cases, it may be appropriate to look for both Faults and Fixes before comparing the two lists and making a decision.

The Pros-Cons-Faults-and-Fixes technique does not tell an analyst whether the Pros or the Cons have the strongest argument. That answer is still based on the analyst's professional judgment. The role of the technique is to offset any

Figure 11.4

Pros-Cons-Faults-and-Fixes Analysis

Faults	Pros	Cons	Fixes
Fault Pro A	Pro A	Con A	Fix Con A
	Pro B	Con B	Fix Con B
Fault Pro C	Pro C	Con C	
Fault Pro D	Pro D	Con D	Fix Con D

A **Fault** is any argument that the option is unrealistic, won't work, or will have unacceptable side effects. Identifying faults allows you to troubleshoot your Pros.

A **Fix** is any argument or plan of action that would neutralize or miminize a Con, or even change it into a Pro. Identifying fixes allows you to improve the chances of success for an option by removing possible obstacles.

tendency to rush to judgment. It also organizes the elements of the problem in a logical manner that can help the decision maker make a carefully considered choice. Writing things down in this manner helps the analyst and the decision maker see things more clearly and become more objective and emotionally detached from the decision. (See Figure 11.4.)

▶ **The Method**
Start by clearly defining the proposed action or choice. Then follow these steps:

＊ List the Pros in favor of the decision or choice. Think broadly and creatively and list as many benefits, advantages, or other positives as possible.

＊ List the Cons, or arguments against what is proposed. There are usually more Cons than Pros, as most humans are naturally critical. It is easier to think of arguments against a new idea than to imagine how the new idea might work. This is why it is often difficult to get careful consideration of a new idea.

＊ Review and consolidate the list. If two Pros are similar or overlapping, consider merging them to eliminate any redundancy. Do the same for any overlapping Cons.

* If the choice is between two clearly defined options, go through the previous steps for the second option. If there are more than two options, a technique such as Decision Matrix may be more appropriate than Pros-Cons-Faults-and-Fixes.

* At this point you must make a choice. If the goal is to challenge an initial judgment that the idea won't work, take the Cons, one at a time, and see if they can be "Fixed." That means trying to figure a way to neutralize their adverse influence or even to convert them into Pros. This exercise is intended to counter any unnecessary or biased negativity about the idea. There are at least four ways an argument listed as a Con might be Fixed:
  - Propose a modification of the Con that would significantly lower the risk of the Con being a problem.
  - Identify a preventive measure that would significantly reduce the chances of the Con being a problem.
  - Do contingency planning that includes a change of course if certain indicators are observed.
  - Identify a need for further research or information gathering to confirm or refute the assumption that the Con is a problem.

* If the goal is to challenge an initial optimistic assumption that the idea will work and should be pursued, take the Pros, one at a time, and see if they can be "Faulted." That means to try and figure out how the Pro might fail to materialize or have undesirable consequences. This exercise is intended to counter any wishful thinking or unjustified optimism about the idea. There are at least three ways a Pro might be Faulted:
  - Identify a reason why the Pro would not work or why the benefit would not be received.
  - Identify an undesirable side effect that might accompany the benefit.
  - Identify a need for further research or information gathering to confirm or refute the assumption that the Pro will work or be beneficial.

* A third option is to combine both approaches, to Fault the Pros and Fix the Cons.

* Compare the Pros, including any Faults, against the Cons, including the Fixes. Weigh the balance of one against the other, and make the choice. The choice is based on your professional judgment, not on any numerical calculation of the number or value of Pros versus Cons.

Pros-Cons-Faults-and-Fixes is Richards Heuer's adaptation of the Pros-Cons-and-Fixes technique described by Morgan D. Jones in *The Thinker's Toolkit: Fourteen Powerful Techniques for Problem Solving* (New York: Three Rivers Press, 1998), 72–79. Jones assumed that humans are "compulsively negative," and that "negative thoughts defeat creative objective thinking." Thus his technique focused only on Fixes for the Cons. The technique that we describe here recognizes that analysts and decision makers can also be biased by overconfidence, in which case Faulting the Pros may be more important than Fixing the Cons.

11.5   SWOT ANALYSIS

SWOT is commonly used by all types of organizations to evaluate the Strengths, Weaknesses, Opportunities, and Threats involved in any project or plan of action. The strengths and weaknesses are internal to the organization, while the opportunities and threats are characteristics of the external environment.

▶ When to Use It

After setting a goal or objective, use SWOT as a framework for collecting and organizing information in support of strategic planning and decision making to achieve the goal or objective. Information is collected to analyze the plan's strengths and weaknesses and the opportunities and threats present in the external environment that might have an impact on the ability to achieve the goal.

SWOT is easy to use. It can be used by a single analyst, although it is usually a group process. It is particularly effective as a cross-functional team-building exercise at the start of a new project. Businesses and organizations of all types use SWOT so frequently that a Google search on "SWOT Analysis" turns up more than five million hits.

▶ Value Added

SWOT can generate useful information with relatively little effort, and it brings that information together in a framework that provides a good base for further analysis. It often points to specific actions that can or should be taken. Because the technique matches an organization's or plan's strengths and weaknesses against the opportunities and threats in the environment in which it operates, the plans or action recommendations that develop from the use of this technique are often quite practical.

▶ Potential Pitfalls

This technique has been criticized for providing too easy a path to what is actually a more difficult planning decision. SWOT focuses on a single goal without weighing the costs and benefits of alternative means of achieving the same goal. In other words, SWOT is a useful technique as long as the analyst recognizes that it does not necessarily tell the full story of what decision should or will be made. There may be other equally good or better courses of action.

Figure 11.5   SWOT Analysis

Strengths	**W**eaknesses
List attributes of the organization that are helpful in achieving the objective.	List attributes of the organization that are detrimental to achieving the objective.
Opportunities	**T**hreats
List external conditions that are helpful to achieving the objective.	List external conditions that could be detrimental to achieving the objective.

Another strategic planning technique, the TOWS Matrix, remedies one of the limitations of SWOT. The factors listed under Threats, Opportunities, Weaknesses, and Strengths are combined to identify multiple alternative strategies that an organization might pursue.[8]

▷ **The Method**

  * Define the objective.

  * Fill in the SWOT table by listing Strengths, Weaknesses, Opportunities, and Threats that are expected to facilitate or hinder achievement of the objective. (See Figure 11.5.) The significance of the attributes' and conditions' impact on achievement of the objective is far more important than the length of the list. It is often desirable to list the items in each quadrant in order of their significance or to assign them values on a scale of 1 to 5.

  * Identify possible strategies for achieving the objective. This is done by asking the following questions:
    - How can we use each *Strength*?
    - How can we improve each *Weakness*?
    - How can we exploit each *Opportunity*?
    - How can we mitigate each *Threat*?

---

8. Heinz Weihrich, "The TOWS Matrix—A Tool for Situational Analysis," *Long Range Planning* 15, no. 2 (April 1982): 54–66.

An alternative approach is to apply "matching and converting" techniques. Matching refers to matching strengths with opportunities to make the strengths even stronger. Converting refers to matching opportunities with weaknesses in order to convert the weaknesses into strengths.

▶ **Relationship to Other Techniques**
The factors listed in the Opportunities and Threats quadrants of a SWOT Analysis are the same as the outside or external factors the analyst seeks to identify during Outside-In Thinking (chapter 8). In that sense, there is some overlap between the two techniques.

▶ **Origins of This Technique**
The SWOT technique was developed in the late 1960s at Stanford Research Institute as part of a decade-long research project on why corporate planning fails. It is the first part of a more comprehensive strategic planning program. It has been so heavily used over such a long period of time that several versions have evolved. Richards Heuer has selected the version he believes most appropriate for intelligence analysis. It comes from multiple Internet sites, including the following: www.businessballs.com/swotanalysisfreetemplate.htm, http://en.wikipedia.org/wiki/SWOT_analysis, www.mindtools.com, www.valuebasedmanagement.net, and www.mycoted.com.

12

Practitioner's Guide to Collaboration

Practitioner's Guide to Collaboration

12.1 Social Networks and Analytic Teams   [294]

12.2 Dividing the Work   [297]

12.3 Common Pitfalls with Small Groups   [300]

12.4 Benefiting from Diversity   [301]

12.5 Advocacy vs. Objective Inquiry   [302]

12.6 Leadership and Training   [304]

CHAPTER 12

Practitioner's Guide to Collaboration

Analysis in the U.S. Intelligence Community is now in a transitional stage from being predominantly a mental activity done by a solo analyst to becoming a collaborative or group activity. The increasing use of structured analytic techniques is central to this transition. Many things change when the internal thought process of analysts can be externalized in a transparent manner so that ideas can be shared, built on, and easily critiqued by others.

This chapter provides practical guidance on how to take advantage of the collaborative environment while preventing or avoiding the many well-known problems associated with small-group processes. It starts by describing three different types of groups that engage in intelligence analysis—two types of teams and a type of group that is described here as a "social network." The rapid growth of social networks across organizational boundaries and the consequent geographic distribution of their members are changing how analysis needs to be done. We propose that much analysis should be done in two phases: a divergent analysis phase conducted by a geographically distributed social network and a convergent analysis phase and final report done by a small analytic team.

The chapter then reviews briefly a number of problems known to impair the performance of teams and small groups and concludes with some practical measures for limiting the occurrence of such problems. This chapter is not intended to describe collaboration as it exists today. It is a visionary attempt to foresee how collaboration might be put into practice in the future when interagency collaboration is the norm and the younger generation of analysts has had even more time to imprint its social networking practices on the Intelligence Community.

12.1 SOCIAL NETWORKS AND ANALYTIC TEAMS

There are several ways to categorize teams and groups. When discussing the U.S. Intelligence Community, it seems most useful to deal with three types: the traditional analytic team, the special project team, and social network. Analytic teams, supported by social networks, can operate effectively in both co-located and geographically distributed modes. The special project team is most effective when its members are co-located. These three types of groups differ in the nature of their leadership, frequency of face-to-face and virtual meetings, breadth of the analytic activity, and amount of time pressure they work under.[1]

＊ Traditional analytic team: This is the typical work team assigned to perform a specific task. It has a leader appointed by a manager or chosen by the team, and all members of the team are collectively accountable for the team's product. The team may work jointly to develop the entire product or, as is commonly done for National Intelligence Estimates, each team member may be responsible for a specific section of the work. Historically, many teams were composed of analysts from a single agency, and involvement of other agencies was through coordination during the latter part of the process rather than collaboration from the beginning. That way is now changing as a consequence of changes in policy and easier access to secure interagency communications and collaboration software. Figure 12.1a shows how the traditional analytic team works. The core analytic team, with participants usually working at the same agency, drafts a paper and sends it to other members of the government community for comment and coordination. Ideally, the core team will alert other stakeholders in the community of their intent to write on a specific topic, but more often such dialogue occurs much later when they are coordinating the draft. In most cases, specific permissions are required, or established procedures must be followed to reach out and tap the expertise of nongovernment experts.

＊ Special project team: Such a team is usually formed to provide decision makers with near–real time analytic support during a crisis or an ongoing operation. A crisis support task force or field-deployed interagency intelligence team that supports a military operation exemplifies this type of team. Members typically are located in the same physical office space or are connected by video communications. There is strong team leadership, often with close personal interaction

---

1. This chapter was inspired by and draws on the research done by the Group Brain Project at Harvard University. That project was supported by the National Science Foundation and the CIA Intelligence Technology Innovation Center. See in particular J. Richard Hackman and Anita W. Woolley, "Creating and Leading Analytic Teams," *Technical Report* 5 (February 2007), http://groupbrain.wjh.harvard.edu/publications.html. The graphics were created by Sarah Beebe, Pherson Associates, LLC.

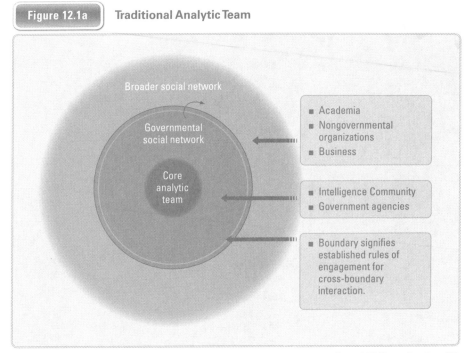

Figure 12.1a   Traditional Analytic Team

- Academia
- Nongovernmental organizations
- Business

- Intelligence Community
- Government agencies

- Boundary signifies established rules of engagement for cross-boundary interaction.

Broader social network

Governmental social network

Core analytic team

Source: 2009 Pherson Associates, LLC.

between team members. Because the team is created to deal with a specific situation, its work has a narrower focus than a social network or regular analytic team and its duration is limited. There is usually intense time pressure, and around-the-clock operation may be required. Figure 12.1b is a diagram of a special project team.

  ✳ Social networks: Experienced analysts have always had their own network of experts in their field or related fields with whom they consult from time to time and whom they may recruit to work with them on a specific analytic project. Social networks are critical to the analytic business. They do the day-to-day monitoring of events, produce routine products as needed, and may recommend the formation of a more formal analytic team to handle a specific project. The social network is the form of group activity that is now changing dramatically with the growing ease of cross-agency secure communications and the availability of social networking software. Social networks are expanding exponentially across organization boundaries. The term "social network" as used here includes all analysts working anywhere in the world on a particular country, such as Brazil, or on an issue, such as the development of chemical weapons. It can be limited to a small

Figure 12.1b   Special Project Team

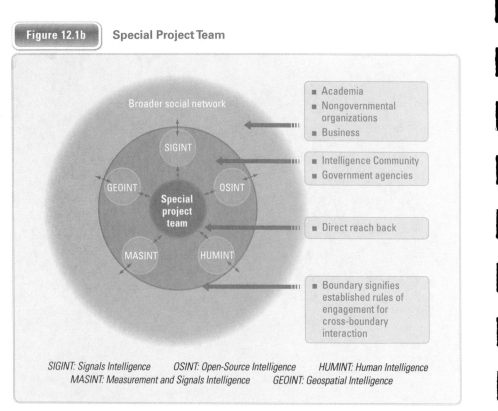

SIGINT: *Signals Intelligence*   OSINT: *Open-Source Intelligence*   HUMINT: *Human Intelligence*
MASINT: *Measurement and Signals Intelligence*   GEOINT: *Geospatial Intelligence*

Source: 2009 Pherson Associates, LLC.

group with special clearances or comprise a broad array of government, nongovernment, and academic experts.

The key problem that arises with social networks is the geographic distribution of their members. Even within the Washington, D.C., metropolitan area, distance is a factor that limits the frequency of face-to-face meetings. From their study of teams in diverse organizations, which included teams in the Intelligence Community, Richard Hackman and Anita Woolley came to this conclusion:

> Distributed teams do relatively well on innovation tasks for which ideas and solutions need to be generated, for example, but generally underperform face-to-face teams on decision-making tasks. Although decision support systems can improve performance slightly, decisions made from afar still tend to take more time, involve less exchange of

information, make error detection and correction more difficult, and can result in less participant satisfaction with the outcome than is the case for face-to-face teams. . . . In sum, distributed teams are appropriate for many, but not all, team tasks. Using them well requires careful attention to team structure, a face-to-face launch when members initially come together, and leadership support throughout the life of the team to keep members engaged and aligned with collective purposes.[2]

Research on effective collaborative practices has shown that geographically distributed teams are most likely to succeed when they satisfy six key imperatives. Participants must

* Know and trust each other; this usually requires that they meet face-to-face at least once.

* Feel a personal need to engage the group in order to perform a critical task.

* Derive mutual benefits from working together.

* Connect with each other virtually on demand and easily add new members.

* Perceive incentives for participating in the group, such as saving time, gaining new insights from interaction with other knowledgeable analysts, or increasing the impact of their contribution.

* Share a common understanding of the problem with agreed lists of common terms and definitions.[3]

12.2 DIVIDING THE WORK

Managing the geographic distribution of the social network can also be addressed effectively by dividing the analytic task into two parts—first exploiting the strengths of the social network for divergent or creative analysis to identify ideas and gather information, and, second, forming a small analytic team that employs convergent analysis to meld these ideas into an analytic product. When the draft is

---

2. Ibid, 8.
3. Randolph Pherson and Joan McIntyre, "The Essence of Collaboration: The IC Experience," in *Scientific Underpinnings of 'Collaboration' in the National Security Arena: Myths and Reality—What Science and Experience Can Contribute to Its Success,* ed. Nancy Chesser (Washington, D.C.: Strategic Multi-Layer Assessment Office, Office of the Secretary of Defense DDR&E RRTO, June 2009).

Figure 12.2 | **Wikis as Collaboration Enablers**

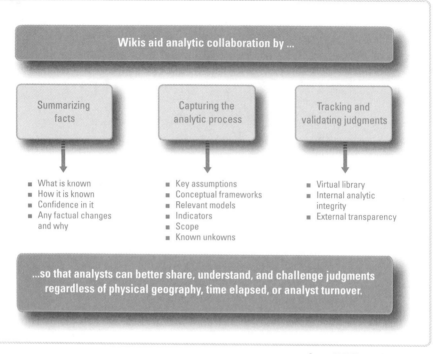

Source: 2009 Pherson Associates LLC.

completed, it goes back for review to all members of the social network who contributed during the first phase of the analysis, and then back to the team to edit and produce the final product.

Structured analytic techniques and collaborative software work very well with this two-part approach to analysis. A series of basic techniques used for divergent analysis early in the analytic process works well for a geographically distributed social network communicating via a wiki. This provides a solid foundation for subsequent convergent analysis by a small analytic team. In other words, each type of group performs the type of task for which it is best qualified. This process is applicable to most analytic projects. Figure 12.2 shows how it can work.

A project leader informs a social network of an impending project and provides a tentative project description, target audience, scope, and process to be followed. The leader also gives the name of the wiki to be used and invites interested analysts knowledgeable in that area to participate. Any analyst with access to the secure network also has access to the wiki and is authorized to add information and ideas to it. Any or all of the following techniques, as well as others, may come into play during the divergent analysis phase as specified by the project leader:

* Issue Redefinition as described in chapter 4.

* Collaboration in sharing and processing data using other techniques such as timelines, sorting, networking, mapping, and charting as described in chapter 4.

* Some form of brainstorming, as described in chapter 5, to generate a list of driving forces, variables, players, etc.

* Ranking or prioritizing this list, as described in chapter 4.

* Putting this list into a Cross-Impact Matrix, as described in chapter 5, and then discussing and recording in the wiki the relationship, if any, between each pair of driving forces, variables, or players in that matrix.

* Developing a list of alternative explanations or outcomes (hypotheses) to be considered (chapter 7).

* Developing a list of items of evidence available to be considered when evaluating these hypotheses (chapter 7).

* Doing a Key Assumptions Check (chapter 8). This will be less effective when done on a wiki than in a face-to-face meeting, but it would be useful to learn the network's thinking about key assumptions.

Most of these steps involve making lists, which can be done quite effectively with a wiki. Making such input via a wiki can be even more productive than a face-to-face meeting, because analysts have more time to think about and write up their thoughts and are able to look at their contribution over several days and make additions or changes as new ideas come to them.

The process should be overseen and guided by a project leader. In addition to providing a sound foundation for further analysis, this process enables the project leader to identify the best analysts to be included in the smaller team that conducts the second phase of the project—making analytic judgments and drafting the report. Team members should be selected to maximize the following criteria: level of expertise on the subject, level of interest in the outcome of the analysis, and diversity of opinions and thinking styles among the group. The action then moves from the social network to a small, trusted team (preferably no larger than eight analysts) to complete the project, perhaps using other techniques such as Analysis of Competing Hypotheses or What If? Analysis. Face-to-face meetings should be held as needed. Software used for exchanging ideas and revising text should be a system like Microsoft SharePoint rather than a wiki, because a SharePoint-type system allows for privacy of deliberations and the wiki does not. The draft report is best done by a single person. That person can work from other team members' inputs, but the report usually reads better if it is crafted in one voice. As noted earlier, the working draft should be reviewed by those members of the social network who participated in the first phase of the analysis.

12.3 COMMON PITFALLS WITH SMALL GROUPS

As more analysis is done collaboratively, the quality of intelligence products is increasingly influenced by the success or failure of small-group processes. The various problems that afflict small-group processes are well known and have been the subject of considerable research.[4] One might reasonably be concerned that more collaboration will just mean more problems, more interagency battles. However, as we explain here, it turns out that the use of structured analytic techniques frequently helps analysts *avoid* many of the common pitfalls of the small-group process.

Some group process problems are obvious to anyone who has participated in trying to arrive at decisions or judgments in a group meeting. Guidelines for how to run meetings effectively are widely available, but many group leaders fail to follow them.[5] Key individuals are absent or late, and participants are unprepared. Meetings are often dominated by senior members or strong personalities, while some participants are reluctant to speak up or to express their true beliefs. Discussion can get stuck on several salient aspects of a problem, rather than covering all aspects of the subject. Decisions may not be reached, and if they are reached, may wind up not being implemented.

> *If you had to identify, in one word, the reason that the human race has not achieved, and never will achieve, its full potential, that word would be meetings.*[6]
>
> Dave Barry, American humorist

Academic studies show that "the order in which people speak has a profound effect on the course of a discussion. Earlier comments are more influential, and they tend to provide a framework within which the discussion occurs."[7] Once that

---

4. For example, Paul B. Paulus and Bernard A. Nijstad, *Group Creativity: Innovation Through Collaboration* (New York: Oxford University Press, 2003).

5. J. Scott Armstrong, "How to Make Better Forecasts and Decisions: Avoid Face-to-Face Meetings," *Foresight* 5 (Fall 2006).

6. Dave Barry, *Dave Barry Turns 50* (Ballantine Books, 1999).

7. James Surowiecki, *The Wisdom of Crowds* (New York: Doubleday, 2004), 184.

framework is in place, discussion tends to center on that framework to the exclusion of other options.

Much research documents that the desire for consensus is an important cause of poor group decisions. Development of a group consensus is usually perceived as success, but, in reality, it is often indicative of failure. Premature consensus is one of the more common causes of suboptimal group performance. It leads to failure to identify or seriously consider alternatives, failure to examine the negative aspects of the preferred position, and failure to consider the consequences that might follow if the preferred position is wrong.[8] This phenomenon is what is commonly called groupthink.

Other problems that are less obvious but no less significant have been documented extensively by academic researchers. It frequently happens that some reasonably satisfactory solution is proposed that all members can agree with, and the discussion is ended without further search to see if there may be a better answer. Such a decision often falls short of the optimum that might be achieved with further inquiry. A phenomenon known as group "polarization" leads, in certain predictable circumstances, to a group decision that is more extreme than the average group member's view prior to the discussion. "Social loafing" is the phenomenon that people working in a group will often expend less effort than if they were working to accomplish the same task on their own. In any of these situations, the result is often an inferior product that suffers from a lack of analytic rigor.

12.4 BENEFITING FROM DIVERSITY

Improvement of group performance requires an understanding of these problems and a conscientious effort to avoid or mitigate them. The literature on small-group performance is virtually unanimous in emphasizing that groups make better decisions when their members bring to the table a diverse set of ideas, opinions, and perspectives. What premature consensus, groupthink, and polarization all have in common is a failure to recognize assumptions and a failure to adequately identify and consider alternative points of view. Laboratory experiments have shown that even a single dissenting opinion, all by itself, makes a group's decisions more nuanced and its decision-making process more rigorous.[9] "The research also shows that these benefits from dissenting opinions occur regardless of whether or not the dissenter is correct. The dissent stimulates a reappraisal

---

8. Charlan J. Nemeth and Brendan Nemeth-Brown, "Better than Individuals? The Potential Benefits of Dissent and Diversity for Group Creativity," in *Group Creativity: Innovation Through Collaboration*, ed. Paul B. Paulus and Bernard A Nijstad (New York: Oxford University Press, 2003), 63–64.

9. Surowiecki, *The Wisdom of Crowds*, 183–184.

of the situation and identification of options that otherwise would have gone undetected."[10]

To be effective, however, dissent must be genuine, not generated artificially as in some applications of the Devil's Advocacy technique.[11] It should also be reasonable. If the person voicing dissenting views is known to the group as a habitual contrarian or maverick, his or her comments run the risk of being dismissed by the group regardless of merit.

Briefly, then, the route to better analysis is to create small groups of analysts who are strongly encouraged by their leader to speak up and express a wide range of ideas, opinions, and perspectives. The use of structured analytic techniques generally ensures that this happens. These techniques guide the dialogue between analysts as they share evidence and alternative perspectives on the meaning and significance of the evidence. Each step in the technique prompts relevant discussion within the team, and such discussion can generate and evaluate substantially more divergent information and new ideas than can a group that does not use such a structured process.

With any heterogeneous group, this reduces the risk of premature consensus, group think, and polarization. Use of a structured technique also sets a clear step-by-step agenda for any meeting where that technique is used. This makes it easier for a group leader to keep a meeting on track to achieve its goal.[12]

12.5 ADVOCACY VS. OBJECTIVE INQUIRY

The desired diversity of opinion is, of course, a double-edged sword, as it can become a source of conflict which degrades group effectiveness.[13] It is not easy to introduce true collaboration and teamwork into a community with a history of organizational rivalry and mistrust. Analysts must engage in inquiry, not advocacy, and they must be critical of ideas but not critical of people.

In a task-oriented team environment, advocacy of a specific position can lead to emotional conflict and reduced team effectiveness. Advocates tend to examine evidence in a biased manner, accepting at face value information that seems to confirm their own point of view and subjecting any contrary evidence to highly critical evaluation. Advocacy is appropriate in a meeting of stakeholders that one is attending for the purpose of representing a specific interest. It is also "an effective

---

10. Nemeth and Nemeth-Brown, "Better than Individuals?" 73.

11. Ibid, 76–78.

12. This paragraph and the previous paragraph express the authors' professional judgment based on personal experience and anecdotal evidence gained in discussion with other experienced analysts. As discussed in chapter 13, there is a clear need for systematic research on this topic and other variables related to the effectiveness of structured analytic techniques.

13. Frances J. Milliken, Caroline A. Bartel, and Terri R. Kurtzberg, "Diversity and Creativity in Work Groups," in *Group Creativity: Innovation Through Collaboration*, ed. Paul B. Paulus and Bernard A Nijstad (New York: Oxford University Press, 2003), 33.

Figure 12.5   Advocacy vs. Inquiry in Small-Group Processes

	Advocacy	Inquiry
Concept of decision making	A contest	Collaborative problem solving
Purpose of discussion	Persuasion and lobbying	Testing and evaluation
Participants' role	Spokespeople	Critical thinkers
Pattern of behavior	Strive to persuade others Defend your position Downplay weaknesses	Present balanced arguments Remain open to alternatives Accept constructive criticism
Minority views	Discouraged or dismissed	Cultivated and valued
Outcome	Winners and losers	Collective ownership

Source: 2009 Pherson Associates, LLC.

method for making decisions in a courtroom when both sides are effectively represented, or in an election when the decision is made by a vote of the people." [14] However, it is not an appropriate method of discourse within a team "when power is unequally distributed among the participants, when information is unequally distributed, and when there are no clear rules of engagement—especially about how the final decision will be made." [15] An effective resolution may be found only through the creative synergy of alternative perspectives.

Figure 12.5 displays the differences between advocacy and the objective inquiry expected from a team member or a colleague. [16] When advocacy leads to emotional conflict, it can lower team effectiveness by provoking hostility, distrust, cynicism, and apathy among team members. On the other hand, objective inquiry, which often leads to cognitive conflict, can lead to new and creative solutions to

---

14. Martha Lagace, "Four Questions for David Garvin and Michael Roberto," *Working Knowledge: A First Look at Faculty Research*, Harvard Business School weekly newsletter, October 15, 2001, http://hbswk.hbs.edu/item/3568.html.

15. Ibid.

16. The table is from David A. Garvin and Michael A. Roberto, "What You Don't Know About Making Decisions," *Working Knowledge: A First Look at Faculty Research*, Harvard Business School weekly newsletter, October 15, 2001, http://hbswk.hbs.edu/item/2544.html.

problems, especially when it occurs in an atmosphere of civility, collaboration, and common purpose.

A team or group using structured analytic techniques is believed to be less vulnerable to these group process traps than is a comparable group doing traditional analysis, because the techniques move analysts away from advocacy and toward inquiry. This idea has not yet been tested and demonstrated empirically, but the rationale is clear. As we have stated repeatedly throughout the eight chapters on structured techniques, these techniques work best when an analyst is collaborating with a small group of other analysts. Just as these techniques provide structure to our individual thought processes, they also provide structure to the interaction of analysts within a small team or group.[17]

Some techniques, such as Key Assumptions Check and Analysis of Competing Hypotheses (ACH), help analysts gain a clear understanding of how and exactly why they disagree. For example, many CIA and FBI analysts report that their preferred use of ACH is to gain a better understanding of the differences of opinion between them and other analysts or between analytic offices. The process of creating an ACH matrix requires identification of the evidence and arguments being used and determining how these are interpreted as either consistent or inconsistent with the various hypotheses. Review of this matrix provides a systematic basis for identification and discussion of differences between two or more analysts. CIA and FBI analysts also note that referring to the matrix helps to depersonalize the argumentation when there are differences of opinion.[18] In other words, ACH can help analysts learn from their differences rather than fight over them, and other structured techniques do this as well. The set of techniques discussed in chapter 10 is intended to stimulate or to resolve *productive* conflict rather than emotional conflict.

12.6 LEADERSHIP AND TRAINING

Considerable research on virtual teaming shows that leadership effectiveness is a major factor in the success or failure of a virtual team.[19] Although leadership usually is provided by a group's appointed leader, it can also emerge as a more distributed peer process and is greatly aided by the use of a trained facilitator (see Figure 12.6). When face-to-face contact is limited, leaders, facilitators, and

---

17. This paragraph expresses our professional judgment based on personal experience and anecdotal evidence gained in discussion with other experienced analysts. As we discuss in chapter 13, there is a clear need for systematic research on this topic and other variables related to the effectiveness of structured analytic techniques.

18. This information was provided by two senior educators in the Intelligence Community.

19. Jonathan N. Cummings, "Leading Groups from a Distance: How to Mitigate Consequences of Geographic Dispersion," in *Leading Groups from a Distance: Consequences of Geographic Dispersion*, ed. Susan Weisband (New York: Routledge, 2007).

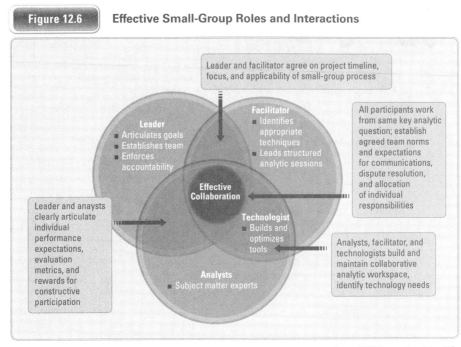

Figure 12.6   **Effective Small-Group Roles and Interactions**

Leader and facilitator agree on project timeline, focus, and applicability of small-group process

Leader
- Articulates goals
- Establishes team
- Enforces accountability

Facilitator
- Identifies appropriate techniques
- Leads structured analytic sessions

All participants work from same key analytic question; establish agreed team norms and expectations for communications, dispute resolution, and allocation of individual responsibilities

Effective Collaboration

Leader and anaysts clearly articulate individual performance expectations, evaluation metrics, and rewards for constructive participation

Technologist
- Builds and optimizes tools

Analysts
- Subject matter experts

Analysts, facilitator, and technologists build and maintain collaborative analytic workspace, identify technology needs

Source: 2009 Pherson Associates, LLC.

team members must compensate by paying more attention than they might otherwise devote to the following tasks:

* Articulating a clear mission, goals, specific tasks, and procedures for evaluating results.

* Defining measurable objectives with milestones and timelines for achieving them.

* Identifying clear and complementary roles and responsibilities.

* Building relationships with and between team members and with stakeholders.

* Agreeing on team norms and expected behaviors.

* Defining conflict resolution procedures.

* Developing specific communication protocols and practices.[20]

---

20. Sage Freechild, "Team Building and Team Performance Management." Originally online at www.phoenixrisingcoaching.com. This article is no longer available online.

As illustrated in Figure 12.6, the interactions between the various types of team participants—whether analyst, leader, facilitator, or technologist—are as important as the individual roles played by each. For example, analysts on a team will be most effective not only when they have subject matter expertise or knowledge that lends a new viewpoint but also when the rewards for their participation are clearly defined by their manager. Likewise, a facilitator's effectiveness is greatly increased when the goals, timeline, and general focus of the project are agreed to with the leader in advance. When roles and interactions are explicitly defined and functioning, the group can more easily turn to the more challenging analytic tasks at hand.

As the Intelligence Community places greater emphasis on interagency collaboration, and more work is done through computer-mediated communications, it becomes increasingly important that analysts be trained in the knowledge, skills, and abilities required for facilitation and management of both face-to-face and virtual team or group meetings, with a strong emphasis on conflict management during such meetings. Training is more effective when it is made available just before the skills and knowledge must be put to use. It is most effective when it is fully integrated into the work process with instructors acting in the roles of coaches, mentors, and facilitators.

An Intelligence Community–wide training program of this sort could provide substantial support to interagency collaboration and the formation of virtual teams. Whenever a new interagency or virtual team or work group is formed, it would be advantageous to ensure that all members have the same training in understanding the pitfalls of group processes, performance expectations, standards of conduct, and conflict resolution procedures. Standardization of this training across the Intelligence Community would accelerate the development of a shared experience and culture and reduce start-up time for any new interagency group.

13

Evaluation of
Structured
Analytic
Techniques

Evaluation of Structured Analytic Techniques

13.1   Establishing Face Validity   [310]

13.2   Limits of Empirical Testing   [312]

13.3   A New Approach to Evaluation   [317]

13.4   Recommended Research Program   [321]

Evaluation of Structured Analytic Techniques

The Intelligence Community has had nearly a decade of experience in using structured analytic techniques, but it has no systematic program for evaluating or validating the effectiveness of these techniques. The absence of hard proof that structured techniques provide better results than unaided expert judgment is often cited by analysts who are reluctant to change their long-established analytic habits.

How can we know that the use of structured analytic techniques does, in fact, provide the claimed benefits for intelligence analysis? There are two approaches to answering this question: logical reasoning and empiricism. The logical reasoning approach starts with an extensive body of psychological research on the limitations of human perception and memory and pitfalls in human thought processes. The impact of these cognitive limitations on intelligence analysis is described in Richards Heuer's book, *Psychology of Intelligence Analysis*. If a structured analytic technique is specifically designed to mitigate or avoid one of the proven problems in human thought processes, and if the technique appears to be successful in doing so, that technique can be said to have face validity. In the next section we discuss a number of such structured techniques and the rationale for their face validity. This logical reasoning creates a strong presumption that the use of structured analytic techniques in general will usually contribute to better analysis, but it does not constitute empirical proof of better analysis.

Another approach to evaluating these techniques is to conduct experiments that compare analyses in which a specific technique is used with analyses in which the technique is not used, and then to judge which approach best meets some criterion for quality of analysis. In theory, such empirical testing can assess the utility, or lack of utility, of any specific technique. In practice, however, it can be very difficult. Our review of a sample of such research found that the results have been of limited value, because the tests did not simulate the conditions in which the techniques are used in the Intelligence Community. This is discussed in the section called "Limits of Empirical Testing."

To examine the effectiveness of structured analytic techniques, we need a new approach that is embedded in the reality of how structured analysis is actually done. The standard practice of conducting empirical experiments to test the accuracy of judgments will not meet many of our needs. The new approach needs to focus on the multiple benefits derived from the use of structured techniques at various stages of an analytic project, not only on the accuracy of an analytic report. And the methodology for evaluating structured techniques needs to include observation, interviews, and surveys as well as experiments. The third section of this chapter, "A New Approach to Evaluation," provides examples of how this approach could be applied to three specific structured techniques. In the final section we present a recommended research program.

13.1 ESTABLISHING FACE VALIDITY

The taxonomy of structured analytic techniques presents each category of structured technique in the context of how it is intended to mitigate or avoid a specific cognitive or group process problem. In other words, each structured analytic technique has face validity because there is a rational reason for expecting it to help mitigate or avoid a recognized problem that can occur when one is doing intelligence analysis. For example, a great deal of research in human cognition during the past sixty years shows the limits of working memory and suggests that one can manage a complex problem most effectively by breaking it down into smaller pieces. That is, in fact, the dictionary definition of analysis,[1] and that is what all the techniques that involve making a list, tree, matrix, diagram, map, or model do. It is reasonable to expect, therefore, that an analyst who uses such tools for organization or visualization of information will in most cases do a better job than an analyst who does not.

Similarly, much empirical evidence suggests that the human mind tends to see what it is looking for and often misses what it is not looking for. This is why it is useful to develop scenarios and indicators of possible future events for which intelligence needs to provide early warning. These techniques can help collectors target needed information, and, for analysts, they prepare the mind to recognize the early signs of significant change.

"Satisficing" is the term Herbert Simon invented to describe the act of selecting the first identified alternative that appears "good enough" rather than

---

1. *Merriam-Webster Online*, www.m-w.com/dictionary/analysis.

evaluating all the likely alternatives and identifying the best one (see chapter 7). Satisficing is a common analytic shortcut that people use in making everyday decisions when there are multiple possible answers. It saves a lot of time when you are making judgments or decisions of little consequence, but it is ill-advised when making judgments or decisions with significant consequences for national security. It seems self-evident that an analyst who deliberately identifies and analyzes alternative hypotheses before reaching a conclusion is more likely to find a better answer than an analyst who does not.

Given the necessary role that assumptions play when making intelligence judgments based on incomplete and ambiguous information, it seems likely that an analyst who uses the Key Assumptions Check technique will, on average, do a better job than an analyst who makes no effort to identify and validate assumptions. There is also extensive empirical evidence that reframing a question helps to unblock the mind and enables one to see other perspectives.

The empirical research on small-group performance is virtually unanimous in emphasizing that groups make better decisions when their members bring to the table a diverse set of ideas, experiences, opinions, and perspectives.[2] Looking at these research findings, one may conclude that the use of any structured technique in a group process is likely to improve the quality of analysis as compared with analysis by a single individual using that technique or by a group that does not use any structured process for eliciting divergent ideas or opinions. The experience of Intelligence Community analysts using the Analysis of Competing Hypotheses (ACH) software—and similar computer-aided analytic tools—in their work provides anecdotal evidence to support this conclusion. One of their goals in using ACH is to gain a better understanding of the differences of opinion with other analysts or between analytic offices.[3] The creation of an ACH matrix requires step-by-step discussion of the evidence and arguments being used and deliberation about how these are interpreted as either consistent or inconsistent with each of the hypotheses. This process takes time, but many analysts apparently believe it is time well spent; they say it saves time in the long run once they have learned this technique.

Randy Pherson, who has conducted ACH exercises with more than 3,000 students in multiple federal agencies, found that students disagree on how to rate the evidence in about 20–30 percent of the cells in a matrix. The differences are usually traced to students interpreting the data differently, bringing different

2. Charlan J. Nemeth and Brendan Nemeth-Brown, "Better than Individuals: The Potential Benefits of Dissent and Diversity for Group Creativity," in *Group Creativity: Innovation Through Collaboration*, ed. Paul B. Paulus and Bernard A. Nijstad (New York: Oxford University Press, 2003), 63–64.

3. This information was provided by a senior Intelligence Community educator, December 2006.

experiences to the table, or simply not considering a key fact that another student points out to them. If the students in these exercises had not engaged their colleagues in a discussion before filling out the matrix, 10–15 percent of the judgments they entered would have been incorrect!

These experiences in teaching ACH to Intelligence Community analysts illustrate how structured techniques can elicit significantly more divergent information when used as a group process. Intelligence Community and law enforcement analysts consider this group discussion the most valuable part of the ACH process. The ACH process does not guarantee a correct judgment, but this anecdotal evidence suggests that ACH does make a significant contribution to better analysis.

13.2 LIMITS OF EMPIRICAL TESTING

Findings from empirical experiments can be generalized to apply to intelligence analysis only if the test conditions match relevant conditions in which intelligence analysis is conducted. There are so many variables that can affect the research results that it is very difficult to control for all or even most of them. These variables include the purpose for which a technique is used, implementation procedures, context of the experiment, nature of the analytic task, differences in analytic experience and skill, and whether the analysis is done by a single analyst or as a group process. All of these variables affect the outcome of any experiment that ostensibly tests the utility of an analytic technique. In a number of readily available examples of research on structured analytic techniques, we identified serious questions about the applicability of the research findings to intelligence analysis.[4] Some of these cases are described in this section.

This problem could largely be resolved if experiments were conducted with intelligence analysts using techniques as they are used within the Intelligence Community to analyze typical intelligence issues. But even if such conditions were met, another obstacle would still remain. The conventional criterion for validating an analytic technique is the accuracy of the answers it provides. However, it is almost impossible, even in retrospect, to judge the accuracy of an intelligence product. This is because intelligence analysis usually contains judgments that cannot be proved true or false within the time frame of an experiment. Intelligence analysis does make forecasts and estimates, but these are usually probablistic judgments conditioned on the continued presence or absence of certain other events or trends.

---

4. One of the best examples of research that does meet this comparability standard is MSgt Robert D. Folker Jr., *Intelligence Analysis in Theater Joint Intelligence Centers: An Experiment in Applying Structured Methods* (Washington, D.C.: Joint Military Intelligence College, 2000).

On the other hand, if an experiment is structured in such a way that the accuracy of the conclusion can be measured, that experiment is probably not using the kinds of incomplete, ambiguous, and potentially deceptive information that intelligence analysts typically work with. Test participants are often asked to perform tasks that are so different from what most experienced analysts ordinarily do that any generalizations relating the experimental results to actual intelligence analysis is questionable. Such findings should not be ignored, but they are not persuasive enough to overturn a strong case for the face validity of a technique. The following examples illustrate the difficulty of conducting experiments in a manner that makes the findings generalizable to intelligence analysis.

Different Purpose or Goal

Many structured analytic techniques can be used for several different purposes, and research findings on the effectiveness of these techniques can be generalized and applied to the Intelligence Community only if the technique is used in the same way and for the same purpose as in the actual practice of the Intelligence Community. For example, Philip Tetlock, in his important book *Expert Political Judgment,* describes two experiments showing that scenario development may not be an effective technique. The experiments compared judgments on a political issue before and after the test subjects prepared scenarios in an effort to gain a better understanding of the issues.[5] The experiments showed that the predictions by both experts and nonexperts were more accurate *before* generating the scenarios; in other words, the generation of scenarios actually *reduced* the accuracy of their predictions. Several experienced analysts have separately cited this finding as evidence that scenario development may not be a useful method for intelligence analysis.[6]

However, Tetlock's conclusions should not be generalized to apply to intelligence analysis, as those experiments tested scenarios as a predictive tool. The Intelligence Community does not use scenarios for prediction. The purpose of scenario development is to describe several outcomes or futures that a decision maker should consider because intelligence is unable to predict a single outcome with reasonable certainty. Another major purpose of scenario development is to identify indicators and milestones for each potential scenario. The indicators and milestones can then be monitored to gain early warning of the direction in which events seem to be heading. Tetlock's experiments did not use scenarios in this way.

---

5. Philip Tetlock, *Expert Political Judgment* (Princeton: Princeton University Press, 2005), 190–202.
6. These judgments have been made in public statements and in personal communications to the authors.

Different Implementation Procedures

There are specific procedures for implementing many structured techniques. If research on the effectiveness of a specific technique is to be applicable to intelligence analysis, the research should use the same implementing procedure(s) for that technique as those used by the Intelligence Community. Use of a different procedure is another limitation on the conclusions that can be drawn from Tetlock's experiments in scenario development. His experiments apparently did not use a structured process for generating the scenarios, whereas Intelligence Community guidance does stipulate a specific structured process. Randy Pherson believes this structured process is what makes the difference between success and failure in developing useful scenarios.

Different Environment

When evaluating the validity of a technique, it is necessary to control for the environment in which the technique is used. If this is not done, the research findings may not always apply to intelligence analysis. For example, it is now conventional wisdom that the effectiveness of a brainstorming session is measured by the quantity of ideas generated. This quantity standard is the metric used when researchers conduct empirical experiments to determine which procedures for collecting, recording, and discussing ideas in a brainstorming session are the most effective. However, the quantity standard is appropriate only when the goal is creativity and the number of possibilities is infinite, such as when generating a new advertising slogan. (The advertising world indeed was the environment in which the brainstorming technique was invented by Alex Osborn in the 1930s.) However, for many intelligence analysis purposes—such as brainstorming to identify key drivers that will influence events five years from now—the quality of ideas may be a better measure of effectiveness than the quantity of ideas. In such cases, the optimal procedures for collecting, recording, and discussing ideas during brainstorming as published in research findings may not be the best procedures for intelligence analysis.

This is by no means intended to suggest that techniques developed for use in other domains should not be used in intelligence analysis. On the contrary, other domains are a productive source of such techniques, but the best way to apply them to intelligence analysis needs to be carefully evaluated.

Misleading Test Scenario

Empirical testing of a structured analytic technique requires developing a realistic test scenario. The test group analyzes this scenario using the structured technique while the control group analyzes the scenario without the benefit of any such technique. The MITRE Corporation conducted an experiment to test the ability of the Analysis of Competing Hypotheses (ACH) technique to prevent confirmation bias.[7] Confirmation bias is the tendency of people to seek information or assign greater weight to information that confirms what they already believe and to underweight or not seek information that supports an alternative belief.

The experimental task was to analyze the relative likelihood of three hypothesized causes of an explosion on the battleship USS *Iowa* in April 1989. Analysts in the test group were asked to read a tutorial on the manual version of ACH. They were then given four rounds of evidence, fifteen items of evidence per round, and asked to assess the relative probability of the three hypotheses after each round. The goal was to determine the extent to which their initial evaluation of the hypotheses was modified in response to the successive rounds of evidence. In other words, did they overweight evidence confirming their initial assessment and underweight contrary evidence? The control group analysts performed the same functions but without any prior ACH training.

The experiment found that ACH did reduce the confirmation bias, but the effect was limited to participants without professional analysis experience. This experiment was interesting and useful for several reasons, but the findings cannot be generalized as applicable to use of ACH by intelligence analysts for two reasons. First, the test group had minimal training or practice in the use of ACH. Second, the test group and the control group were both given at the start of the exercise the three hypotheses to be evaluated, rather than being required to develop the hypotheses themselves. Typically, intelligence analysts do not begin the process of attacking an intelligence problem by developing a full set of hypotheses. Richards Heuer, who developed the ACH methodology, has always believed that a principal benefit of ACH in mitigating confirmation bias is that it does requires analysts to develop a full set of hypotheses before evaluating any of them. The MITRE experiment was constructed in a way that precluded measurement of this benefit of ACH.

Differences in Analytic Experience and Skill

There is a difference between structured techniques in the skill level and amount of training that is required to implement them effectively. For example, Analysis of Competing Hypothesis and the Policy Outcomes Forecasting Model (described in chapter 8) require a moderately high skill level, while structured brainstorming has relatively low skill requirements. When one is evaluating any technique, the level of skill and training required is an important variable. Any empirical testing needs

---

7. Brant A. Cheikes, Mark J. Brown, Paul E. Lehner, and Leonard Adelman, *Confirmation Bias in Complex Analyses* (Bedford, Miss.: MITRE Corporation, October 2004), www.mitre.org/work/tech_papers/tech_papers_04/04_0985/04_0985.pdf.

to control for this variable, which suggests that testing of any medium- to high-skill technique should be done with current or former intelligence analysts, including analysts at different skill levels.

Stanley Feder, a veteran CIA methodologist and author of the Policon/Factions tool (the precursor of the Policy Outcomes Forecasting Model) for assessing political instability, observes that "it took me a year of assisting and then leading analytic sessions using the method before I fully understood the constraints imposed by the assumptions on which the method was based. But one payoff of persistence in using the method was that after a few years of using it I began to see ways in which the method could be applied to a broader domain of questions and provide insights that were of great value to other analysts and to policymakers."[8] This observation led Feder to note that "methods are only tools. In the hands of a novice they can produce ugly, and useless, results. But they can give an experienced 'craftsman' great analytic powers. Applications of a method cannot be evaluated without evaluating the people who were using the method and the ways they were applying it."[9] In other words, an analytic tool is not like a machine that works whenever it is turned on. It is a strategy for achieving a goal. Whether or not one reaches the goal depends in part upon the skill of the person executing the strategy.

Single Analyst or Group Process

Research on small-group performance makes a strong case that a structured technique employed as a group process will be more productive than the same technique used by a single analyst. Although most techniques will provide valuable benefits when used by an individual analyst, research on group processes indicates that they will provide significantly more benefits when used by a small group. The reason is that the group process generates more new or divergent information for the group to consider. Unfortunately, it is far more expensive to research group performance than individual performance while using a specific technique, as the former requires so many more test subjects.

Conclusion

Using empirical experiments to evaluate structured techniques is difficult because the outcome of any experiment is influenced by so many variables. Experiments conducted outside the Intelligence Community typically fail to replicate the important conditions that influence the outcome of analysis within the community.

---

8. Stanley Feder, personal e-mail to Richards Heuer, November 26, 2007.
9. Ibid.

13.3 A NEW APPROACH TO EVALUATION

There is a better way to evaluate structured analytic techniques. In this section we outline a new approach that is embedded in the reality of how analysis is actually done in the Intelligence Community. We then show how this approach might be applied to the analysis of three specific techniques.

Step 1 is to identify what we know, or think we know, about the benefits from using any particular structured technique. This is the face validity as described earlier in this chapter plus whatever analysts believe they have learned from frequent use of a technique. For example, we think we know that ACH provides several benefits that help produce a better intelligence product. A full analysis of ACH would consider each of the following potential benefits:

* It requires analysts to start by developing a full set of alternative hypotheses. This reduces the risk of satisficing.

* It enables analysts to manage and sort evidence in analytically useful ways.

* It requires analysts to try to refute hypotheses rather than to support a single hypothesis. This process reduces confirmation bias and helps to ensure that all alternatives are fully considered.

* It can help a small group of analysts identify new and divergent information as they fill out the matrix, and it depersonalizes the discussion when conflicting opinions are identified.

* It spurs analysts to present conclusions in a way that is better organized and more transparent as to how these conclusions were reached.

* It can provide a foundation for identifying indicators that can be monitored to determine the direction in which events are heading.

* It leaves a clear audit trail as to how the analysis was done.

Step 2 is to obtain evidence to test whether or not a technique actually provides the expected benefits. Acquisition of evidence for or against these benefits is not limited to the results of empirical experiments. It includes structured interviews of analysts, managers, and customers; observations of meetings of analysts as they use these techniques; and surveys as well as experiments.

Step 3 is to obtain evidence of whether or not these benefits actually lead to higher quality analysis. Quality of analysis is not limited to accuracy. Other measures of quality include clarity of presentation, transparency in how the conclusion was reached, and construction of an audit trail for subsequent review, all of which are benefits that might be gained, for example, by use of ACH. Evidence of higher quality might come from independent evaluation of quality standards or interviews of customers receiving the reports. Cost effectiveness, including cost in analyst time as well as money, is another criterion of interest. As stated previously in this book, we claim that the use of a structured technique often saves analysts time in the long run. That claim should also be subjected to empirical analysis.

In the following sections we show how this three-step process might be applied to three other analytic techniques. See Figure 13.3.

Key Assumptions Check

The Key Assumptions Check described in chapter 8 is one of the most important and most commonly used techniques. Its purpose is to make explicit and then to evaluate the assumptions that underlie any specific analytic judgment or analytic approach. The evaluation questions are (1) How successful is the technique in achieving this goal, and (2) How does that improve the quality of analysis? The following is a list of studies that might answer these questions:

  * Survey analysts to determine how often they use a particular technique, their criteria for when to use it, procedures for using it, what they see as the benefits gained from using it, and what impact it had on their report.

  * Compare the quality of a random sample of reports written without having done a Key Assumptions Check with reports written after such a check.

  * Interview customers to determine whether identification of key assumptions is something they want to see in intelligence reports. How frequently do they see such a list?

  * Can a single analyst effectively identify his or her own assumptions, or should this always be done as a small-group process? The answer seems obvious, but it is easy to document the magnitude of the difference with a before-and-after comparison. Analysts are commonly asked to develop their own set of assumptions prior to coming to a meeting to do the Key Assumptions Check. Compare these initial lists with the list developed as a result of the meeting.

  * Observe several groups as they conduct a Key Assumptions Check. Interview all analysts afterward to determine how they perceive their learning experience during the meeting. Did it affect their thinking about the most likely hypothesis? Will their experience make them more likely or less likely to want to use this technique in the future? Conduct an experiment to explore the impact of different procedures for implementing this technique.

  * Research the literature on the impact of assumptions (mental models), both good and bad, on various types of analysis.

Figure 13.3   Three Approaches to Evaluation

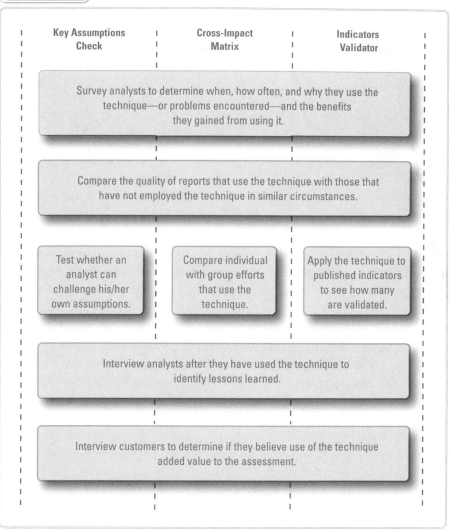

Key Assumptions Check	Cross-Impact Matrix	Indicators Validator
Survey analysts to determine when, how often, and why they use the technique—or problems encountered—and the benefits they gained from using it.		
Compare the quality of reports that use the technique with those that have not employed the technique in similar circumstances.		
Test whether an analyst can challenge his/her own assumptions.	Compare individual with group efforts that use the technique.	Apply the technique to published indicators to see how many are validated.
Interview analysts after they have used the technique to identify lessons learned.		
Interview customers to determine if they believe use of the technique added value to the assessment.		

Source: 2009 Pherson Associates, LLC.

Cross-Impact Matrix

A Cross-Impact Matrix (described in chapter 5) is an old technique that Richards Heuer tested many years ago, but as far as both of us know it is not now being used in the Intelligence Community. It is described in chapter 5. Heuer recommends that it become part of the standard drill early in a project when an analyst is still in a learning mode trying to sort out a complex situation. It is the next logical step after a brainstorming session is used to identify all the relevant factors or variables that may influence a situation. All the factors identified by the brainstorming are put into a Cross-Impact Matrix, which is then used systematically in discussing how each factor influences all other factors to which it is judged to be related in the context of a particular problem. Such a group discussion of how each pair of variables interacts is an enlightening learning experience and a good basis on which to build further analysis and ongoing collaboration.

Cross-Impact Matrix is a simple technique with obvious benefits, but like any technique its utility can and should be tested. There are several viable ways to do that:

* Interview or survey analysts after the cross-impact discussion to gain their judgment of its value as a learning exercise.

* Ask each analyst individually to analyze the interrelationships among the various factors prior to a cross-impact discussion. Then compare these individual efforts with the group effort. This is expected to show the benefits of the group process.

* Develop a scenario and conduct an experiment. Compare the conclusions and quality of a report prepared by one team that was unaware of the concept of a Cross-Impact Matrix with that of another team that was instructed to use this technique as a basis for discussion. Is the analysis prepared by the team that used the Cross-Impact Matrix more complete and thorough than the analysis by the other team?

Indicators Validator

The Indicators Validator described in chapter 6 is a new technique developed by Randy Pherson to test the power of a set of indicators to provide early warning of future developments, such as which of several potential scenarios seems to be developing. It uses a matrix similar to an ACH matrix with scenarios listed across the top and indicators down the left side. For each combination of indicator and scenario, the analyst rates on a five-point scale the likelihood that this indicator will or will not be seen if that scenario is developing. This rating measures the diagnostic value of each indicator or its ability to diagnose which scenario is becoming most likely.

It is often found that indicators have little or no value because they are consistent with multiple scenarios. The explanation for this phenomenon is that when analysts are identifying indicators, they typically look for indicators that are consistent with the scenario they are concerned about identifying. They don't think about the value of an indicator being diminished if it is also consistent with other hypotheses.

The Indicators Validator was developed to meet a perceived need for analysts to better understand the requirements for a good indicator. Ideally, however, the need for this technique and its effectiveness should be tested before all analysts working with indicators are encouraged to use it. Such testing might be done as follows:

* Check the need for the new technique. Select a sample of intelligence reports that include an indicators list and apply the Indicators Validator to each indicator on the list. How often does this test identify indicators that have been put forward despite their having little or no diagnostic value?

* Do a before-and-after comparison. Identify analysts who have developed a set of indicators during the course of their work. Then have them apply the Indicators Validator to their work and see how much difference it makes.

13.4 RECOMMENDED RESEARCH PROGRAM

Steven Rieber and Neil Thomason recommended in 2005 the creation of a National Institute for Analytic Methods to improve intelligence analysis by conducting empirical research to learn which methods work best. They support this recommendation by pointing out that "the opinions of experts regarding which methods work may be misleading or seriously wrong."[10] That observation is true. It often happens that things are not what they appear to be, and many research efforts to correct for cognitive biases have been unsuccessful.

A 2005 RAND Corporation study by Gregory Treverton and C. Bryan Gabbard concludes that "the analytic community badly needs a common focal point for assessing and developing tradecraft." Treverton and Gabbard state further that this focal point "probably should be a virtual center, perhaps managed by outside consultants, not a bricks-and-mortar operation. Ultimately, that virtual center might become part of a National Intelligence University that is both virtual and physical. Or, the community might delegate one agency or school as the lead."[11]

10. Steven Rieber and Neil Thomason, "Creation of a National Institute for Analytic Methods," *Studies in Intelligence* 49, no. 4 (2005).

11. Gregory F. Treverton and C. Bryan Gabbard, *Assessing the Tradecraft of Intelligence Analysis*, RAND Corporation Technical Report (Santa Monica, Calif.: RAND, 2008).

An organizational unit with Intelligence Community–wide responsibilities for research on analytic tradecraft is certainly needed. We are very skeptical, however, about the benefits of establishing either a national institute or a virtual center managed by consultants. The prior history of research to improve intelligence analysis would argue that either of those options is likely to serve primarily as a magnet for expensive contract proposals and have only a marginal impact, if any, on how the average analyst does his or her job.

Nancy Dixon recently conducted a study for the Defense Intelligence Agency on the "lessons learned problem" across the Intelligence Community and within the DIA specifically. This study confirmed a disconnect between the so-called lessons learned and the implementation of these lessons. Dixon found that "the most frequent concern expressed across the IC is the difficulty of getting lessons implemented." She attributes this to two major factors:

> First, those responsible for producing lessons are seldom accountable for the implementation of what has been learned…. Under the best of circumstances this handoff of findings from studies and reports to ownership by operations is notoriously difficult to accomplish.

> Secondly, most lessons learned efforts lack the initial identification of a specific target audience…. Without a pre-designated mutually agreed upon target audience for the lessons, recommendations necessarily lack context that would otherwise make them actionable.[12]

If the research that we recommended in the previous section of this chapter is to be done effectively and have a significant effect on how analysis is actually done, we believe it should be conducted by an operational component within the Intelligence Community, or work in close collaboration with such an operational component that has some responsibility for implementing its findings. We make two recommendations:

＊ The Director of National Intelligence should form within the Office of the Deputy for Analysis a center for analytic tradecraft that has broad responsibility for improving the quality of intelligence analysis. One principal responsibility of this center should be research to test the validity and value added of existing analytic techniques and to develop new techniques as needed. A second major

---

12. Nancy Dixon, "The Problem and the Fix for the US Intelligence Agencies' Lessons Learned," July 1, 2009, www.nancydixonblog. com/2009/07/the-problem-and-the-fix-for-the-us-intelligence-agencies-lessons-learned.html.

function should be to support the creation of tradecraft cells throughout the Intelligence Community and then have responsibility for guiding and assisting them as needed. We have in mind a proliferation of tradecraft cells comparable to those already in operation within the CIA. The new center for analytic tradecraft, or whatever it might be called, should also be responsible for establishing and managing an IC-wide knowledge management system for the creation, capture, storage, and sharing of lessons learned about the use of various analytic methods and techniques. It should also help and encourage analytic "communities of interest" as needed, for example, ensuring that these communities have appropriate technical support.

∗ The DNI should also create a position on the National Intelligence Council (NIC) that might be called a vice chair for analytic tradecraft. The vice chair should oversee and assist in the appropriate collaboration and use of appropriate methods or techniques in all analytic projects for which the NIC has oversight. It may be advisable for the NIC's new vice chair for analytic tradecraft to be dual-hatted, also assuming the role of deputy chief of the new center for analytic tradecraft. This would ensure that the new center would remain attuned to the NIC's analytic needs. The vice chair should also manage an after-action review of lessons learned after each major NIC project, basing the review on input from all who contributed to the project. Dixon makes a strong case that organizational learning should be embedded in the workflow process.[13]

At present, structured analytic techniques are generally used within a single office or agency rather than as an element of interagency collaboration. Implementation of the recommendations we describe in this chapter, combined with increasing activity on A-Space, would put structured analysis at the forefront of interagency collaboration.

13. Ibid.

14 Vision of the Future

14 Vision of the Future

14.1 Structuring the Data   [328]

14.2 Analyzing the Data   [331]

14.3 Conclusions Drawn from This Analysis   [339]

14.4 Imagining the Future: 2015   [340]

CHAPTER 14

Vision of the Future

The Intelligence Community is pursuing several paths in its efforts to improve the quality of intelligence analysis. One of these paths is the increased use of structured analytic techniques, and this book is intended to encourage and support that effort. The Director of National Intelligence's *Vision 2015* includes the statement that, in 2015, "Analysts will routinely employ advanced analytic techniques, including scenario-based analysis, alternative analysis, and systems thinking. The move toward extensive use of data, tools, and modeling is at the heart of collaborative analytics."[1] *Vision 2015* also foresees more "rigor in our analytic approaches to complexity."[2]

To assess the likelihood of the DNI's vision being realized, the first part of this final chapter is a case study that employs a new technique called Complexity Manager (chapter 11) to address the following questions:

* What is the prognosis for the use of structured analytic techniques in 2015? Will this relatively new approach gain traction and be used with much greater frequency and by all elements of the Intelligence Community? Or will its use remain at current levels, or will it atrophy?

* What forces are supporting increased use of structured analysis, and what opportunities are available to support these forces?

* What obstacles are hindering the increased use of structured analysis, and how might these obstacles be overcome?

The final section of this chapter supposes that it is now the year 2015 and the use of structured analytic techniques is widespread. It presents our vision of what has happened to make this a reality and how the use of structured analytic techniques has transformed the way intelligence analysis is done.

---

1. *Vision 2015: A Globally Networked and Integrated Intelligence Enterprise* (Washington, D.C.: Director of National Intelligence, 2008), 13.
2. Ibid., 9.

The Complexity Manager technique being used here was described in chapter 11, "Decision Support." For the convenience of readers, the mechanics of that technique are repeated here before we describe the specific application of this technique to the growth of structured analytic techniques. Richards Heuer developed the Complexity Manager as a *very* simplified combination of two long-established futures analysis methods, Cross-Impact Analysis and System Dynamics. It is designed to be used by the average intelligence analyst who is not trained to use such advanced, quantitative techniques.

There is reason to expect that the Complexity Manager will, in many cases, provide much of the benefit one could gain from a more sophisticated computer modeling and simulation without the substantial time and cost usually required for such a project. This is because the benefits come from reducing a problem to its fundamentals in a manner that enables the average analyst to deal with a higher level of complexity. Complexity Manager identifies the relevant variables, assesses interactions among the variables, assigns a weight to each interaction, and then focuses on those variables that are changing or could be changed. These are the things that Complexity Manager does, and they are also the initial steps in developing a computer model and simulation. As we noted in chapter 11, modeling and simulation experts report that the most important insights in their work often come from these initial steps.

Since complexity analysis is itself complex, even in its most simple form as presented here, we request your patience as you read this case study.

14.1 STRUCTURING THE DATA

The analysis for the case study starts with a brainstormed list of variables that will impact, or be impacted by, the extent to which the use of structured analytic techniques increases during the coming five years. The first variable listed here is the target variable, followed by nine other variables related to it.

A. Increased use of structured analytic techniques

B. DNI's promotion of information sharing, interagency collaboration, and structured analytic techniques

C. Availability of technical infrastructure for sharing and collaboration

D. Generational change among intelligence analysts

E. Availability and depth of analytic support for structured analytic techniques

F. Reduction of budget for analysis

G. Change in customer needs and preferences

H. Research on effectiveness of structured techniques

I. Analysts' perception of time pressure

J. Lack of openness to change among senior analysts and managers

The next step in Complexity Manager is to put these ten variables into a Cross-Impact Matrix. This is a tool for the systematic description of the two-way interaction between each pair of variables. Each pair of variables is assessed by asking the following question: Does this variable impact the paired variable in a manner that will contribute either to increased or decreased use of structured analytic techniques in 2015? The completed matrix is shown in Figure 14.1. This is the same matrix shown in chapter 11. The following paragraphs describe how the matrix was created.

Again, the goal of this analysis is to assess the likelihood of a substantial increase in the use of structured analytic techniques by 2015, while identifying any side effects that might be associated with such an increase. That is why increased use of structured analytic techniques is the lead variable, variable A, which forms the first column and top row of the matrix. The letters across the top of the matrix are abbreviations of the same variables listed down the left side.

To fill in the matrix, one starts with *column* A to assess the impact of each of the variables listed down the left side of the matrix on the frequency of use of structured analysis. This exercise provides an overview of all the variables that will impact positively or negatively on the use of structured analysis. Next, one fills in *row* A across the top of the matrix. This shows the reverse impact—the impact of increased use of structured analysis on the other variables listed across the top of the matrix. Here one identifies side effects. Does the growing use of structured analytic techniques impact any of these other variables in ways that one needs to be aware of?

The remainder of the matrix is then completed in a similar manner, one variable at a time, while also identifying and making notes on potentially significant secondary effects. A secondary effect is when one variable strengthens or weakens another variable, which in turn impacts on or is impacted by structured analytic techniques.

The plus and minus signs in the matrix show the nature of the impact or influence that one variable has on the other variable with which it is paired. For example, a plus sign signifies a positive impact on the other variable, while a minus sign

Figure 14.1   Variables Affecting the Future Use of Structured Analysis

	A	B	C	D	E	F	G	H	I	J
A Increased use of Structured Analytic Techniques		+			+	–	+	+	+	–
B DNI promotes sharing, collaboration	+		+	+	+	–	+	+	+	–
C Availability of technical infrastructure	+	+		+	+		+	+	+	+
D Generational change of analysts	+	+	+		+			+	–	–
E Availability/depth of analytic support	+−	+−	+				+	+	–	–
F Reduced budget for analysis	−	–	–	–	–			−		–
G Change in customer needs/ preferences	+−	+			+			+	–	–
H Research on effectiveness of Structured Analytic Techniques	+−	+−			+		+		+−	+−
I Analyst perception of time pressure	–	–								+
J Lack of openness to change among senior analysts and managers	–	−							+	

Reading the Matrix: The cells in each *row* show the impact of the variable represented by that row on each of the variables listed across the top of the matrix. The cells in each *column* show the impact of each variable listed down the left side of the matrix on the variable represented by the column.

Direction and magnitude of the impact:

− strong negative impact
– medium negative impact
- weak negative impact

= strong positive impact
+ medium positive impact
+ weak positive impact

Combination of + and - means impact could go either direction.
Empty cell = no impact

signifies a negative impact. The varying size of the plus or minus sign signifies the strength of the positive or negative impact on a three-point scale. The large plus or minus sign shows a strong positive or negative impact, while the middle and smaller sizes indicate a medium or weak impact. If a variable has no influence or only trivial influence on the other variable, that cell is left blank. If one variable might change in a way that could reverse the impact from positive to negative, or vice versa, the plus and minus signs are both entered to show that the impact could go either way.

The relationship between each pair of variables can also be shown with the letters *P* and *M* for plus and minus, and the level of impact that one variable has on the other with the numbers 3, 2, and 1 rather than by varying the size of the plus and minus signs. This may be preferable when first populating the matrix with these judgments about direction and impact of each relationship, especially if you want to enter information about whether the impact is positive or negative before making the more difficult judgments about the strength of the impact that one variable has on another. We use plus and minus signs in Figure 14.1 because they look nicer and take up less room, making it easier to fit the graphic on the book page.

The principal benefit of the Cross-Impact Matrix is gained in the act of creating it. It requires the analyst to think about and record all of these interactions, and the matrix then serves as a memory jogger throughout the analysis. The matrix enables the analyst to mentally process a much higher level of complexity than would be possible if the analysis were unstructured. It is also a reminder to consider the side effects of every change. When the matrix is created by a team, which is the preferred process, there will be differences of opinion about some of the ratings. If these differences are not resolved during the group discussion, they can be noted in the written summary about that interaction.

The Complexity Manager does not involve any mathematical calculation of the likelihood or magnitude of change in any particular variable or the probability of any specific outcome. Adding these elements would require a more careful wording of the variables, a more systematic procedure for assigning values, sophisticated mathematical calculations, and software for visualization of complex interactions. Again, this technique is for use by the average intelligence analyst who is not trained in quantitative analysis. A full System Dynamics Analysis may be preferable when time and resources are available for that.

14.2 ANALYZING THE DATA

The following sections discuss each of the ten variables, including how each variable impacts other variables and how other variables impact the variable being discussed. This assessment of each interaction becomes the database that the analyst subsequently utilizes to identify alternative outcomes and draw conclusions. The goal of this analysis is to foresee what future progress might be expected in the use of structured analytic techniques. We also take this opportunity to identify opportunities to support increased use of such techniques and to identify obstacles to use of these techniques that might be overcome.

A. Increased Use of Structured Analytic Techniques

Impacts on Other Variables: The effects of increased use of structured analysis on each of the other variables are shown in row A of the matrix. Increased use of structured analysis provides strong support to the DNI policy for increased information sharing and collaboration because structured analysis is the process by which much collaboration is done. It increases the pressure to provide more support for analysts using structured analysis (E) and for research on the effectiveness of these techniques (H). It may have a little effect on reducing pressures to cut funding for analysis (F). To the extent that structured analysis is perceived as increasingly successful, it may diminish the influence of two variables that discourage use of structured analysis, analysts' perception of time pressure (I) and lack of openness to change among senior analysts and managers (J).

Impacts on This Variable: The impact of other variables on the use of structured analysis is shown in column A of the matrix. Variables with a strong favorable impact on the use of structured analysis include the DNI's promotion of information sharing and interagency collaboration (B), availability of a new technical infrastructure for sharing and collaboration (C), and generational change among intelligence analysts (D). Although the DNI has developed and is supporting the use of collaborative information sharing systems such as Intellipedia and Share-Point, its influence on the use of structured techniques is potentially far greater once the A-Space platform for interagency information sharing and collaboration becomes fully operational.

Availability and depth of analytic support for structured analysis (E) and research that validates the asserted benefits of structured analysis (H) have a potentially strong favorable impact on the use of structured analysis, but the impact would clearly be unfavorable if no action is taken to enhance the support and assess the effectiveness of these techniques. The fact that the impact of these variables could go either way is shown in the matrix by the combination of both plus and minus signs. Change in customer needs and preferences (G) could also go in either direction, as discussed under that variable.

The dominant threat to further growth in the use of structured analysis is clearly the anticipated reduction of the budget for analysis (F). Because of the increase in the national debt, due to the wars in Iraq and Afghanistan and continuing after effects of the 2008 financial collapse, some budget reductions are expected throughout the Intelligence Community. Any failure to fund support for structured analysis (E) would have a significant adverse impact on the growth of structured analysis. Budget limitations could also preclude the research needed to assess the benefits of structured techniques (H), and that loss would hinder any increase in structured analysis.

Analysts' concerns about the multiple pressures on their time (I) and lack of openness to change by senior analysts and managers (J) discourage the use of structured analysis. These are both ranked as a medium negative rather than a strong negative in the matrix because, at least at some agencies, the use of structured techniques has grown despite these factors. In other words, these are obstacles to be overcome, but they are not show stoppers, and there is no indication that either of them is getting stronger.

B. DNI's Promotion of Information Sharing, Interagency Collaboration, and Structured Analytic Techniques

Impacts on Other Variables: DNI support of information sharing and collaboration strongly supports the use of structured analytic techniques (A), as these techniques are the process by which much collaboration occurs. However, the greatest impact of DNI policies on the use of structured analytic techniques is indirect, through its support and funding of the technical infrastructure for sharing and collaboration (C). The A-Space collaboration platform should enhance the effectiveness of DNI policies for promoting information sharing, collaboration, and use of structured analytic techniques. The DNI support for sharing and collaboration supports the social networking practices of the new generation of analysts (D) and has most of the same strongly favorable impact on other variables as that of increased use of structured analysis (A).

Impacts on This Variable: Increased use of structured analysis (A), availability of technical infrastructure (C) and generational change (D) all have a strongly favorable impact on the DNI effort to promote increased information sharing and collaboration. However, reduction of budget resources (F) is a significant threat to this DNI goal.

C. Availability of Technical Infrastructure for Sharing and Collaboration

Impacts on Other Variables: A-Space is a common workspace for the Intelligence Community that enables analysts in different agencies to share information and collaborate across organizational borders. A-Space has encountered delays; so to date it has only limited effect on the use of structured analysis. This analysis assumes that use of A-Space will grow steadily over the coming years.

The ratings in row C of the matrix reflect the transformational influence that this platform for interagency communication will have on the use of structured analysis (A), enabling the implementation of DNI policy on information sharing and collaboration (B) and enabling the new generation of analysts to use their social networking skills to support closer collaboration (D). As discussed later in this chapter under the section on changes in customer needs and preferences (G), A-Space may fundamentally change the relationship between analysts and their customers. It might also undercut the two variables that are obstacles to increased use of structured analysis—analysts' concern about the pressures on their time (I) and the lack of openness to change by some senior analysts and managers.

Impacts on This Variable: As shown in column C of the matrix, the main variable with a positive impact on availability of the new technical infrastructure (C) is DNI policy support for sharing and collaboration (B). That policy is driving the development of this technical infrastructure, but the new technical infrastructure also gets firm support from pressures generated by the new generation of analysts (D).

Two factors could conceivably undermine the benefits anticipated from A-Space. One is the anticipated budget cuts (F) if these are so severe as to interfere with the full development of this system. The other is the boomerang effect that could follow if a series of major espionage cases shows that the security costs of increased information sharing may be greater than its benefits. This low-probability scenario is not included in the matrix, but it cannot be entirely discounted.

D. Generational Change among Intelligence Analysts

Impacts on Other Variables: The incoming younger generation of analysts has grown up with the Internet and, more recently, with MySpace, FaceBook, Linked-In, instant messaging, texting, wikis, and blogs. This generation has already had an impact by forcing improvements in technical infrastructure such as Intellipedia (C). As the generation of analysts that is dependent on social networking and instant communications becomes more dominant, the analytic community will become increasingly amenable to sharing of information and expectant of interagency collaboration (B). By 2015, this could have a very favorable impact on collaboration, including the use of structured analytic techniques as a collaborative process.

Impacts on This Variable: There is a positive feedback loop between generational change (D) and DNI policies (B) and enhancements of the technical infrastructure (C). The three variables all support each other, thus strengthening each of them.

E. Availability and Depth of Analytic Support for Structured Analysis

Impacts on Other Variables: This variable includes several activities and programs that for the convenience of discussion we have combined into a single variable. It includes on-the-job-mentoring and coaching of analysts in the use of the techniques, facilitation of team projects, and an online knowledge management system in addition to training classes. Most agencies provide some classroom training. The CIA has formed embedded tradecraft cells for on-the-job mentoring and facilitation in the use of structured analytic techniques. Other agencies, including the National Geospatial-Intelligence Agency, the Department of Homeland Security, and the Office of Naval Intelligence, also provide some coaching and facilitation support. The CIA initiative has been successful, and it is difficult to imagine more widespread collaborative use of structured analysis without this type of support becoming available in other major agencies. That support plays an important role in helping analysts overcome the initial inertia and uncertainty associated with doing something different from their past practices.

Increased on-the-job mentoring and facilitation of team projects would have a strong favorable impact on the use of structured analysis and collaboration (A, B). An Intelligence Community–wide knowledge management system to share lessons learned or provide other online support would surely broaden the use of structured analytic techniques.

Impacts on This Variable: The matrix ratings for this variable include both medium and strong ratings that are both positive and negative, indicating that the impact of this variable can be either advantageous or detrimental to other variables, depending upon whether analytic support for structured analysis is increased or decreased. What happens with respect to analytic support for structured analysis will be a telling indicator of the direction in which events are moving.

The biggest threat to the continuation and expansion of the support structure for structured techniques is a cut in the budget for intelligence analysis (F). If the support structure is not expanded, especially to other agencies in addition to the CIA, the chances for a significant increase in the use of structured techniques as a common ground for interagency collaboration is significantly diminished (A, B).

F. Reduction of Budget Resources for Analysis

Impacts on Other Variables: With the serious budget deficits resulting from the financial crisis of 2008 and the wars in Iraq and Afghanistan, the Intelligence Community's budget is expected to diminish. How much might be cut from analysis versus operations and administration is uncertain. If these cuts adversely affect funding of the technical infrastructure for sharing and collaboration (C), availability and depth of analytic support for structured analytic techniques (E), or research on the effectiveness of structured analytic techniques (H), the adverse impact on the growth of structured analysis could be significant. For example, elimination or reduction of the tradecraft cells and support for facilitation of structured analysis at any agency would have a significant adverse impact. So would the inability to initiate funding for services at agencies lacking such services at present; these will become even more necessary after the A-Space platform becomes fully available and collaboration becomes more widespread.

Impacts on This Variable: One might hope that the benefits to be gained from structured analytic techniques, especially when combined with DNI promotion of information sharing and collaboration (B) and the transformative impact of technical infrastructure for sharing and collaboration (C) may reduce the likelihood of these programs being impaired by budget reductions. However, that is a hope, not a forecast.

G. Change in Customer Needs and Preferences

Impacts on Other Variables: Changes in focus or priority on the types of analytic products that are needed can have a significant influence on the use of structured analytic techniques. Historically, the priorities and preferences have cycled back and forth over the years depending, in part, on the style of presidential leadership and at what point the administration is located in its four-year cycle. A new administration is more likely to ask strategic and estimative questions than one that has been in power for three years. One might speculate that President Barack Obama's administration will have a continuing interest in substantial analytic papers on fundamental issues. Such an interest might have a supportive impact on the use of structured analytic techniques (A), DNI policies to promote information sharing and collaboration (B), availability of analytic support for structured techniques (E), and research on the effectiveness of structured techniques (H).

Impacts on This Variable: One side effect of A-Space and the use of structured analytic techniques as a basis for online interagency collaboration is that they create the potential for fundamental change in the analyst-customer relationship. The customer might request a report that uses a specific policy support technique, such as Complexity Manager, Analysis of Competing Hypotheses, or a scenario technique with indicators to monitor which future is emerging. Such a project could be worked in a controlled access compartment of A-Space. A decision maker, such as a senior State Department official or an analyst in the department's intelligence arm, the Bureau on Intelligence and Research, might request access to observe or to participate in such an analysis as it evolves online.

The use of Intellipedia or A-Space combined with structured analytic techniques might even change the definition of an intelligence "product." An ongoing project that tracks a development of interest over time might never need to be finalized as a written report. It might simply be available online as needed by anyone with approved access. Those on the access list might automatically receive e-mail notification whenever there is a significant update. This availability of access might apply, for example, to a group project monitoring indicators of alternative scenarios or an analyst tracking the development of a weapons system in a foreign country. Any interested customers, or an intelligence officer supporting that customer, might be approved for observer status so that the latest information can be viewed whenever desired.

H. Extent to Which Benefits of Structured Techniques Are Proven

Impacts on Other Variables: Analysts who do not use structured analysis often justify their decision by claiming there is no hard evidence that these techniques improve analysis. It is true that little has been done to validate empirically the utility of these techniques as used in intelligence analysis, to formally assess the impact on the workload of analysts using these techniques or their supervisors, or to conduct systematic customer evaluation of products that have used structured techniques. This absence of proof of effectiveness makes it harder to "sell" analysts on the use of these techniques, especially analysts who claim they do not have enough time to use structured analytic techniques (I).

The current situation supports the status quo. Failure to fund such research raises questions about the effectiveness of structured techniques (A) and about the value of programs that provide support to analytic techniques (E). There is good reason to expect, however, that research would document the effectiveness of many structured techniques and would provide a major boost to the use of structured techniques throughout the Intelligence Community. Hence the matrix ratings for variable H include both pluses and minuses—the impact could go either way.

Impacts on This Variable: A reduced budget for analysis (F) may have a significant adverse impact on any research program to evaluate the effectiveness of structured analytic techniques.

I. Analysts' Perception of Time Pressure

Impacts on Other Variables: Most intelligence analysts are constantly multitasking and under time pressure to meet deadlines. "I don't have time to use structured techniques" is a common refrain. The experience of many analysts who have learned how to use structured techniques is that these techniques actually save time rather than cost time. But those analysts who have not used the structured approach are unlikely to be convinced that it saves time until that claim is documented by systematic research and the results of this research are widely distributed. The argument that it does save time is twofold. First, there are many structured techniques that take very little time at all. Second, structuring the analysis gives it a clear direction, and the increased rigor involved usually means that less time is spent in editing the original draft and coordination is faster. In other words, the structured process helps analysts get it right the first time, thus saving time in the long run as well as producing better products.

In some offices, the concern about time pressure is enhanced by a perception that promotions tend to be based more on quantity of analytic products than on quality. Quantity is easier to measure and thus a more "objective" standard. Analysts who believe they don't have time to use structured analytic techniques may regard such techniques as not career enhancing, because they would have fewer products to their credit. Agencies that effectively promote and support the use of structured techniques are creating incentives for analysts to seek quality as well as quantity. For example, some analysts now use structured techniques because they see them as a means to get ahead in their careers.

This variable has a direct adverse impact on the frequency of use of structured techniques (A) and an indirect impact on the availability of analytic support for structured techniques (E).

Impacts on This Variable: Favorable findings from a research program on the substantive effectiveness, and the cost and time efficiency, of structured analytic techniques (H) would significantly diminish the influence of this variable. Several other variables are also expected to gradually erode the ranks of those who say, "I don't have time to use structured techniques." These include the increased use of structured analysis (A), increased availability of support for analysts using structured analysis (E), growing influence over time of the new generation of analysts (D), and perhaps changes in customer needs and preferences (G).

J. Lack of Openness to Change among Senior Analysts and Management

Impacts on Other Variables: Long-standing analytic habits that come naturally and are ingrained in the organizational culture are not changed by fiat from on high or by a few days or few weeks of training. The cultural heritage of traditional analysis done in independent agencies is a strong obstacle to spreading the use of structured techniques to other agencies (A) and to interagency collaboration (B). These habits are reinforced by the alleged lack of time needed for analysts to use the techniques and analysts' concerns about promotion based on quantity rather than quality (I).

Although many senior personnel are strongly supportive of structured analytic techniques, quite a few are unfamiliar with these tradecraft tools and perhaps are reluctant to change the analytic culture that enabled them to achieve a senior position. They may be concerned that using, or managing analysts who are using, techniques they are not familiar with will put them at a disadvantage.

Impacts on This Variable: The strength of this variable will be weakened over time by the gradual advancement of a younger generation trained in structured analysis, but that evolution will still be at a fairly early stage in 2015. Favorable research results on the effectiveness of structured analytic techniques might help to change the views of those who are still most comfortable with traditional analysis.

14.3 CONCLUSIONS DRAWN FROM THIS ANALYSIS

Using the information about the individual variables, we can draw some conclusions about the system as a whole. We will focus on those variables that are changing, or that have the potential to change, and that have the greatest impact on other significant variables.

The principal drivers of the system—and indeed the variables with the most cross-impact on other variables as shown in the matrix—are the extent to which the Intelligence Community, led by the Office of the Director of National Intelligence, adopts a culture of sharing and collaboration and the extent to which A-Space is widely accepted and used as a medium for interagency collaboration. These drivers provide strong support to structured analysis through their endorsement of and support for collaboration, and structured analysis reinforces them in turn by providing an optimal process through which collaboration occurs.

A fourth variable, the new generation of analysts accustomed to social networking, is strongly supportive of information sharing and collaboration and therefore indirectly supportive of structured analytic techniques. This new generation is important, because it means time is not neutral. In other words, with the new generation, time is now on the side of change. The interaction of these four variables, all reinforcing each other and moving in the same direction, is sufficient to signal the direction in which the future is headed.

Other variables play an important role. They identify opportunities to facilitate or expedite the change, or they present obstacles that need to be minimized. The speed and ease of the change throughout the Intelligence Community will be significantly influenced by the support, or lack of support, for structured techniques and for collaboration in the form of tradecraft cells for on-the-job mentoring, facilitators to assist in team or group processes using structured techniques, and a knowledge management system for recording lessons learned and for self-learning. A research program on the effectiveness of structured techniques is needed to optimize their use and to counter the opposition from those who "don't have the time to use structured techniques" or who are uncomfortable using the techniques.

The odds seem to favor a fundamental change in how analysis is done. However, any change is far from guaranteed, because the outcome depends upon three assumptions, any one of which, if it turned out to be wrong, would preclude the desired outcome. One is the assumption that budgets for analysis during the next few years will be sufficient to provide tradecraft cells or collaboration support cells, facilitators, a knowledge management system, research on the effectiveness of structured analytic techniques, and other support for the learning and use of structured analysis throughout the Intelligence Community. A second assumption is that Intelligence Community managers will have the wisdom and incentives to allocate the necessary personnel, funding, and training to support collaboration and a broader use of structured techniques across the community. A third assumption is that A-Space will be successful and widely adopted.

14.4 IMAGINING THE FUTURE: 2015

Imagine it is now 2015. Our three assumptions have turned out to be accurate, and collaboration in the use of structured analytic techniques is now widespread. What has happened to make this outcome possible, and how has it transformed the way intelligence analysis is done in 2015? This is our vision of what could be happening by that date.

The use of A-Space has been growing for the past five years. Younger analysts in particular have embraced it in addition to Intellipedia as a channel for secure collaboration with their colleagues working on related topics in other offices and agencies. Analysts in different geographic locations arrange to meet as a group from time to time, but most of the ongoing interaction is accomplished via collaborative tools such as A-Space, communities of interest, and Intellipedia.

Structured analytic techniques are a major part of the process by which information is shared and analysts in different units work together toward a common goal. There is a basic set of techniques and critical thinking skills that collaborating teams or groups commonly use at the beginning of most projects to establish a common foundation for their communication and work together. This includes Virtual Brainstorming to identify a list of relevant variables to be tracked and considered; Cross-Impact Matrix as a basis for discussion and learning from each other about the relationships between key variables; and Key Assumptions Check to discuss assumptions about how things normally work in the topic area of common interest. Judgments about the cross-impacts between variables and the key assumptions are drafted collaboratively in a wiki. This process establishes a common base of knowledge and understanding about a topic of interest. It also identifies at an early stage of the collaborative process any potential differences of opinion, ascertains gaps in available information, and determines which analysts are most knowledgeable about various aspects of the project.

The National Intelligence Council (NIC) has become a leader in the use of structured analytic techniques, as most of its products are of a type that benefits from the use of these techniques. National Intelligence Officers (NIOs) and several DNI Mission Managers began back in 2010 to take on increasing responsibility for overseeing the application of analytic tradecraft. This effort received a major boost when two analysts in the Exceptional Analyst Program published papers establishing the validity of two widely used techniques—the Key Assumptions Check and Indicators Validator. The ability of individual NIOs and Mission Managers to perform this new aspect of their job varied considerably, and some new appointees still came into the NIC with no experience using structured analytic techniques. In 2011, a new position was created under the Director of National Intelligence with the title Vice Chair for Analytic Tradecraft to oversee the use of appropriate tradecraft in all major Intelligence Community analytic papers and projects, including National Intelligence Estimates. The new Vice Chair also became responsible for oversight and improvement of the overall process by which NIC analytic reports are produced. This includes an after-action review of lessons learned after each major DNI project.[3]

By 2012, all the principal elements of the Intelligence Community had created tradecraft or collaboration support cells in their analytic components. Analysts with experience in using structured techniques are now helping other analysts overcome their uncertainty when using a technique for the first time; helping others decide which techniques are most appropriate for their particular needs; providing oversight when needed to ensure that a technique is being used

3. See the recommendation in Nancy Dixon's blog, "The Problem and the Fix for the US Intelligence Agencies' Lessons Learned," July 1, 2009, www.nancydixonblog.com/2009/07/the-problem-and-the-fix-for-the-us-intelligence-agencies-lessons-learned.html.

appropriately; and through example and on-the-job training teaching other analysts how to effectively facilitate team or group meetings.

The DNI's Analytic Transformation Cell, formed in 2011, was instrumental in helping some of these tradecraft cells get started.[4] It provided guidance and in some cases an experienced analyst on temporary assignment to provide on-the-job training to members of the new tradecraft cells. The DNI cell maintained a list of analysts who are knowledgeable about various techniques and willing to provide informal guidance to others who want to use a specific technique.

Funding for expanding the Analytic Transformation Cell into a new Center for Analytic Tradecraft was not approved until 2013, but now, in 2015, the new center is in full operation conducting research to validate and establish best practices for the use of various analytic techniques, creating a knowledge management system for the Intelligence Community, and continuing to assist the tradecraft cells in individual agencies.

The process for coordinating a National Intelligence Estimate (NIE) has changed dramatically. Formal coordination prior to publication of an NIE is now usually a formality, as there has been collaboration among interested parties from the inception, and all relevant intelligence is shared. The Key Assumptions Check and other basic critical thinking and structured analytic techniques have identified and explored differences of opinion early in the preparation of an estimate, and new analysis techniques, such as Premortem Analysis, Structured Self-Critique, and Adversarial Collaboration—all now described and discussed in the DNI knowledge management system—are being employed to define and resolve disagreements as much as possible prior to the final coordination.

Exploitation of outside expertise, especially cultural expertise, has increased significantly. Panels of experts in various Middle Eastern and Asian cultures are used routinely to support Red Hat Analysis or Red Team Analysis, trying to envision how leaders or groups in another culture will react in various circumstances. The Delphi Method is used extensively as a very flexible procedure for obtaining ideas, judgments, or forecasts electronically from geographically dispersed panels of experts. Under the management of the Center for Analytic Tradecraft, the recruitment and management of these panels has become a centralized service available to all members of the Intelligence Community.

By 2015, the use of structured analytic techniques has expanded well beyond the United States. The British, Canadian, Australian, and several other foreign intelligence services increasingly incorporate structured techniques into their training programs and their processes for conducting analysis. After the global financial

---

4. This idea is explored in more detail in Randolph Pherson, "Transformation Cells: An Innovative Way to Institutionalize Collaboration," June 2009, www.pherson.org/library/OP.pdf.

crisis that began in 2008, a number of international financial and business consulting firms adapted several of the core intelligence analysis techniques to their business needs, concluding that they could no longer afford multi-million dollar mistakes that could have been avoided by engaging in more rigorous analysis as part of their business processes.

One no longer hears the old claim that there is no proof that the use of structured analytic techniques actually improves analysis. The widespread use of structured techniques in 2015 is partially attributable to the debunking of that claim, which not so long ago was offered by analysts who just didn't want to change their long-established practices. One of the first studies conducted by the new Center for Analytic Tradecraft involved a sample of reports prepared with the assistance of several structured techniques and a comparable sample of reports where structured techniques had not been used. Researchers interviewed the authors of the reports, their managers, and the customers who received these reports. This initial study confirmed that reports prepared with the assistance of the selected structured techniques were more thorough, provided better accounts of how the conclusions were reached, and generated greater confidence in the conclusions than did reports for which such techniques were not used. These findings were replicated by other friendly intelligence services that were using these techniques, and this was sufficient to quiet most of the doubters.

The collective result of all these developments is an analytic climate in 2015 that produces more rigorous, constructive, and informative analysis—a development that decision makers have noted and are making use of as they face increasingly complex and interrelated policy challenges. As a result, policymakers are increasing their demand for analyses that, for example, consider multiple scenarios or challenge the conventional wisdom. Techniques like the Complexity Manager are commonly discussed among analysts and decision makers alike. In some cases, decision makers or their aides even observe or participate in collaborative processes via Intellipedia or A-Space. These interactions help both customers and analysts understand the benefits and limitations of using collaborative processes and tools to produce analysis that informs and augments policy deliberations.

This vision of a robust and policy-relevant analytic climate in 2015 is achievable. But it is predicated on the Intelligence Community's willingness and ability to foster a collaborative environment that encourages the use of structured analytic techniques. Achieving this goal will require an infusion of resources for tradecraft centers, facilitators, training, and methodology development and testing. It will also require patience and a willingness to accept a modest failure rate as analysts become familiar with the techniques and collaborative tools. We believe the outcome will definitely be worth the risk involved in charting a new analytic frontier.

Structured Analytic Techniques: Families and Linkages

The structured analytic techniques presented in this book can be used independently or in concert with other techniques. For ease of presentation, we have
sorted the techniques into eight groups, or domains, based on the predominant
focus and purpose of each technique. The graphic on the opposing page illustrates the relationships among the techniques. Mapping the techniques in this
manner reveals less obvious connections and highlights the mutually reinforcing
nature of many of the techniques.

▬▬▬ Connections within a domain are shown by a thick blue line.

───── Connections to techniques in other domains are shown by a thin gray
line.

(CORE) "Core" techniques, or "hubs," are highlighted in blue circles because of
the strong connections they have across more than one domain. These
core techniques have been cited by many Intelligence Community and
business analysts as the tools they are most likely to use in their analyses.

✳ Structured analytic techniques in six different domains often make use
of indicators and are indicated by stars.

Most techniques are also enhanced by brainstorming. The art and science of
analysis is dynamic, however, and we expect the list of techniques to change over
time.

Please send ideas on how this chart can be improved to pherson@pherson.org.